BLEEDING KANSAS

Bleeding Kansas

BY

ALICE NICHOLS

NEW YORK

OXFORD UNIVERSITY PRESS

1954

TO JEB PATTERSON

This book is dedicated to Jeb Patterson because the typecases of his *Parkville Luminary* were dumped into the icy Missouri River in March 1855.

Many of Jeb Patterson's contemporaries I know better than I know him. I could write a book about free-soilism's Huey Long, General James H. Lane, or about pro-slavery's Nero, Sheriff Samuel J. Jones. I can tell you the color of Charles Robinson's eyes and considerable about the color of the deals that built him, a thousand-dollar-a-year agent of the New England Emigrant Aid Society, into the richest man in the new state of Kansas.

I know more about most of the characters, major and minor, in America's least-known historical drama—The Struggle for Kansas—than I do about Jeb Patterson, the man to whom I dedicate this book. I can review the brief but bloody works of the sainted hatchet-murderer, John Brown, and the bloody words of Dr. John Stringfellow who let his junior editor say, in print, 'I'd as lief kill a babe in its cradle if I knew it would grow up to be an abolitionist.' But I know only this about Jeb Patterson: He was a man who believed and had the courage to say that Right is a middle way.

Contents

Prologue

THIS IS THE STORY of the birth of Kansas. It was a seven-year labor of great violence and historical import, for Kansas had a twin and its twin was Civil War.

So bitter was the struggle over the Territory of Kansas, so deliberately was it used to arouse and spread hatred that even the Northerners, who had done so much to make a peaceful solution to the slavery problem impossible, came to realize that they had gone too far. When Kansas was finally admitted to the Union after four Southern states had withdrawn from it, early in 1861, Congress, as if aghast at the tragic consequences that threatened from this final defiance of the South's States' Rights stand, jointly resolved to submit an amendment to the Constitution designed to establish slavery in the United States forever.

This proposed Thirteenth Amendment, signed by James Buchanan two days before Lincoln's inauguration, forbade the Constitution's ever being amended to 'give to Congress the power to abolish or interfere within any State with the domestic institutions thereof, including that of persons held to labor or service by the laws of said State.' Lincoln's home state, Illinois, was one of three states to ratify this amendent in a last-minute attempt to undo the damage deliberately done through seven bloody years in Kansas Territory.

The contest between North and South for the possession of the Territory of Kansas was a crucial chapter in our history and it has been as distorted in its telling as it was in its making. If a song had never been sung about John Brown's body a-moldering in its grave, chances are the truth would have lain forever buried under the lies that were megaphoned by press and pulpit in this first great propaganda prelude to war. The canonization of John Brown and the linking of his name to Kansas brought a rash of I-Done-It books by men who thought all credit for winning Kansas for the North should be theirs. That made other Northerners mad and they wrote books. When these versions of events are checked against what was written at the time by propagandists as well as by relatively impartial observers and against what was claimed by Southerners, a picture close to the truth emerges. It is not a pretty picture.

It is a colorful picture and an instructive one. It shows how an honest approach might have prevented the Civil War, leaving slavery an evil to be legislated out of existence as have been other forms of human bondage.

An Acknowledgment

EASTERN NEWSPAPERS sent correspondents to cover the troubles in Kansas Territory and to them we are indebted for colorful writing. There may be invented dialogues in this book, invented quotations, even invented appraisals of the Kansas weather and the Kansas countryside, but, if so, they are the inventions of reporters and diarists who lived a hundred years ago. To these vivid writers, I wish to express my gratitude.

BLEEDING KANSAS

1

Family Tree

THERE WAS A TIME when the institution of slavery was a mutually shared responsibility between North and South, a mutually recognized evil. Northerners were well aware that Yankee fortunes had been built on the slave trade, and Southerners, on whom slavery had been foisted by the Duke of York's Royal African Company, knew as well as anyone that slavery was in violation of democratic government and the very dignity of man.

Thomas Jefferson of Virginia fought to denounce the institution of slavery in the Declaration of Independence. He lost this fight. And, in 1784, his proposal to exclude slavery from all new states was defeated by only one vote and that happened to be a Northern vote. Congress unanimously agreed to exclude slavery from the Northwest Territory in 1787, and the constitutional convention, which met that year, outlawed the importation of slaves after 1 January 1808.

No more men and women were to be brought in chains from Africa, it was hoped, but the problem of what to do about the thousands of Negroes already in bondage remained. Anti-slavery societies sprang up all over the new nation. Two hundred and fifty societies were flourishing by 1826, and all but thirty-eight of them were below the Mason-Dixon Line. Quaker Benjamin Lundy's *Genius of Universal Emancipation* was sustained by Southern subscribers and Southern advertisers. And a Virginian, James Madison, proposed that monies accrued from the sale of public lands be used to compensate owners as slaves were freed. This proposal raised grave problems of relocation or assimilation of the slave population that could be solved only by a concentration of the national mind and heart upon them. But few Northerners were concerned over slavery at that time. Their concern came only after the protective tariff revealed Northern and Southern economic interests as irreconcilable, and then it was a concern over slavery's evils with little thought to the factors complicating its solution.

South Carolina's John Calhoun was a strong advocate of the first protective tariff. He had seen in New England's protests over the embargo of the War of 1812 'a new and terrible danger — disunion.' A protective tariff, he argued, would foster 'manufactures to bind together more closely our widely spread Republic.' It was a maritime New England that had threatened a walkout over the embargo, and it was a maritime-minded Daniel Webster who opposed the first protective tariff in 1816.

Twelve years later positions were reversed, for the most part because of Eli Whitney. The full effect of his cotton gin was being felt. It had industrialized the North and had nailed the South to the soil and a dependence on slave labor. The greatly expanded acreages of the South fed the textile mills of the North and supplied nearly two-thirds of the new nation's exports. England was the South's best customer. If the high prices set by high duties cut off England's American market, as New England hoped they would, the South would lose her best customer. Moreover, agriculture would still be 'taxed' for the benefit of industry, since American manufacturers could keep prices of goods high, though below those of imports.

The South framed the Tariff of 1828 for defeat, but it was passed and became 'the tariff of abominations.' Now, Calhoun formulated his doctrine of nullification, asserting the right of a state to veto Federal action.

When the North tenaciously hung onto high duties on textiles in 1832, Calhoun's South Carolina declared the tariff unconstitutional and threatened secession from the Union if an attempt was made to enforce the tariff there. The possibility that Charleston might become a free port probably influenced the quick acceptance of Henry Clay's compromise tariff, which provided for a gradual reduction of duties during the next eight years. But hatred had been established and it was being pushed from another direction. 'The basis for Southern union must be shifted to the slavery question,' Calhoun told his constituents.

For it chanced, in the fateful year of 1828, that Benjamin Lundy, who had gained Southern converts to the anti-slavery cause by his ability to attack slavery without laying blame for it, met up with a young printer by the name of William Lloyd Garrison. Lundy had gone to Boston to arouse support there for his anti-slavery movement, and he just happened to stay at the rooming house where Garrison lived. The printer became a Lundy convert. He went to Baltimore as associate editor of *The Genius,* and when he took up pen, the kind of name calling it takes to start a fight began.

Garrison laid full blame for slavery on the South. 'He attacks individuals as if they were personally responsible for the status of slavery,' said the *Boston Globe* of Garrison, after he had been run out of Baltimore and had returned to Boston to establish his own organ, *The Liberator.*

Southern voices struck back, but few with such cool-headed argument as Savannah's *Daily Georgian,* which compared the lot of the Southern slave with that of the Northern mill worker. When a master became unable to feed and clothe his slaves, he had to sell them to someone who could care for them, said the *Daily Georgian,* while Northern laborers in hard times were thrown out of their jobs and left to starve or freeze. And slaves did not have to worry about their old age, were not faced with the poorhouse as mill workers were.

There were slaves up North, too, and some Northerners admitted it. Listen to the Lowell, Massachusetts, *Voice of Industry* in 1856: 'Observing a singular-looking long, low, black wagon passing along the street, we made inquiries respecting it and were informed that it was what we term a "slaver." She makes regular trips to the north of the states, cruising around

Vermont and New Hampshire, with a "commander" whose heart must be as black as his craft, who is paid a dollar a head for all he brings to market, and more in proportion to the distance — if he brings them from such a distance that they cannot easily get back. This is done by "hoisting false colors," and representing to the girls that they can tend more machinery than is possible, and that the work is very neat, and the wages such that they can dress in silks and spend half their time in reading. Now is this true? Let the girls who have been thus deceived answer.'

Moderate voices were raised south and north, in reasoned argument and self-criticism, but they were lost in the screams of the name-callers. Garrison's small but vociferous band of abolitionists ignored dawn-to-dark mill slavery as they ignored the outfitting of slave-runners in Northern ports where smuggling continued to the eve of the Civil War, with eighty-three slavers outfitted in the port of New York alone in 1859 and 1860. They ignored, too, the social and economic factors complicating solution of the slavery problem. They sent a rising, pounding tide of blame and abuse against taut Southern nerves, demanded a dissolution of the Union if Southerners persisted in their evil ways.

Anti-slavery societies disappeared from the South. Inflamed slaveholders, harassed by their own enslavement to King Cotton with his insatiable appetite for high-priced slaves and new unplundered soils, flocked to John Calhoun's States' Rights banner. They swore to protect their property rights and to protect the institution of slavery by expanding the South, by taking slavery into new territories.

With the admission of Arkansas in 1836, the South had thirteen states to the North's twelve. The next year, when Michigan was admitted to even things up, the South secured passage of a resolution by Henry Clay which viewed with alarm any attempt Congress might make to abolish slavery in the territories where it existed. The South had its eyes on Florida and Texas. Their admission in 1845 gave the South a four-seat advantage in the

Senate, but to re-establish the customary balance of power, Iowa was admitted in 1846 and Wisconsin in 1848. Then, in 1850, California prayed for admission as a free state. Her admission would give the North sixteen states to the South's fifteen. And the South had run out of territory into which to expand, for Missouri had been admitted as a slave state in 1820 only on the South's agreement that any other new states to be carved out of territory above the 36-30 parallel, which bounds Missouri on the south, would be free.

The time had come for another compromise and again Henry Clay set to work. California was admitted free in exchange for several concessions to the South, one of which was a provision for the organization of New Mexico and Utah as territories with no reservations about slavery.

The Compromise of 1850 was everywhere hailed as an end to slavery as a political issue. Never again, said both Whigs and Democrats in their national conventions in 1852, would there be a renewal of sectional controversy on the subject. And the Whigs, to show their good faith, helped elect the Democratic candidate, Franklin Pierce of New Hampshire, President of the United States.

The controversy was not renewed for more than a year. Then on 4 December 1853 A. C. Dodge of Iowa introduced the Kansas-Nebraska Bill and a month later, when the Committee on Territories reported the bill, the long, bombastic, and bloody battle for Kansas began.

The bill, as clarified by Senator Stephen A. Douglas, Chairman of the Committee on Territories, in effect, pronounced the Missouri Compromise dead. The Compromise of 1850, Douglas said, had established the principle of popular sovereignty. If settlers of New Mexico and Utah could determine whether their lands were to be slave or free, then settlers of all new territories, no matter where they were located, must be allowed to make the same decision.

The North was shocked. The dead Missouri Compromise was revived but after six months of oratorical torture was killed again — this time for good. On 30 May 1854, President Pierce signed the Kansas-Nebraska Bill.

Squatter sovereignty had been written into the law. Kansas Territory was thrown open for settlement. The side that got there first with the most settlers would win — or should.

2

The Parent Stock

THE NIGHT of 30 May 1854 became a night of riotous celebration in the border counties of Missouri, as self-appointed couriers spread the news that the Kansas-Nebraska Bill had been signed by Franklin Pierce.

Men gathered in the barroom of the St. Georges Hotel in Weston, in the saloons of Westport and Independence, of Parkville, Lexington, and Platte City to celebrate. Toasts were drunk in every crossroads grocery store reached by the word, brought so miraculously from Washington to their own Boonville by telegraph. The President of the United States was honored, as was Missouri's Senator David R. Atchison, who had fought hard for this bill that meant survival to the South.

Atchison had warned Missourians to be prepared to rush across the border to settle Kansas Territory and secure her for the South the moment the lands to the west were opened. There were fifty thousand slaves in Missouri's border counties, representing some thirty million dollars in investment. 'To have a free state as our western neighbor would spell disaster,' Atchison had written, adding that the Yankees were prepared for an organized emigration.

Now the time had come for action. Every night became a rally night. 'If I had my way, I'd hang every damned abolitionist!' cried Dr. John Stringfellow of Weston. 'And everyone born north of the Mason-Dixon Line is an abolitionist.' So saying, he became a tireless procurer for the virgin land that lay across the border. At rally after rally, he extolled its great promise for those who were men enough to take it. And Missouri bordermen, by and large, were men — men who had gone with Doniphan to Chihuahua, men who had bullwhacked to Santa Fe, trapped fur in the mountains of the Northwest. They were buffalo hunters, Indian fighters, scrappers. They liked the idea of taking Kansas.

Border towns buzzed with talk and activity. Reading matter fluttered in the air, made an autumnal rustling under foot, each leaf a handbill proclaiming the great advantage of this proposed townsite or that as a place to invest in, a place to squat near. Copper ore from Marysville on the Big Blue; town shares only $100 apiece! Fortunes ahead at Kickapoo; coal beds underlie the city! Leavenworth, near the Fort, bound to be a metropolis, $400 the town share — (no title, but the Delawares, like all Indians, could be swindled). And on 10 June, a party of horsemen ferried the Missouri and rode to Salt Creek Valley, there to make fiery pronouncement that slavery was thereby instituted in the Territory of Kansas.

They issued the proclamation, then rode back.

Missourians liked the idea of taking Kansas — as an idea. They took her with a storm of words, but it was a marriage in name only. Virgin sod was tough to break, hard to subdue, and as for a place to live — well, these Missourians liked Missouri just fine.

'We must have settlers,' Stringfellow cried again and again. 'We must have men to live on the land; voters. And Kansas, gentlemen, is a land of infinite promise, a land of opportunity . . .'

Then at a meeting at Lexington, a great lanky fellow with a slow drawl and a tobacco-stained beard got to his feet, spat deliberately, and said, 'If this here Kansas is such a daggone dreadful nice place to live in, why ain't you a-livin' there?'

Stringfellow's answer was not reported, but that jibe may have prompted him to establish a newspaper at Atchison, K.T., 'Future Home of the Vice President of the United States! All Mormon trains will outfit here.'

Someone was going to have to move across the river.

Bordermen loved rallies, would ride fifty miles to one, but the border counties were just wild enough, and just civilized enough, to suit their tall-talking, short-working ways.

Rally riders, by and large, were the itchy-footed fellows who were to become known as Border Ruffians. The more solid citizens, the actual farmers, had little time for traipsing about to meetings, and though they cursed abolitionism as a matter of form, their talk was of more immediate things when they gathered in the grocery stores on Saturday night — the way the rains had gummed the bottoms, the countless hazards of farming.

Close to home was the talk on Saturday night, when many men drifted into the stores and few drifted out. For the grocery of that time and place had much more to offer than a potbellied stove and a cracker barrel. Its cash leader, season in and season out, was whisky, barreled and spigoted and bursting to be drawn. Always 'highly rectified,' for those who believed in signs, it might be rye but usually it was corn, for the 'Old Monongahela' more closely met border specifications with its 'strength of forty jack-asses, guaranteed to kill forty rods around the corner.'

Spigots were turned and turned again, for a Missourian, one drink gone, was always ready to allow that he was dry as a powder horn. 'Step up hoss, and liquor,' was the standard invitation.

Border Missouri was still new country, and there was no reason that the bordermen could see to leave it.

Some did leave that first summer, it is true, seeing the move as an opportunity or a patriotic duty. But most men simply crossed the Missouri line to lay claim, in the fair name of the South, to the virgin acres. Along the Missouri's west bank, along the Little Stranger and the Big Stranger, as far west as the Kickapoo lands beyond the Grasshopper, many of the best pieces of land were soon marked with 'improvements.' More often than not, these consisted of four logs laid together to form a rectangle. There was no sign of life about them except in posted warnings. 'If I find any damned rascal tearing this foundation down, I'll cut his liver out,' one early 'settler' had written.

'Citizens of the West, South, and Illinois!' cried Senator

Atchison's *Platte Argus*. 'Stake out your claims and woe be to the Abolitionist or Mormon who shall intrude upon it or come within reach of your long and true rifles, or within point blank shot of your revolvers.'

Enough bordermen responded to such appeals to establish the proslavery towns of Leavenworth, Kickapoo, and Atchison on the west bank of the Missouri that first summer.

II

NEW ENGLANDERS were no more eager to leave their homes than were border Missourians. There were those who liked where they lived. There were those too inured to human drudgery, on rocky fields or in dawn-to-dark mills, to feel much concern over the question of human bondage. And there were those who felt with Daniel Webster that the tendency of the anti-slavery movement had been 'not to set free, but to bind faster the slave population of the South.' William Lloyd Garrison, with his fiery demands for abolition and disunion, had done a better job of antagonizing the South than of rousing the North.

Even the Northern clergy and press decried the fanaticism of the abolitionists, though they wanted the North to have Kansas for either humane or economic reasons. Their congressmen put up a hard fight against the bill that gave the South a chance at her. The day before the passage of the Kansas-Nebraska Bill was a day of swan-song oratory. 'Tomorrow,' said Senator Benjamin F. Wade, 'I believe there is to be an eclipse of the sun and I think that the sun in the heavens and the glory of this republic should both go into obscurity and darkness together. Let the bill pass then. It is a proper occasion for so dark and damning a deed.'

And Senator William H. Seward cried, 'Come on then, gentlemen of the slave states! Since there is no escaping your challenge, I accept it, in behalf of freedom. We will engage in competition for the virgin soil of Kansas and God give victory to the side that is stronger in numbers, as it is in right.'

By this challenge, Seward came to be credited with in-augurating the contest for Kansas. One man resented this. He also resented postwar praise of William Lloyd Garrison, Wen-dell Phillips, and John Brown. He wrote letters to the press, leaflets, and finally a book to prove that it was he, Eli Thayer, who won Kansas for the North, thereby bringing about the Civil War and emancipation of the slaves. And certainly he deserved a share of such credit.

Eli Thayer anticipated that Northerners would have no sweeping moral urge to move westward when the Kansas-Nebraska Bill became a law. Weeks before Seward flung his challenge, Thayer had hatched a crafty plan for colonizing the new lands. It had a sure-fire Yankee appeal. It was a low-cost, promised-profit way of exerting virtue.

Thayer believed that the North could outcolonize the South in Kansas Territory, despite Missouri's closeness, if there was 'an organized emigration, guided and guarded by a responsible business company.' As representative from Worcester to the Massachusetts State Legislature, he got that body to grant his Massachusetts Emigrant Aid Society a charter to raise a capital of $5,000,000.

The money would be spent, Thayer said, to construct re-ceiving houses to give temporary accommodations to emigrants to Kansas, to set up grist mills and steam sawmills to be leased or run by company agents, and to establish newspapers 'to be organs of the company and from the very first an index to that love of freedom and good morals which it is to be hoped may characterize the state now to be formed.'

The corporation would spend money, but it would also make money. Company agents would 'locate and take up for the company's benefit the section of land in which the boarding houses and mills are located.' When the Territory became a state, the directors would dispose of these company holdings, 're-place the money laid out and declare a dividend to stockholders.' By that time, Thayer pointed out, 'the company would possess several reservations of 640 acres each, on which are boarding

houses and mills, and the churches and schools which it has rendered necessary. In other words, these points will then be the
large commercial positions of the new State.'

The dividends on investments would, in brief, be good.

The charter granted, sales of stock began. The clergy
responded fairly well to the first circularization, but several
sour notes were struck when the second came around. Reverend
Joseph Chandler of West Brattleboro, Vermont, came right to
the point. 'Is the company purely a benevolent, or is it a commercial property, a holding and money making company? Is it
expected that the stock of the company will be worth its par
value or is this matter of shares to be owned by the ministers a
mere ruse to get more money?' he asked. 'There is an apparent
mixture of benevolence, patriotism, and speculation in this enterprise that makes me a little suspicious.' And one of the directors, Dr. Samuel Cabot, even protested the bills submitted by a
fellow director, Edward Everett Hale, saying that they 'were
larger than we anticipated.'

L. B. Russell, writing more than a year after the company's
founding and concerned with the criticisms that were being
leveled against it, disapproved of the emphasis its promoters
were putting on the speculative phase. 'Our friend, Mr. Thayer,'
he said, 'represents the company's stock as a great speculation,
likely to pay 100 per cent or more profit.' And he criticized the
Society for exaggerating its success in Kansas. By July 1855,
more than a year after the Territory's opening, it had sent only
1,216 settlers, he said.

The Society was mistrusted by the very men it sought as
sponsors, by the men morally concerned over slavery yet un-
sympathetic toward the fanaticism of abolitionism. And its representatives managed to alienate, on the field of battle, those
who should have been allies, the Northern men from Western
states. Thayer's agents took a monopolistic attitude toward winning Kansas for the North. At a 'Territorial Indignation Meeting' held in January 1855, the Society's Kansas agent, Dr.
Charles H. Robinson, was called a "False Belshazzar' and
charged with stealing timber for his mill. He was said to go

about with armed patrols cutting trees on claims of men from west of the Alleghenies. Reporting the meeting, the *Kansas Free State* said, 'C. W. Babcock charged that "the Emigrant Aid Company of Boston is a swindle on the public, the principal object of those concerned being that of making a grand land speculation under the guise of making Kansas a free state." '

With all these things against it, the enterprise would have failed had not Amos A. Lawrence of Boston advanced out of his own pocket the funds necessary to revive it. The name was changed to the New England Emigrant Aid Society and it was to play, by its very aggressiveness, an important role in the seven-year struggle for Kansas Territory.

One of the Society's claims was that it made the first free-soil settlement in the new Territory. On 17 July 1854, twenty-nine New England men were sent off from Boston with much the same fanfare with which heroes are sent to war. They were met by company agent Charles Branscomb in St. Louis and conducted to a spot which Thayer claimed Branscomb had picked from a Thayer description of a perfect townsite — and which agent Charles Robinson claimed to have spotted on his way to California in 1849.

Robinson never mentioned the fact that free-soil men were living on this location when his party arrived, so histories and encyclopedias credit him with founding the first free-soil community in Kansas Territory. Perhaps the reason Dr. Charles Robinson made no mention of Dr. John Doy and the fifteen other men from upstate New York who were squatting on the land he wanted was that he had to cheat them to get the land. On Robinson's promise of share and share alike, Doy relinquished his squatter rights to one hundred sixty acres of land and ended up with title to one town lot.

By such shenanigans, a Yankee town was founded some forty miles upriver from the juncture of the Kansas and Missouri Rivers in that first summer of 1854. It was variously called Wakarusa, after a creek which ran not far away, New Boston, and, by Missourians, Yankee Town. 'I think I was first to suggest your name for the city,' agent Charles Robinson wrote to Amos Lawrence, savior and treasurer of the New England Emigrant Aid Society, when the town was officially named that fall and Lawrence, K.T., became a name destined to be written on history's pages in fire and blood.

3

Seedbed

KANSAS IN 1854 was a land of great beauty, a grassland heavily fenced with timber. Walnut, hickory, elm and oak, buttonwood, cottonwood, and willow marked the course of creeks as they cut through the limestone hills in their search for a way to the Father of All Waters. Flowers bloomed everywhere and the wild blossom fragrance of elderberry, gooseberry, plum, of mandrake, raspberry, apple, and grape lingered in the air that rose cool from the ground toward the warming sun. On rivers trapped by the Chouteaus — *père, fils,* and *frères* — for a golden decade, game still abounded. The fur bearers were gone, it is true; no beavers were to be seen, few otters, or muskrats. And the animals with a price on their hides, a good part of the deer, and all of the buffalo had fled to west Kansas. But walk anywhere and you would hear the sudden whir of wings as quail, prairie chickens, and wild turkeys sought new cover.

This was virgin land that had felt the fevered hand of man but was yet to be ravished by him. The soil lay deep and firmly textured upon its rock-ribbed frame — soil virgin to man yet burgeoning from its timeless marriage with the sun. It was a land eternally renewed by life's happy cycle of birth, growth, seeding, death, and decay. It was a living soil, veined by clear waters, with a perpetual youth that only man, with his thoughtless haste and relentless steel, could destroy.

Far to the east, and to the north and south, were lands

once as untouched that now lay dying, worn and wrinkled with rivers drying, clogged by their own once-living soil.

And the run-off of men from these lands was beginning to trickle to the virgin domain. Men looking for a new start, or easier plundering, were on their way westward. They came bringing cows, mules, plows — and those who had them brought slaves.

Men of the land were on their way, but not in the numbers a new country needs. This was not the usual surge westward. It was a ballyhoo boom and one of the many handbooks written to entice settlers from the North made a frank appeal to farmers and other producers. In a chapter headed 'What business will pay best?' the author, Nathan Parker, said, 'Physicians, lawyers, clergymen, real-estate brokers and the like, had better stay home; for the Territory is already bountifully supplied with them.' It was Mr. Parker's way of saying that Kansas Territory had a bigger dose of politicians than it could swallow.

The men who came with an eye to farming saw a rich land where bottomland grass grew higher than a horseman's head, a land of open and rolling uplands. It was a land bright with the bloom of flowers under a limitless sky, a land where clear springs gushed in rock ravines.

Kansas Territory was a park-like land in its eastern reaches, a vast land that lifted to great flat stretches of treeless plains and, across them, to the summits of the Rocky Mountains that mark the Great Divide. It had been separated from Nebraska upon passage of the bill that linked their names, but still it was a huge spread of land, 200 miles wide and nearly 700 miles long. And though the first white men had come to it as early as 1542, when Coronado was seeking the fabled Quivira, and though the Chouteaus and other trappers had grown rich on its furs, there were, in May 1854, less than 800 white people living in its 126,000 square miles.

Kansas had been a way to other places.

A great road led out from Westport, Missouri, into the Territory and, after a few miles, forked.

One fork, called the California Road, followed the Kansas,

or Kaw, River for more than fifty miles, crossed it either at the ferry run by Jules Pappan, Chouteau kinsman and grandson-in-law of Chief White Plume of the Kanzas, or farther west at the Great Crossing, then headed north to meet a northern branch called the Oregon Trail (route of the Mormon flight from Missouri in 1844) at Marysville, K.T., on the Big Blue. Over the California Road, missionary Marcus Whitman had guided the first families of Oregon in 1843. And this had been the route for many of the 50,000 gold rushers of 1849, as well as for other parties of coast-bound homeseekers, including the Donner Party doomed to fame through freezing to death.

The other fork cut southwest to Santa Fe and it was called the Santa Fe Trail. Along it — in the thirty years since Miss Fanny Marshall of Arrow Rock, Missouri, had invested $60 in William Becknell's first wagon expedition and realized a 1500 per cent profit — hundreds of wagon trains had traveled. By 1848, Santa Fe trade profits were down to less than 100 per cent, but that was enough to inspire one of the most famous horseback rides in all history — Little Aubrey's 5-day-16-hour sprint back the 775 miles to Independence for more goods. Just what the trade margin of profit was by 1854 has not been recorded, but it was good enough that Majors & Russell of Westport could have in their employ 1000 bullwhackers or teamsters to drive their 7000 oxen and mules.

Kansas was still to be a way to other places, but now it was also to become a place to stay. It was a seedbed of giant proportions and in it North and South now met, to plant such seed as only violence could nurture and deliver.

Kansas Territory was a vast and lonely land, a land that by one treaty was to have belonged to the red man 'as long as grass grows and water flows.'

'Quivira,' Coronado's Spaniards called the land, reporting the name as it was pronounced to them. It was the land of the Kanzas, or Kaws, but by 1854 that tribe had been treatied almost to death. However irresistible the tide of westward migration, no Great White Father in Washington had been able to dull his conscience enough to send displaced tribes to lands that

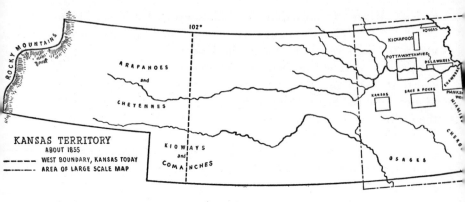

KANSAS TERRITORY
ABOUT 1855
----- WEST BOUNDARY, KANSAS TODAY
-·-·- AREA OF LARGE SCALE MAP

did not hold at least some potential for cultivation and civilization. The land of the Kaws held promise, so in it were crowded the remnants of many tribes of the East and the near West. Now that these lands were to be opened to white settlement as Kansas Territory, President Franklin Pierce, as Great White Father incumbent, had to deal with the situation. Beginning early in 1854, he called many Indian chiefs to his wigwam in Washington.

By June, whittling treaties had been made with the Otoes, Ioways, and Missourias; with the Kickapoos, the Kaskaskias, the Weas, Peorias, and Piankeshaws; with the Shawnees, Senecas, and Quapaws; the Delawares, the Wyandottes, the Chippewas; with the Osages, Pottawatomies, Sacs, and Foxes. The Apaches and Comanches, the Cheyennes and Arapahoes, the Kiowas, Pawnees, and Sioux could keep the Great American Desert, as the western reaches of the new territory were called.

It was announced, with no mention of method, that these Indian tribes had ceded such and such lands. Millions of deep-loamed acres were thrown open for settlement.

The land was there for the claiming. Shake together a cabin or pitch a tent, break half an acre of sod and fence it, file a notice of intention to pre-empt your chosen 160 acres at the nearest sutler's office. The price, $1.25 an acre, but you will have months or years of free use of the land to help you raise the money, since the land cannot be sold until government surveys

are completed. Then, for $200, that quarter-section piece of God's earth will be assigned to you and your heirs forever.

This was the well-established pre-emption routine, but for Northeasterners there were added inducements. The dozen plus connecting railroads of the Northern states offered a 25 per cent reduction in fare to St. Louis, which was as far as rails were laid in 1854. Except during a few deep-winter months, the rest of the trip to the United States border could be made by boat, up the Missouri. Combination fare from Boston, Massachusetts, to Leavenworth, Kansas Territory, first class, was $34.

Eastern newspapers, North and South, were filled with go-West exhortations, but all the inducements and all the political need produced only a trickling settlement that first year. It was a trickling settlement at best and most of it came from near by, from across the borders of proslavery Missouri and Arkansas, or from free-soil Western states such as Illinois and Indiana. Nearly as many trickled out as trickled in.

For all the fanfare, nine months after the new lands were thrown open for settlement, there were, according to the Territory's first census, only 8,501 settlers, including women, children, and 242 slaves. Of the 2,905 American-born males of voting age, more than 62 per cent were from the slave states.

The South had a clear majority. In the fall of 1854, it elected its candidate, J. W. Whitfield, as the Territory's delegate to Congress. A later Congressional Investigating Committee, free-soil in its leanings, had to admit that in that first election 'of the legal votes cast, General Whitfield received a majority.' But it was true that some illegal votes had been cast. Some Missourians had crossed the border to cast ballots, giving a pre-taste of the ardor that was to cost the South so heavily in the years to follow. It was an ardor that was to be met with ardor, the one naked, the other clothed.

4

The Mighty Seed

THE FIRST GOVERNOR of Kansas Territory, Andrew H. Reeder, arrived in October 1854. He was welcomed with bouquets of full-blown words and then duly forgotten. There was building to be done before the winter came.

Leavenworth City, aspirant territorial capital, did not look, in September 1854, as if it could grow to be the capital of anything. It consisted of four tents and a steam engine sawing out wood the day representatives of Cincinnati's free-soil Kansas League visited it. 'Under a tree, a type-sticker had his case before him, was at work on the first number of the newspaper; within a frame, without a board on the side or roof, was the editor's desk and sanctum,' the committee reported. 'When we returned from the Territory to Weston, we saw a notice stating that the editor had removed his office from under the elm tree to the corner of "Broadway and the Levee." This Broadway was, at that time, much broader than the streets of old Babylon, for, with the exception of the Fort, there was probably not a house on either side for thirty miles.'

But the steam engine was making lumber and the Leavenworth House had been thrown together by the time Governor Reeder arrived to take up his duties. He preferred to stay, however, a couple of miles upriver at Fort Leavenworth, established since 1827. The Leavenworth House, with its balloon frame and cottonwood siding, one of the warpingest of woods, was not a

first-class hostelry. One of its early guests, John McNamara,
said of it, 'The daylight sought us through a thousand holes in
the morning.' That was in the upstairs dormitory. Downstairs:
'The room we sat in was barroom, dining room, smoking room,
whittling room, sitting room, coughing room and spitting room,
reading room and writing room, committee room and debating
room.'

McNamara was a preacher on his way to claim a block of
land that a Mr. Boyd, real-estate promoter at Kickapoo, K.T.,
had given for a church in Martinsburg, a town he was promoting
on the Stranger. This town-to-be had even scantier accommodations for the newcomer than Leavenworth. McNamara, his
brother, and two cousins tented in the snow as they set to work
to build a cabin. When their neighbor, Azariah Martin, charged
them 80 cents to make a loaf of bread, they established this
standard menu: 'Bacon and corn meal bread for breakfast,
bacon and corn meal bread for dinner and, for variety, corn meal
bread and bacon for supper.'

And back in Kickapoo, the McNamara benefactor, Mr.
Boyd, had joined him in the open-air way of living. When Blue
Lodge members at Weston, Missouri, heard that the real-estate
promoter had given land to a preacher who was not 'sound on
the goose,' they crossed the Missouri to burn down the Boyd
office, which was also the Boyd home.

The passage of the Kansas-Nebraska Bill had created a
great fraternal spirit stateside of the border. Hundreds of
Missourians joined a new brotherhood, the Blue Lodge, variously called The Social Band, Friends' Society, Sons of the
South, The Self-Defensives. The avowed purpose of the Lodge
was to extend slavery into Kansas. The password was the phrase,
'Sound on the goose,' but if it was supposed to be secret the secret
was soon out. Every man, resident or newcomer, was judged by
his 'soundness on the goose.' Every man judged not 'sound'
was called an abolitionist, even though he might be a Southerner
who simply disapproved extreme methods. The fraternal em-
blem was a bit of hemp, worn in the lapel buttonhole. Hemp
makes nooses.

The free-soilers had a secret organization, too, so secret that its existence was repeatedly denied by free-soil protagonists, even after a disgruntled member told all about it. Secret sign was given with the right hand, thumb under chin as forefinger scratched the nose; countersign was made by rubbing the lower lip with forefinger and thumb of the left hand. The Kansas Regulators, sometimes called the Kansas Legion, used military titles and insignia in their secret meetings — and they were armed by men in the East.

The destiny of Kansas Territory was shaped by men who never lived there.

II

THE WINTER OF 1854 was an open and peaceful one. The Yankees had founded a piddling town or two, taken over some land, but no more than enough to heat mildly the talk that rose with the pipe smoke in border grocery stores. Squatters had time to tighten their cabins, chink in the cracks that the cold winds discovered. Some settlers rode the winter out in tents with boarded sides, though they made progress in constructing more permanent dwellings. The ring of the McNamara axes as they felled trees along the Stranger, notched and saddled them, was echoed in the ravines of Salt Creek, Grasshopper Creek, of the Wakarusa, and in the valley of the Kaw.

On 23 February 1855, the *Leavenworth Herald*, of elm-birth fame, could say, 'Five months ago there was not a building in the place. The town had just been laid off and the brush cut down. Leavenworth now has a hotel, a saw mill, a tailor's shop, a shoemaker, a barber, two blacksmiths, three carpenter shops, several law and two doctor's offices.'

And the Territory, by then, had five other newspapers. Each side — for this is a history of sides — had three. Leavenworth's *Herald* and Atchison's *Squatter Sovereign* had joined Kickapoo's *Kansas Pioneer* in the Southern chorus. The *Herald of Freedom*, voice of the New England Emigrant Aid Society but published in Pennsylvania, and the *Kansas Tribune*, expression of Ohio free-soilism and printed there, were distributed in Lawrence along with the locally printed *Kansas Free State*.

All were soon to have vital news to report. The results of the first census were announced on the last day of February and the date for the first general election was set for a month later, on 30 March. Kansas Territory was about to elect a legislative body to create the laws by which it would be governed and might, in time, become a state.

The announcement of the election date made more of a stir across the border than in the Territory. Dr. John Stringfellow, senior editor of Atchison's *Squatter Sovereign*, had much business back in Missouri. It was so newsworthy that other newspapers reported it.

'I tell you to mark every scoundrel among you that is the least tainted with freesoilism, or abolitionism, and exterminate him,' Stringfellow exhorted a crowd at St. Joseph, Missouri, according to the *Leavenworth Herald*. 'To those having qualms of conscience, as to violating laws, state or national, the time has come when such impositions must be disregarded, as your lives and property are in danger, and I advise you one and all to enter every election district in Kansas, in defiance of Reeder and his vile myrmidons, and vote at the point of Bowie knife or revolver!'

When a similar speech was given in Boonville, a planter responded by going up to the speaker's table and plunking down $1000 in crisp greenbacks. 'I just sold a nigger for that, and I reckon that's about my share for cleaning out them daggone Yankees,' he said.

Such contributions were welcome. 'Free ferry, a dollar a day, and liquor, gentlemen.' That was the Blue Lodge promise to Missourians willing to travel across the United States border to vote in the coming Kansas election. It would take money to keep that promise. It would take thousands of dollars to put an army of voters in the field, but that was not the reason some Missourians were against the idea. Middle-of-the-road men foresaw that a wholesale casting of illegal votes would prejudice the Southern cause in the eyes of the nation.

Jeb Patterson came right out and protested in print, and an armed mob wrecked the office of the *Parkville Luminary*, which he edited. Cases of type were carried down to the Missouri and dumped into the chill waters. The mob uncoiled a length of hemp. It planned to swing Jeb and would have done it had not his beautiful young wife flung her arms about his neck. Border respect for womanhood was a shade stronger than its contempt for a mugwump. Jeb's life was spared. Another man with 'his mug on one side of the fence and his wump on the other,' was the editor of the *Jefferson Inquirer*. He protested the voting invasion and was branded 'a negro-stealer at heart' by his Missouri colleague, the editor of *The Brunswicker*.

And old Tom Thorpe, who farmed out Platte City way, was to tell the Congressional Investigating Committee how his nephew Jem had come knocking on his door one night toward election eve. 'Who's there?' Tom said he had called.

'It's Jem, your brother Hank's boy.'

Tom opened the door. 'Jem boy!' he exclaimed. 'What in thunderation brings you out from Howard County at this hour?'

'I'm on my way to Kansas to vote.'

That made Tom Thorpe mad. 'Then you can't stay here,' he said.

'But Uncle Tom, a dollar a day and — '

'I'm agin it!' Tom cried. 'I tell you, I'm agin it. They been a-jawin' me, wantin' wagons, but I don't subscribe to such doins and you ain't a-going out there to vote.'

'I'm a-going,' Jem said.

And Tom Thorpe slammed the door in his nephew's face.

'I'm no abolitionist,' Tom told the committee. 'I tell you I'm pro-slave. I'm dyed-in-the-wool and can never make a free-soiler. But this going over there to vote ain't right, and it's going to make trouble.'

Missouri men of action, however, looked forward to the Kansas elections, the men who had with Doniphan raped Chihuahua, the luckless prospectors, the winter-bound bull-whackers. And a dollar a day looked good to many farmers whose land lay locked in hibernal lassitude.

The ferries from Rialto, the Weston landing, to Kickapoo and Fort Leavenworth on the Kansas bank of the Missouri could not handle the crowds. The river boat, the *New Lucy*, was pressed into ferry service. And, to the south, the great road that led out from Westport was crowded with traffic, all headed west on the California Road. An army of voters a thousand strong was marching on Lawrence to stuff the ballot boxes in that free-soil section.

Men on horses, men on mules, men in a hundred wagons; men with guns across the knees of their butternut breeches, red shirts flaming beneath their sky-blue mackinaws. Border men, bearded giants, they came with banners flying, to the music of fifes and fiddles. They came singing, with guffaws ringing, passing the jug from man to man, toasting the strength of their arms, their delight in their two cannons, loaded with musket balls.

It was election eve and this contingent of the great voting army Missouri had put in the field pitched camp on the Wakarusa, some six miles from Lawrence. The commanders, Colonel Samuel Young and Captain Claiborne Jackson, planned their campaign. They decided they had more than enough force to carry the Lawrence election and deployed groups of volunteers to the neighboring towns of Tecumseh, Bloomington, and Hickory Point.

It was a tactical move of great sagacity. The South carried the election, even in this free-soil section of the Territory. And without bloodshed, though there was much cocking of revolvers to convince election judges they should waive the oath of residence. 'Cut his throat!' 'Tear his heart out!' 'Kill the damned nigger thief!' Thus were the leaders encouraged by their men.

On the last day of March, a month after the completion of the first census, which showed a voting population of 2,905, a total of 6,307 ballots were cast in the first general territorial election. Thirty-six proslavery legislators were elected, and three free-soilers.

Jeb Patterson got into trouble because he pointed out that the results would have been about the same without the voting invasion, since the South-North ratio of legal voters, qualified residents of Kansas Territory, was at the time close to two to one.

III

'ALL HAIL! Proslavery Party Victorious!' The border press was jubilant. 'Come on, Southern men!' cried the *Leavenworth Herald*. 'Bring your slaves and fill up the Territory. Kansas is saved. Abolitionism is rebuked, her fortress stormed, her flag is draggling in the dust!'

Kansas was, they said, 'S.G.Q.' — sound on the goose question.

And it was, in 1855. The voting army from Missouri invaded all but four of the Territory's eighteen election districts, yet only six districts sent protests to the governor. The others apparently were satisfied with the way the election went, and when new elections were held in the six protested districts, proslavery men did not bother to go to the polls, except in Leavenworth, where, with some unnecessary help from the boys across the river, the same proslavery ticket was elected.

The Jeb Pattersons were right. The South could have won the election fairly, supplied no ammunition for the North's oratorical guns, which immediately opened fire on what was forever to be called 'The Bogus Legislature.'

There was, however, little regret along the border. The few Southerners who felt that any justification for the voting invasion was needed said that the North had imported voters, too. And the *Kansas Free State*, voice of the free-soil settlers from Western states, frankly admitted in its post-election issue, that from seventy-five to a hundred Eastern immigrants, just arrived, had voted the Free State ticket in Lawrence. 'This we tried to prevent, but could not,' wrote honest editor Josiah Miller. 'The Proslavery-imported voters use this as their great argument, that if Eastern persons have a right to come in just before election and vote, persons of other States have also the same right.'

This excuse was used, but most bordermen were not interested in finding excuses for their acts. They were interested in finding more reasons to act. When Governor Reeder ordered new elections in the six protesting districts, the editor of *The Brunswicker* again dipped his pen in red to write, 'This infernal scoundrel will have to be hemped yet.' And William Phillips, Leavenworth lawyer who instigated the protest from that district, was taken on a skiff across the river to Weston, where a new touch was added to the old tar-and-feather formula. His ride on a rail ended at an auction block, where he was sold by a clowning Negro; high bid was a dollar.

The *Leavenworth Herald* 'emphatically endorsed' this action. 'The joy, exultation, and glorification produced by it in our community are unparalleled,' it said.

South and North had met and the mighty seed was planted.

5

One Governor Down and Five To Go

APRIL RAN OUT and May came. Governor Reeder, on a trip back East, ignored broad hints that his resignation would be in order. Free-soiler Cole McCrea killed proslavery Malcolm Clark in an argument over a claim on Salt Creek. But aside from these events, not much happened.

Leavenworth was growing. John Keller had finished his two-story hotel and now that river traffic was open again, the Leavenworth House, at the corner of Main and Delaware, was always filled to capacity. Majors & Russell had moved from Westport to Leavenworth to become purveyors to the Interior Basin and were building a great blacksmith shop to service their thousand wagons. The *Polar Star* made the trip up the river from St. Louis in less than four days and the *Martha Jewell* unloaded the first of the town's prefabricated houses. But the arrival of that ready-built house from St. Louis did not worry the Skinner Lumberyard at the foot of Cherokee Street. It was doing a boom business and there was no man in town with less time on his hands than Samuel Lynn, house joiner and carpenter. Dr. Charles Lieb, moved from his office in the 'first tent north of the Big Elm' to more permanent quarters, was chairman of the Citizens' Committee, organized to importune Congress to open the Delaware lands, on which the settlers had illegally built their town, to pre-emption. Values were rising and they wanted clear title.

Lawrence was growing, too. Charles Robinson, Aid Society agent, brought his wife and a party of two hundred in the first contingent from Boston that year. Others were on their way. Every river boat that lowered its gangplank to the levee of bluff-perched Kansas City debarked some free-soilers with their trunks and carpetsacks. And in May, three boats made their way up the Kaw to the Lawrence landing. There, tent homes had been replaced by grass-thatched mud huts, shake cabins of cottonwood, and squat mud-chinked log cabins. The town's most imposing structure was a two-story building which served as meeting place and church. Its cottonwood siding was already sun-curled and cracked, but solid foundations were being laid for buildings of lasting stone — the largest to be the New England Emigrant Aid Society's Free State Hotel, on broad Massachusetts Street. Down on the river, the steam sawmill was cutting sturdier woods than cottonwood — black walnut, hickory, and oak — but it could not keep pace with demand. A Boston couple went back home because they were so far down on the lumber waiting list. Building was the big activity. Stores were going up, and homes. Agent Charles Robinson was building his residence on a commanding site south of the town, high on the side of Mt. Oread.

It was May, a month of sunshine and shadow, a month of bright days and sudden, crashing thunderstorms. The grass grew deep. Sunny slopes were red with wild strawberries and flowers bloomed everywhere — straw-colored evening primroses, the bright yellow blossom of the compass plant, pink running roses, blue lupine. Farmers had put aside their hammers. Time and time again they sharpened the shares of their sod-busters to turn under this brightly patterned carpet of green that was Kansas Territory. 'We have revelled,' Mrs. Robinson wrote in her diary, 'in flowers under our windows and at our doors, which, with much tending, we have tempted to bloom meagerly in garden-borders and green-houses in New England, such as verbenas — velvet and sweet-scented — petunias, foxgloves, flox, larkspurs, spiderwort, etc., an endless variety.'

June came in with a drop in temperature that reminded

New Englanders of October at home. After being kept awake by the cold wind and the bark of coyotes, the Robinsons rose to find a rattlesnake curled under their stove for warmth. Another pioneer couple found one of the critters snuggled between them in bed.

June came and the free-staters held the first of their many powwows. A memorial protesting that 'men, armed with guns, revolvers, and bowie knives, from another State,' had carried the election was sent to Congress. Among the many resolutions passed was this one: 'In reply to the threats of war so frequently made in our neighboring State, our answer is, "We Are Ready!"'

June came and Governor Reeder returned to the headquarters he had established in one of the brick buildings of Shawnee Mission, across the border from Westport. His first act was to deny a charge made against him by W. L. Marcy, United States Secretary of State. He had not, he said, been party to any irregularities in the purchase of Indian lands.

The lands in question lay just east of Fort Riley. It was upon them that the new town of Pawnee was supposed to be building, and Pawnee was the place Governor Reeder had designated as the capital of Kansas Territory. The Legislature would convene there, he announced, on the first Monday in July, in a building 'to be provided for that purpose.'

It was toward this place that the legislators set out late in June. They had to make an early start, for Pawnee lay some 125 miles from the Missouri border and, therefore, almost that far from the Territory's center of population. And they could not travel light, for scouts had warned them that Pawnee was a 'paper town.' They carried tents, pots, provisions.

'And the Governor says he don't go in for real estate on the side!'

This became the greeting when legislators met up with each other along the way. And it was repeated when, at last, they came to the capital city, which still existed largely in its promoters' imaginations. Two half-finished shacks and a windowless, doorless, two-story stone capitol building were all that marred the beauty of the rim-nested spot. 'It was a novel sight,' reported James Christian, 'to see grave Councilmen and brilliant orators of the House of Representatives cooking their food by the side of a log, or sleeping on a buffalo robe in the open air, with the broad canopy of heaven for covering.' The only two things that were plentiful in the new capital, he said, were 'rocky mounds and highly rectified whiskey.' Pawnee was a long way from anywhere.

But if Governor Reeder himself found the journey from Shawnee Mission long, he did not show it. He could summon the zeal, on the sultry second day of July, to exhort the assembled solons to their high duty. Looking much cooler than he must have felt in his high stock and best black broadcloth, he lifted his not inconsiderable weight from his chair and faced his unfriendly audience. He stood before it, his gray moustache curling in magnificent defiance of the wilting heat and, speaking with all the oratory befitting the time and the occasion, he came at last to this concluding plea: 'I ask you, then, gentlemen, to lay aside all selfish and equivocal motives, to discard all unworthy ends and, in the spirit of justice and charity toward each other, with pure hearts, tempered feelings, and sober judgments to enter upon your duties.' The assembly politely applauded and set about — with impetuous feelings and rash judgments — to attain perfect unanimity. The ten free-soil members were invited, much as sinners are invited to be saved, to stand and resign like gentlemen.

An eleventh free-soil member, Martin Conway, had resigned by letter, in accordance with a free-soil strategy planned by Charles Robinson and Colonel Kersey Coates of Kansas City, a free-soil leader who lived in Missouri throughout the territorial days yet was to be called by Robinson, in 1892, 'the brainiest man and shrewdest manager in Kansas.' These two selected Martin Conway to put the free-soil view on record. Conway wrote that he declined to participate in the proceedings of a Legislature 'derogatory to the respectability of popular government.' He went on at some length, then concluded: 'I am so unfortunate as to have been trained to some notions of human rights, some such notions as those for which, in ages past, our foolish ancestry periled their lives in revolutionary fields. Simply as a citizen and a man, therefore, I shall yield no submission to this alien legislature. On the contrary, I am ready to set its assumed authority at defiance, and shall be prompt to spurn and trample under my feet its insolent enactments, whenever they conflict with my rights or inclinations.'

The legislators tossed Conway's letter aside, checked him off the list of men it had to unseat, and set to work on the others. One by one, they found the free-soil members irregularly elected and voted them out, giving their seats to the proslave men who had been elected at the time of the voting invasion. Only one, S. D. Houston of the Big Blue district, could not be thus ousted. He had been elected in the first voting. He finally resigned, however, of his own accord, saying that the retention of a seat in such a body was a 'condescension too inglorious for the spirit of an American freeman.'

By that time, Pawnee was no longer the territorial capital. It had lasted as that only four days. The legislators, having accomplished their first aim — unanimity — adjourned. They were tired of cooking over campfires and of having to jump up in the night to seek some kind of shelter from soaking thunderstorms. Reports of death from cholera in the vicinity heightened their homesickness. And they were homesick, according to Mr. Christian — who was one of those rarities, a moderate proslavery man — for Missouri. He upheld the Northern claim that most of these legislators still lived in Missouri, and certainly the place they chose to reconvene was within walking distance of that State. They adjourned to meet again, after ten days, at Shawnee Mission.

Governor Reeder promptly vetoed the resolution to change the place of meeting. Any enactments of the legislature in any place other than Pawnee would be illegal, he said, since 'federally-appointed officers must keep the seat of government where they are best able to attend to their duties and the wants of the Territory.' The legislators passed the resolution over his veto and the federally appointed members of the Territorial

Supreme Court upheld the right of the Legislature to change capitals in mid-session.

This was the last straw for Governor Reeder. His law-makers damned themselves forever with him when, as Senator Robert Toombs of Georgia put it, 'they moved from his town to somebody else's town.' There would be no boom in Pawnee building lots. Reeder had lost a dream of wealth and was to lose the governorship, while his real-estate partner, the commandant of Fort Riley, Major W. R. Montgomery, lost a dream of wealth and his commission in the United States Army. Reeder was never prosecuted, but the major was found guilty of irregu-larities in the purchase of Indian lands and was court-martialed by a board which had as one of its members Lieutenant Colonel Robert E. Lee.

6

False Virtue

NEGRO STEVEDORES that spring and summer carried heavy boxes marked 'books' down the planks of side-wheelers arrived from St. Louis. The boxes went into Kansas City warehouses and, from there, by freight stage to the various learned citizens of Lawrence, K.T., to whom they were addressed.

'Those damn Yankees aim to do a powerful lot of reading.'

'They sure as shootin' do.'

'Sure as *shootin'!*'

Border men had their suspicions. Things had not gone so far that they dared to confirm them by opening freight, but there was no law against saying what you thought. The *Democratic Review* pondered the heaviness of the boxes and said, 'Sharp's rifles are the religious tracts of the new Free Soil System.'

It was true. The boxes marked 'books' were filled with Sharp's rifles, repeating guns, the newest thing in weapons. The Fourth of July entry in Mrs. Robinson's diary describes the presentation of a flag by the ladies of Lawrence 'to the military companies of Lawrence.' And on 22 July she noted, 'The military companies are on drill today.'

As free-soilers prepared for war, their proslavery lawmakers kept at their peaceable task of establishing a code of laws for all to live by. It was a laborious task. They had to go through the whole Missouri code and substitute 'Territory of

Kansas' for 'State of Missouri.' But it was rewarding. By such diligence these young legislators — more than half of them under thirty and most of the others not much older — discovered that the Missouri laws regarding slavery were much too namby-pamby.

They created their own body of law on that vital question: Residents of the Territory of Kansas could be jailed for reading a paper of free-soil sentiment; they could lose their vote by refusing to take the oath supporting the Fugitive Slave Law, their property for questioning the right of slaveholding, and their lives for aiding a slave to escape.

A rigorous code — and the governor of the Territory could pardon no offense against it.

With both sides so busy, it was a peaceful summer. And it was a wet one. Bright skies would darken as northwest winds drove high-piled thunderheads up over the horizon, flattened and spread them until, with great thrusts of lightning and crashing thunder, they released their drenching burdens. The last week in July was a time of brilliant daytime skies and gentle evening showers. The land burgeoned and fruited. Corn stalks on the Big Blue bottoms shot up to more than three times a man's height. Sweet-meated melons, cantaloupes, and tomatoes were brought to market by those settlers who had found time to plant and tend gardens. Apples had been on the market nearly all month, Mrs. Robinson said, and vines in the wooded ravines were purple with early ripening grapes, not so sweet as those that would ripen in October, but welcome. And to many tongues there was a taste newcomer, the mandrake, which Mrs. Robinson found 'of a pleasant flavor but quite medicinal.' One woman and two of her four children died of eating too freely of this strange fruit. It produced an effect like that of cholera, which was sweeping the countryside that summer, making the cemeteries in some areas grow faster than the towns.

The green, rich land gave forth its fruits while its divided household quietly drew more sharply the lines of division.

'General' Ben Stringfellow, one lawyer who stayed out of Kansas Territory, though he never let that dull his interest in affairs there, looked at the work his brother, Doctor John, had done as Speaker of K.T.'s House of Representatives, and wrote the *Montgomery (Alabama) Register* to say: 'They now have laws more efficient to protect slave property than any State in the Union. These laws have just taken effect, and have already silenced the Abolitionists; for, in spite of their heretofore boasting, they know they will be enforced to the very letter and with utmost vigor. Not only is it profitable for slave holders to go to Kansas, but politically it is all-important.'

The General's enthusiasm over proslavery progress in the new Territory prevailed in the border counties, as free-soilers prepared to give resistance. At a convention of the new Free State Party in mid-August, a time was set for the election of delegates to a constitutional convention to be held at the new town of Topeka on the nineteenth of September. And there would be a preliminary conclave at Big Springs on the fifth, at which the groundwork would be laid for applying to Congress for the admission of Kansas as a free state.

While gloating Southerners sweated and toiled over the transplanting of Missouri law to Kansas Territory, their Northern mates prepared to act as if these lawmakers were nonexistent or there illegally, since the Missouri Compromise had not, in so many words, been repealed.

7

'A Bloody Issue!'

ON THE FIRST DAY of September 1855, the second governor of
Kansas Territory, Wilson Shannon of Ohio, arrived to take
over his duties from Daniel Woodson who, as Secretary of State,
had acted as governor and signed the laws the Legislature had
passed.

Governor Shannon was welcomed by Stringfellow who was
at once doctor, editor, agitator, and Speaker of the House. He
was welcomed to 'the land where the gentle pressure of the hand
attests the warm welcome of the heart.' He was assured, 'Here
no Catalines abound. There are no lean and hungry Italians
with their treacherous smiles, no cowards with their stilettos, no
assassins of reputation. Yes, here, Your Excellency, the morning prayer is heard on every hill, the evening orison is chanted
in every valley and glen.'

Up in Stringfellow's town of Atchison, two weeks
before, a man of the cloth, a Reverend Pardee Butler, had
arrived in town with, as Stringfellow's *Squatter Sovereign* surmised, 'a view of starting for the East, probably for the purpose
of getting a fresh supply of Free-Soilers from the penitentiaries
and pestholes of the Northern States.' Butler had 'gone about
town preaching the foulest sort of Abolitionist heresies,' and,
with more courage than sense, he had refused to sign a memorial
to a border bully who had soundly thrashed free-soiler J. W. B.
Kelley. For these offenses, he was escorted out of town by a
committee of citizens, who painted an 'R' (for Republican) on

his forehead, lashed him to a two-pole cottonwood raft, and shoved him out into the current of the Missouri to the sound of dire threats should he live and dare to return.

Jailed in Leavenworth was free-soiler Cole McCrea for killing proslavery Malcolm Clarke. And in Lawrence, Hickory Point, and Kickapoo; in Tecumseh, Black Jack, and Easton; in Osawatomie and Trading Post, as in Atchison and Leavenworth, mouths that owners insisted on opening were daily closed with fists. The bright Kansas sun was forever glinting on brandished arms and the blue air was made bluer still with oaths and threats.

'I come amongst you not as a mere adventurer to better his fortune, then return home,' said the new governor, accepting the gentle welcome proffered. 'I come as one desiring for himself and family a permanent location.'

In 1855, Wilson Shannon?

Clouds, flat-bottomed billows of white, floated lazily in a sky more azure than other skies, to make a moving pattern of sunlight and shadow on a lovely land. The music of hay cutters rose from the bottomlands as mowing blades cut swatches through grass more than head high and tasseled with red blossoms. The white, arched sail of the prairie schooner was set to a westward course on trails that radiated from Missouri's border ports; and the clear air carried the rhythmic sound of hammers raising homes and stores, hotels and livery stables. Shake cabins, thatched and airy. Mud huts, cottonwood roofed, and log cabins. Frame houses from home-milled lumber and houses of native limestone, beamed with black walnut thick as a man's body. All set on rich land and each of them, for some squatter, home.

The land did have the look and sound of peace, Wilson Shannon, but the things you heard rumored and dismissed as exaggerations were true — first stirrings of a long and violent labor.

II

THE PLACE Big Springs, a four-cabin trading-post stop on the California Road west of Lawrence; the time, 5 September 1855.

Split-log benches were filled. Every tree had its leaner. Free-soil delegates and onlookers had come in spring wagons, lumber wagons, carts, in rockaways and buggies, on horseback, muleback, and afoot. They had come to devise such measures and means as would, in their opinion, best serve the free-soil cause and their own interests.

The leaders had drawn up certain resolutions and were now set to railroad their program through. The proslavery Territorial Legislature had been tagged as 'bogus' at the Fourth of July meeting, decried as that at the August powwow, and now, in September, it was to be openly defied. These free-soilers were determined to set up their own legislature, make their own laws to break.

They were not abolitionists. They denied that charge as 'stale and ridiculous,' disavowed all sympathy with that fanaticism. The South was welcome to her institutions, they said, as long as she kept them within the borders of her states. The simple fact was that these free-soil squatters, working single-handed, had no desire to compete with large holdings using slave labor. Their true feeling for the poor, downtrodden black was reflected in their almost unanimous acceptance of Jim Lane's Black Law.

This free-soil leader, James H. Lane, ex-congressman and Indiana Democrat, had come to Kansas that spring saying he would 'just as soon buy a nigger as a mule.' He had been convinced that Kansas would be slave until he tried to organize the Democratic Party in Kansas, with no success. 'Lane's interest in feeble minorities was very slight,' said a later historian, 'and soon he found his way to the opposition benches.'

He was very much at home 'on the opposition benches' by the time of the Big Springs convention. He sat with his wiry length slumped and sprawled, a perfect specimen of *chameleon politico*. Those interested in the species should study this man, not only as he sat on this day in homespun breeches, buffalo boots, and cowhide vest, hide side out — all so casually frontier and all so carefully chosen as that — but also they should go with him later on his money-raising missions back East, to see

him sit, in impeccable black broadcloth and high white stock,
sipping tea as he bemoaned the fate of the poor black with the
good women of Boston and Providence. 'I never knew a man,
who, when with good men and in refined surroundings, was so
powerfully and wholly under his mother's teachings,' wrote the
Reverend H. D. Fisher, adding, 'In the company of politicians,
his Scotch-Irish pater politician's example lead him and he often
fell into censurable mirthfulness and conversation,' or, as J. M.
Hubbard, who served as a solicitor under him, put it, 'Lane was
by nature an actor.'

Jim Lane had only to rise and slouch forward on the
platform, close his eyes, take a deep chaw on his tobacco, and
spit, preparatory to speaking, to cause an outbreak of stamping
and applause. His audiences always knew they were in for a
show when Jim Lane uncoiled his thin, wiry length — a show
of shout and whisper, of spellbinding, if unreportable, oratory.

There is no record of what he said at Big Springs on
5 September 1855, but it is a matter of record that when he
finished only one of the 100 delegates rose to vote against this
spellbinder's Black Law. Ninety-nine out of 100 free-soil delegates voted that no Negro, slave or free, was ever to live within
the bounds of Kansas when she became a state.

It was no hurdle of conscience for these Americans to ban
the Negro. Massachusetts early had passed a law to discourage
free blacks from residing there, as had other Northern states.
And Eli Thayer, years after the Civil War, applauded the
cleverness of the Free State Party in endorsing Lane's Black
Law — it won so many 'poor whites' to the Free State banner,
he said.

It was a matter of defying the Government of the United
States that struck the first jangling note in the Big Springs
harmony.

A committee appointed to consider a resolution to set up
a free-soil government independent of the federally recognized
proslavery Legislature recommended that the resolution be
killed as untimely and inexpedient.

'Untimely and inexpedient!' a delegate rose to shout. 'As

well say it is untimely and inexpedient for a man to load his
gun when wolves prowl at his door.'

Delegates who agreed with the committee tried to be heard,
but caution has little appeal. A fiery address by ex-Governor
Reeder, who had returned to the Territory with the express goal
of becoming its delegate to Congress on the Free State ticket,
was more to the convention's taste. There were cheers when he
denounced the Territory's legal government as 'the monstrous
consummation of an act of violence, usurpation, and fraud.'
There were more cheers when he said, 'We owe no allegiance or
obedience to the tyrannical enactments of this spurious legislature.' His hour-long speech was split by applause. The resolutions he had written said, 'Whenever peaceful remedies shall
fail and forcible measures shall furnish any reasonable prospect
of success, then let our now shrinking and reluctant hostility be
pushed to a bloody issue!' And it was on such a note that Reeder
ended his speech.

A long deep silence was suddenly shattered with cries.

'Yes, we will strike!'

'White men can never be slaves!'

'Reeder! Reeder!'

'Nine cheers for Reeder and right!'

The Free State Party of the Territory of Kansas resolved
to ignore the enactments of its Territorial Legislature, to set
up its own lawmaking body, and to elect its own delegate to the
United States Congress. The candidate for this office, unanimously chosen, was Andrew H. Reeder, who certainly had ut-
tered one of the most reverberating phrases in history — words
that were to resound for years through the halls of a Congress
which, unable to solve the slavery-veiled economic issues threatening the Union, was striving to keep the opposing forces in
check and balance.

The political fuel that the industrial North had made of
the Missouri ballot invasion of Kansas Territory was nothing
compared to the fire that the agricultural South was to feed with
that 'bloody issue' phrase. It was to take years to exhaust the
oratorical possibilities that Stephen A. Douglas set in motion

with his blast against 'those daring revolutionists in Kansas who plot to overthrow by force the system of law under which they live.'

The South, in its fervor, had gone to one extreme; the North, in its fervor, now went to another. Flint had struck flint and the long powder trail to civil war was lit.

8

The Spark and the Tinder

IT WAS INDIAN SUMMER and the sky lay on the land, so full of light that it hazed the gold, the yellows, the flaming reds, the gleaming bronzes of autumn and painted a paisley landscape. Bittersweet tongued red in the woodlands, where walking was made hazardous by the browning husks of black walnuts and slick little hickories popped from their burs.

Prairie fires burned day and night. 'A grand and sublime sight' to Mrs. Robinson, who said they looked 'like a sea of flame when the fiery billows surge and dash fearfully; or, when the winds are still, like an unruffled, quiet burning lake.'

Rains came and there was a chill spell, then bright warmth again.

That was the weather that busy fall, uneventful in its early stages, with only one killing — a free-soiler named Collins by a free-soil turncoat, Pat Laughlin.

Southerners took a breather after their strenuous legislative labors, but Northerners, assembled in convention, spent a good two weeks working out a constitution.

They met in Topeka and though there was a clash of politics between the conservatives, headquartered at the Garvey House, and the radicals, at Chase House, there was only one near duel and that over a private matter. James H. Lane challenged G. P. Lowry for repeating a scandal about himself and a Mrs. Lindsay. The *Kansas Free State* claimed the convention made Lane its president 'in order to counteract the effect of a true report that was abroad that might injure him.' The *Free State* quoted Lane as saying he 'would rather sink in hell than be defeated' and commented, 'we are rather afraid he will "sink" anyhow, notwithstanding his success.'

Whatever the *Free State's* opinion, Lane dominated the convention, got his Black Law written into the Topeka Constitution as a resolution requiring the first legislature of Kansas State to exclude all Negroes from Kansas. And he defeated a proposal to admit to citizenship 'Indians who conform to the habits of the whites.' One delegate called this a 'singular basis for elective franchise' and suggested that 'the capacity to drink a pint of raw whiskey might be deemed an evidence of conforming.'

The *New York Tribune's* William Phillips reported how votes were secured for the Black Law resolution:

One man would buttonhole another. 'Look here — this black law is a great thing,' he would say. 'They accuse us Kansas folks of being abolitionists. Now we ain't abolitionists, are we?'

'No, *sir!*'

'No, sir—ee. So the thing to do is to vote for the black law and that will prove we're not.'

One of the strongest Black Law men was Reverend J. M. Tutton, who carried a long Western rifle at all times and was 'generally down on anything he pleased to consider abolitionism,' Phillips said. 'He was, singularly enough, opposed to allowing slave owners more than a year to take their slaves from the territory, declaring, "I kem to Kansas to live in a free state and I don't want niggers a-trampin' over my grave!" '

The Topeka convention set 15 December as the date for submission of its constitution to the people and 4 March 1856 as the time when a 'State' government would be set up under that constitution. Then it adjourned.

The South's answer to this defiance of the Territorial government, which it controlled, was a meeting in Leavenworth to which 'all lovers of law and order' were invited.

Governor Wilson Shannon consented to preside. 'The President,' he said, opening the meeting, 'is behind you.'

Under that high aegis, the Topeka constitutional convention — 'a farce had it not been treasonable' — was roundly condemned, and a Law and Order Party was formed to combat the Free State Party. 'I'd rather be a painted slave over in Missouri or a serf to the Czar of Russia than to have abolitionists in power!' cried the Territory's surveyor general, John C. Calhoun, a distantly related namesake of the great statesman. And that meeting adjourned.

If Governor Shannon had had any friends among freesoilers, his presence at the Leavenworth meeting would have lost them.

Free-soilers, particularly those of the New England Aid Society stripe, liked to picture him as an imbibing, pusillanimous weakling. 'Had Governor Shannon been a good disciple of temperance, he would in all probability have been a much better or much worse governor,' commented William Phillips, a reporter as given to editorializing as his famous editor, Horace Greeley.

It was true that Wilson Shannon was not an abstemious man; true, too, that the people of Missouri in cheering his arrival to take up the governorship had, as Mrs. Robinson told her diary, 'expressed their joy that their tool was true.' But the fact that proslavery enthusiasm for him was soon to cool tends to bear out such unprejudiced judgments of the man as those of George Brewerton, self-styled 'war correspondent' for the *New York Herald*, and the historian Leverett Spring. Brewerton found Shannon 'in his anxieties for the best good of Kansas, a very single-hearted man,' and Spring, an objective Northerner, described Shannon as 'genial, companionable, his sympathies and instincts naturally gravitating toward whatever is just and honorable.'

Wilson Shannon, 'a lawyer of good repute,' was a native Ohioan and an unwavering Democrat who had served his state as its governor and representative to Congress, his country as minister to Mexico. He began his career in Kansas Territory by taking his stand with the recognized legal government, however rabidly partisan its legislative enactments. He was, in short, a man who, as Brewerton put it, 'was about to find himself in a devil of a mess.'

II

As THANKSGIVING, 1855, approached, most of the Territory's settlers were still not much concerned with the issues involved in its settlement. Tariff was a word used by congressmen and the institution of slavery was, like the Calvinist creed, something you either did or did not believe in — you might argue your point of view until you were blue in the face, but it was nothing to kill a man over, unless it got mixed up with something more fundamental, like a claim dispute.

If Franklin Coleman had been born in New York state, rather than Virginia, chances are Jacob Branson and his boarder, Charles Dow, would have figured he had as much right as they to jump a bit of the large tract of land an Indiana syndicate had staked at Hickory Point. As it was, there was much bad blood between them. Threats and guns were brandished whenever these men met; then one day, free-soiler Dow took a swing at proslavery Coleman 'with a wagon skein' and got a fatal load of lead in return.

It was a shot that shook the whole community, and was to shake the Nation. Squatter disputes were common enough and this was not the first that had brought sudden death. This one just happened to strike fire.

Hickory Point appeared, to men expert at despoliation, to hold great promise. It was a great grove of hardwood in a land hard pressed for building materials. Missourians had known of this place because Palmyra, at the southern tip of the grove, was on the Santa Fe Trail, and a few dozen serious settlers had brought their families there. Lawrence, however, lay only ten miles to the north and free-soil settlers soon predominated. The local chapter of the secret Kansas Regulators, commanded by the elderly Branson, was strong there and some members considered it their mission in life to badger proslavery families. At the time of the Dow killing, there were some hundred free-soil men in the community and fifteen or twenty pro-slave families. Some Southerners had already gone back to Missouri, where their brightly embroidered stories were relished by the fiery bordermen, who were waiting some pretext to march into Kansas Territory to settle the question of who was to be boss there once and for all.

The Dow killing was to provide the pretext.

The shooting took place on Wednesday, 21 November 1855.

No move was made by Samuel J. Jones, Sheriff of Douglas County, K.T., to arrest the murderer. This may have been a deliberate prod to free-soil emotions; it may have been in simple keeping of territorial custom, since there had been numerous killings and few arrests; or perhaps the strongly proslavery Mr. Jones was just too busy with his duties as postmaster of West-port, Missouri, at the time, to attend to his territorial police duties. Whatever the cause, his ignoring of the murder angered free-soilers. They gathered in knots on the streets of Palmyra and Lawrence and talked of taking steps. They were determined that Coleman should hang.

This made Coleman nervous and he fled the community. Leaving his wife and two children to the care of his proslavery neighbors, Harrison Buckley and Josiah Hargis, he went to Shawnee Mission to give himself up to Governor Shannon. He had killed, he said, in self-defense and was willing to stand trial.

This enraged free-soil men. They felt that Coleman had gone to the governor to seek his protection. And on Saturday night they took things in their own hands. Some seventy-five horsemen rode south from Lawrence.

The pound of hooves became hard and plain to the men, women, and children who had gathered in the cabin of Josiah Hargis to find such feeling of safety as they could in companionship, for they had been warned of this visit from free-soilers.

There was the pound of hooves, a sudden halt, a silence.

Then the men inside heard their names called. There was no choice but to go outside.

The spokesman addressed Buckley. 'We want to know what testimony you plan to give at Coleman's trial,' he said.

Harrison Buckley said he would testify that Coleman killed Dow in self-defense.

The spokesman said that was a lie and he turned to Hargis. 'Dow was unarmed, wasn't he, Hargis?'

"I say the same as Harrison Buckley,' Hargis said.

There was a silence broken only by the click of thumbs pulling back gun hammers.

Finally, the free-soil leader spoke again. 'What you say is false,' he said. 'The circumstances are not so. We will give you until Monday to decide to make a correct statement. If you refuse, we will kill you.'

The threatened men knew that violence has the impatience of passion and they set out that night to take their families back to Missouri. And on Sunday afternoon, the free-soilers did return.

When they found that the threatened men had fled, they chose a small committee to name a secret vigilante committee of twenty-five 'to ferret out and bring the murderers and their accomplices to condign punishment.' A proposition to burn Coleman's cabin and other proslave homes was voted down. But two of the men who favored burning out the Southerners crawled through the fence and went to Coleman's cabin.

'One of the men clubbed his Sharp's rifle and burst open the door; they then set fire to some articles inside,' Albert Bercaw, one of the naming committee, later told Brewerton of the *New York Herald*. When smoke came from the house, the men who had opposed the action rushed forward to put the fire out.

But that night, the cabin was burned to the ground, as were the homes of Coleman's friends, Buckley and Hargis.

Northerners had destroyed Southern homes, but this shocking news was ignored by the free-soil press. The *Herald of Freedom* did carry a brief item about the burnings, but it ended with the editorial surmise that Southerners had set the fires to arouse sympathy for their cause and to give pretext for further violence.

Some free-soilers even accused Buckley and Hargis of setting the fires, though Hargis reported that all his worldly belongings had been lost. It is likely, however, that both men saw the flames of their burning homes light the skies, for that night they rode as reluctant members of a posse for Sheriff Samuel J. Jones.

They had left their families with relatives in Missouri, then had gone to Shawnee Mission to report the threats that had been made against their lives to Governor Shannon.

Unfortunately, the impetuous young sheriff of Douglas County, K.T., was in the governor's office when they appeared. He had long itched for a pretext to arrest a free-soiler and Buckley's story provided it. When Buckley said that the slain Dow's friend, Jacob Branson, had made repeated threats against his own life, the sheriff was very happy. He made an immediate plan to take Buckley to Lecompton, county seat of Douglas County and new capital for the Territory, to obtain a peace warrant against Branson.

As Sheriff Jones was about to start for Lecompton, with Coleman in custody and Buckley and Hargis accompanying, an express arrived from Hickory Point. The rider had been in the saddle all night and he had come to warn Buckley and Hargis not to return to the Hickory Point section, as they would surely be killed. These men changed their minds about wanting Branson arrested, but Jones was not to be thwarted. He promised safe conduct and went to Westport to round up a posse to help keep his promise.

Governor Shannon watched the posse ride off, with great misgivings, he told George Brewerton of the *New York Herald*. He was not surprised to learn later that Branson, dragged from his bed to submit to arrest, had been rescued from the sheriff's posse by free-soilers.

Jones's story was that he and his posse had been set upon at Blanton's Bridge by a mob of fifty men armed with Sharp's rifles. But Captain J. B. Abbott — the man who had put out the first flames in Coleman's house and who, with Samuel N. Wood, led the Branson rescue party — said their company was comprised of only fifteen men and that they had defeated the sheriff with surprise and a volley of words.

The governor did not care which version was correct. By the time he had heard them, Jones had started the thing he wanted most in the world — an organized march on Lawrence.

III

LEAVENWORTH WAS often noisy late at night when bartenders took it into their heads to go to bed and turned their customers out, but never had there been such a hubbub as there was in the early hours of the day that was Thanksgiving Day over in the States. The streets were full of men that morning of 29 November. The air was full of excitement. Campfires and torchlights filled the night with light.

These were self-enlisted troops and there was little of military order about their bivouacking.

News of the Branson arrest and rescue had reached Missouri.

The jubilant Jones, whose avowed ambition was to 'corral all the abolitionists and make pets of them,' had sent couriers to his home state before he communicated with the territorial governor, and bordermen had responded quickly, as if they had been sitting their horses awaiting a summons. All along the road to Lawrence were such bivouacs on this night, two days after the Branson rescue.

'I'm agoin' and my boy's agoin' too,' one old fellow said. 'See this,' and he held an ancient flintlock to the light of the campfire for all to admire. 'This hyar old flintlock was carried by my pa through the dark days of the Revolution, the days that tried men's souls, as I heard one chap say when he was a-makin' a stump speech down in Arkansaw. But I'll be goddamned — yes, I'll be golderned, sir, if ever she was carried in a better cause than this one.'

Jones knew he could count on the bordermen. He did not bother to communicate with Governor Shannon until one of his men, a proslavery man from Iowa, persuaded him to do it.

'We're the Law and Order Party and having got right, we want to keep right,' this man said. 'You ought to have sent your dispatch to the governor and asked him to give you men.'

'Damn the governor,' the sheriff is reported to have said.

'The governor has pledged to support the laws and he is the person to apply to,' the sheriff's deputy insisted. 'He could call out the militia.'

'Where's the militia?' Jones asked.

There was no answer to this question, for though the Territorial Legislature had rewarded certain prominent proslavery men with general rank, no militia had been organized.

But Jones did decide to send a communique to the governor. He exaggerated the incident of free-soil interference and asked for 'a posse of three thousand men to carry out the laws' — a sheriff's dream posse and it was to come close to materialization.

Governor Shannon issued orders to his generals. William P. Richardson, commander of the Northern Division of the Territorial Militia, received an order at his home in Doniphan County to collect as large a force as possible and to move 'with all practical speed' to Lecompton, and his brigadier, H. J. Strickler of Tecumseh, was given temporary command of the general-less Southern Division and ordered to establish headquarters on the Wakarusa.

'I felt I must either furnish Sheriff Jones with a sufficient posse to carry out his instructions or be forced into the disgraceful alternative of surrendering the Territorial government into the hands of an armed and lawless mob,' Governor Shannon told Brewerton. 'I presumed, as a matter of course, and intended, that all these men should be drawn entirely from the citizens subject to militia duty in Kansas Territory. As the seat of the difficulties is some forty miles distant from the State line of Missouri, it never occurred to me that the citizens of that

State would cross into Kansas or volunteer their aid to carry out her laws.'

This was Wilson Shannon's first brush with border tactics and, since he did not know about Sheriff Jones's appeal to Missouri bordermen, he had to find an explanation for the great influx of armed Missourians. Though millions of dollars were invested in slaves in the border counties and though some slaves had already been run off by abolitionists, Wilson Shannon felt that 'the mere pecuniary consideration was the least exciting motive' in causing Missourians to join the posse.

'Their feelings had been worked upon; they had listened to stories of men, women and children who had fled from homes in Kansas, made desolate by the threatened and actual violence of the Free State Party,' he told Brewerton. 'Even granted that these stories were exaggerated by the fancy and indignation of their narrators, there was still enough of truth in their representations to excite a smouldering fire of wrath, which only required some new act of outrage to fan it into an unextinguishable flame; and this came at length in the reports from the town of Lawrence.

'The men of Missouri heard that the Territorial laws were set at defiance; that the sheriff of the county — a Virginian, well-known and highly esteemed, and moreover, a strong pro-slavery man — was actually threatened with death by an armed abolition mob; they heard, too, that these outlaws were fortifying themselves, drilling by day and night, were sending to distant states for men, were amply supplied with the most deadly weapons which modern skill has devised, and even provided with artillery. They knew, too, that this was no disturbance born of transient excitement and nurtured by the passions of the hour. On the contrary, it was understood to be a cold-blooded, long-foreseen, and carefully prepared for thing.

'And what was the most natural result? The gathering in the camp at Wakarusa may be the best answer to that question.' And the governor, puzzled despite his explanation, shook his head. 'They would come; it was impossible to prevent them, so to mitigate an evil I could not suppress, I have ordered these excited and irregular forces incorporated into the organized military commands.'

His problem, he was soon to find, was to control the commanders.

9

'The Wakarusa War'

ON THE FIRST DAY of December 1855, the governor of the
Territory of Kansas drove across the border to the new tele-
graph office at Kansas City to send a telegram to the President
of the United States. He wanted authority to call upon Colonel
Edwin V. Sumner, commanding the First Cavalry at Fort
Leavenworth, for federal military aid 'to protect the Sheriff of
Douglas County in executing the laws and preserving the peace
and good order in the Territory.'

He sent the telegram and, at the same time, dispatched a
rider to inform Colonel Sumner of his request, so the Colonel
would prepare to march with his dragoons.

The situation on that Saturday, four days after the Branson rescue, looked bad. The sheriff's posse, gathered in two
camps near Lawrence — at Lecompton, ten or so miles to the
northwest, and on the Wakarusa, six miles to the southeast —
had swelled to a 1500-man strength. And a like number of free-
soilers were reported gathered in the offending town, well-armed
and prepared to resist any attempt of the sheriff to enter town
to make arrests.

That this might be the beginning of civil war was Governor
Shannon's fear. He believed the Free State Party to be wrong
in attempting to set up its own government and laws in defiance of the constituted Territorial government, but he wanted
to establish the Territorial laws without bloodshed. To do that,

the sheriff would have to have so superior a force that the free-
soilers would not dare resist it. Hence the appeal to the President.

The governor was beset with anxiety when he learned that
his message had been delayed because telegraph wires were down
between Lexington, Missouri, and Jefferson City. He was won-
dering what move to make next when an express came from
Colonel Sumner saying he stood ready to move immediately
upon receipt of orders. Encouraged by this, Shannon dispatched an order to Sheriff Jones to wait for federal help before
attempting to serve his writs. 'This will save any effusion of
blood,' Shannon wrote. 'And it may be a moral influence hereafter, which would prevent any farther resistance to the law;
for when these lawless men find that the forces of the United
States can be used to preserve order, they will not be so ready
to adopt an opposing course.'

The governor was slow to realize that his objective was
not that of the sheriff nor of the Law and Order Party men who
comprised his posse. They wanted to wipe 'that abolitionist
sinkhole,' Lawrence, off the map. 'We mean to have Kansas,'
a border captain told Phillips of the *Tribune*. 'And we are going
to have it, if we have to wade through blood to our knees to get
it.'

The underlying free-soil attitude was also warlike. At the
first meeting after the Branson rescue, Sam Wood, sword belted
to waist, had presided and the men assembled had resolved that
no officer under the Bogus Legislature would be allowed to make
arrests in Lawrence. But clear-headed, cold-eyed Charles
Robinson persuaded free-soilers to a public attitude of non-
resistance. Any action 'with regard to the Bogus laws' should
be left to individual citizens, he said. There should be no general
resistance except in the case of an attack upon their town, and
their strategy should be to give the proslavery forces no apology
for making an attack. Convinced, free-soilers named Robinson
secret commanding general of the spurious Free State Militia,
Chairman of the Safety Committee, thus giving him a title to
put on their memorial to Congress. Citizens of Lawrence de-

clared to the world that they were organizing a force for protection only.

The free-soil tactic was to establish free-soilers as right in the eyes of the nation. Strict orders were never to fire except in extreme emergency. 'If the Missourians, partly from fear and partly from want of pretext, have to go back without striking a blow, it will make them a laughing stock and will redound fearfully against Shannon,' General Robinson told his troops on Saturday night, adding, 'This is the last struggle between freedom and slavery and we must not flatter ourselves that it will be trivial or short.'

II

SUNDAY WAS the day free-soilers expected attack. It was the day, too, that Jones received the governor's order to wait for federal aid. But it was not this order that held the sheriff and his restive posse that day. It was a more potent force — fear of defeat.

The garrison at Lawrence — variously reported at every figure from five hundred to fifteen hundred men — drilled daily and toiled ceaselessly, day and night, building defenses. But neither numbers nor defensive effort gave pause to the bordermen, for the most amateur eye could see that the town's position was indefensible. It stood on an open prairie which sloped to the belt of timber that marked the course of the Kaw, and it was commanded to the west by a bluff which rose precipitously from the town, yet sloped gently to the country approaching. A portion of the bluff's crest was, Brewerton said, 'within five hundred yards — a very neat distance for artillery practice — of the circular forts and earthworks it overlooks.' In addition, a ravine deep enough to cover the approach of troops for a night attack led almost into town from a southerly direction.

The free-soilers were sitting pigeons and the favorite boast of any Border Ruffian was that he could 'scream louder, jump higher, shoot closer, get drunker at night and wake up soberer in the morning than any man this side of the Rocky Mountains.'

A hitch of the britches, then, and some such challenge as, 'I'm easy to whip, I am. Just pitch in, stranger, and don't stand on ceremony.'

Bravado, but it could be backed with lightning action, with flashing Bowie knives quickly unsheathed from boot tops, with quick-drawn Austin pistols, well-aimed Jake Hawkin rifles. The trouble was that such talk could be backed only with these anti-quated arms.

These were men of arms. They never spoke of a weapon without using its given name. It was not fear of men but fear of a weapon that kept them from 'running up the black flag' as a signal for mutiny against the inaction of their leaders. The only thing that held the bordermen was a profound respect for the Sharp's rifle.

'Look here, stranger, did you ever see any of them Sharp's rifles?' a Missourian asked reporter Phillips when he met up with a party of new arrivals and gained their confidence, as he says, by posing as an Illinois sucker.

'Yes, I've seen them,' Phillips said.

'What sort of fixin' are they?'

'Terrible gun,' said Phillips.

'They say they kin load 'em ten times a minute — 's that so?'

'Expect it is.'

'Well, how in thunder kin they do it?'

'It's done by machinery,' Phillips said mysteriously.

'Is it a revolvin' fixin'?' the youngest of the party asked.

'Not exactly.'

'Well, how fur kin they carry?'

'Oh well, I don't believe all the stories they tell of them,' Phillips said. 'Indeed, I am confident they cannot carry a ball with any degree of accuracy for more than a mile, that is, to do close shooting.'

The men looked so anxious at this coolly imparted exagger-ation that Phillips found it hard to suppress a smile. This kind of information could do more than forts to protect Lawrence, and this free-soil partisan knew it. He had heard early arrivals at the camp on the Wakarusa talking about the Sharp's rifle as they rigged their buffalo-robe-draped wagons and their make-shift tents.

Southern guards stood at the shallow ford of the creek, so Phillips had crossed below, tied his horse to a tree, and walked into the camp to listen.

'Look here,' he heard a determined-looking fellow in buck-skin breeches and a red flannel shirt say. 'Look here, if them infernal Yankees should take it into their heads to come down here, we would be in a darned nice scrape.'

'Pshaw!' said another. 'We could use up a nation of them white-livered Yankees.'

'Not so fast, Tom,' said a third. 'If a thousand of them fel-lows was to come down here with them infernal guns of theirn they'd make this patch pretty hot, I tell you.'

This kind of talk was keeping the Border Ruffians in check. There was no attack Sunday. There was no attack Monday. And on Tuesday, 4 December, Charles Robinson wrote to Amos Law-rence, in Boston: 'I have only time to thank you and your friends who sent us the Sharp's rifles, for they will give us vic-tory without firing a shot.'

That was the day Governor Wilson Shannon finally heard from President Franklin Pierce. The President promised fed-eral troops as soon as the proper orders could be made out by Secretary of War Jefferson Davis — a heartening piece of news that the governor passed on to Colonel Sumner. And early next day, the colonel answered: 'I will march with my regiment in a few hours and will meet you at the Delaware Crossing of the Kansas this evening.'

This put the governor in a cheerful frame of mind, but as he was dressing — in the 20 by 20 room that served as guber-natorial mansion and offices — an express arrived from Sheriff Jones.

The rider found the governor putting on his boots, as he sat on a box at the foot of his curled maple four-poster, flanked by a half-gallon bottle of Marquand ink and an old pair of breeches. The governor took the sheriff's dispatch and opened it.

'The volunteer forces, now at this place, are growing weary of inaction,' Jones wrote. 'They will, I presume, remain but a very short time longer, unless a demand for the prisoner is made.' The force in Lawrence was 'not half as strong as reported,' he had learned, and he felt he would have sufficient protection to go in and make his arrest 'on the morrow.' This he intended to do, though he had no wish, he said, to violate the governor's orders.

'This is the morrow!' Shannon exclaimed and, though only half-booted, he went to stand with his back to the rusty, incapable stove. He told the sheriff's rider and his son, who was also his secretary, of the contents of the sheriff's message. Should he wait to meet Sumner, or should he start at once? Would there be any use of his arriving without the federal dragoons?

While he was debating, two men from Lawrence arrived. G. P. Lowry and C. W. Babcock had been sent by the Committee of Safety to appeal for the governor's aid. The city of Lawrence, they said, was no more responsible for the rescue of Branson from the sheriff's posse than it was 'for the procession of the equinoxes.' The rescue had been the action of a handful of men, most of whom were not residents of Lawrence.

'But they are there now,' the governor said, as he rummaged through a pile of old newspapers on the big table that served as his desk and dining table to find the September fifteenth issue of the *Herald of Freedom*. He asked them to read again the Big Springs resolutions and his big forefinger moved for their eyes to follow: 'We owe no obedience to the tyrannical enactments of this spurious legislature . . . will resist them to a bloody issue as soon as we ascertain that peaceable remedies shall fail . . . !' And the governor told the emissaries that he would never have authorized the sheriff's posse had he not believed that the Branson rescue was the commencement of a planned defiance of the Territory's law.

The free-soilers countered with an account of their conduct under the current provocative conditions. They pointed out how their sentries had been fired upon, night after night, and though one free-soiler had had his horse shot out from under him and another had got a bullet hole in his hat, not one shot had been returned. And then they told of an encounter that Phillips of the *Tribune* had had with Sheriff Jones, who mistook him for a scared Yankee on his way back East. Jones, they said, had called all men in Lawrence traitors and had said the town should and would be wiped out. And when Phillips protested that an attack on the place would lead to a war that would endanger the Union, Jones had said, 'Damn the Union. We have gone in for peace long enough. We've got to fight sometime and it might as well be now.'

Governor Shannon was visibly shocked by this report. He assured the free-soilers that his only objective was a peaceful settlement of the difficulties. And they rode westward, impressed with the governor's sincerity and feeling their mission had been successful. Lawrence would be relieved to hear that the President had authorized the use of federal troops. Their only problem, then, was how to get back through the Southern lines. That morning they had pretended to be enraged proslavery officers who had caught sentries napping at their posts. Would as successful a dodge come to them again?

The governor, as he watched them ride away, decided that he must not wait to meet Sumner. There was no time to lose. The sheriff and his men must be controlled.

Shannon sent a note of explanation and apology to Colonel Sumner and dispatched riders to the sheriff and to Generals Richardson and Strickler, ordering them to prevent an attack. Then he sought the aid of influential Missourians. He sent an express to Platte City to ask the proslavery leader of the West, David Atchison, to join him at Camp Wakarusa, and he himself drove across the border to Westport to ask Daniel Boone's grandson, Albert Boone, to go along with him in his carriage.

Colonel Boone hastily packed his carpetsack and the peace party set out.

They had not gone far when a federal dragoon overtook them. He had come from Colonel Sumner, and he must have

passed the governor's courier along the way. The colonel wrote
that 'on sober reflection' he had decided not to move until he
received formal orders from Washington.

This was a setback, for certainly if federal troops could be
stationed in Lawrence, no proslavery faction, however fanatical,
would dare attack.

III

GREAT FIRES BURNED in 'The Athens of Free State Kansas,
Sebastapol of the West,' that night, as labor details, by fifties,
took turns plying the spade and mattock to complete the three
great earthern forts, each 100 feet in diameter, which stood at
the town's approaches, and the entrenchments connecting them.
Candles burned in the southeast rooms, third floor, of the ex-
ternally complete Free State Hotel, for this was defense headquarters. Candles burned, too, in the little shake cabin of Sam
Wood, next door, for there the women of the town were making
cartridges, a day and night activity just resumed, now that materials had been secured by a feminine version of Yankee in-
genuity.

'Our scheme was simply this,' Mrs. Wood later told Brewerton of the *Herald*. 'We knew that powder and lead, together
with a considerable quantity of Sharp's rifle caps and cartridges
were deposited with those favorable to our cause at two separate
points on the Santa Fe Trail. It does not matter as to their
particular whereabouts, but it will do no harm to say they were
to be found within ten miles of where we are now seated. Now,
when a woman makes up her mind to do anything, good or bad,
it is already more than half-accomplished . . .

'I wore two dresses and a petticoat, which, though it went
forth lined with wadding, came back charged with what, if I
were inclined to make a pun, might be called excellent *gun-
cotton. . . .*'

Mrs. Wood and her companion, Mrs. George Brown, hid
'a 25-pound keg of prime rifle powder and a quantity of lead'
about their persons, then squeezed into their buggy. Mrs. Wood

'grasped the reins and whipped up old Sally.' The mare started on a run but soon had to settle down to a long, steady trot. They were within a few miles of home when an exclamation from Mrs. Brown caused the driver to look up and 'there, sure enough, were a party of Border Ruffians on horseback, whose dark figures stood out in bold relief against the wintry sky.'

The ladies were tempted to put their mare 'to her speed,' but they decided that the weight they carried would tell sadly against them in 'a race with twenty-odd well-mounted frontiers-men.' They made themselves keep on 'at an easy jog,' even as two horsemen came galloping across the prairie toward them.

The horsemen reined up sharply. They swept off their hats and with deep bows begged the ladies' pardon, assuring them that they would not have given pursuit had they known there were only ladies in the buggy. They were, Mrs. Wood said, 'very nice Ruffians.'

The heroines drove on to their beleaguered city. 'When I saw those wimmin,' a Western free-soil man told Brewerton, 'I just allowed that bustles had come into fashion again, for they were swelled out awful.'

It was a warming tale to tell and retell on that chill night of expected attack. And when Thursday dawned and all was quiet, free-soilers took new heart.

IV

The governor arrived at three o'clock Thursday morning at Bean's Hotel on the Wakarusa. He was relieved that there had been no attack on Wednesday, but his relief lasted little longer than his nap. After breakfast — during which he wrote a note to General Richardson requesting his presence at a conference that evening — he visited General Strickler's Wakarusa Camp. 'I found,' he wrote the President, 'a deep and settled feeling of hostility against the opposing forces in Lawrence and apparently a fixed determination to attack that place and demolish it.'

The majority feeling of the posse was expressed by a big borderman, quoted by Brewerton. He said he did not care 'whether the whisky give out or not' — he had come for a fight and he was bound to have one. Southerners wanted to strike without further delay and they fanned the fires of their wrath with rumor. The Yankees had hauled down the Stars and Stripes and were flying a red flag and, worse still, the Yankees had smuggled a brass howitzer right through the Southern lines, into Lawrence.

The Stars and Stripes still floated over the Free State headquarters, but it was true about the howitzer. A Southern spy had seen it. It had, in fact, been shown to him, after his capture in a Lawrence rifle pit. General Jim Lane, free-soil field commander, had personally conducted the spy on a tour of the town's defenses, then had given him a pass through the free-soil lines. 'Now go back, sir,' he had said, 'and report yourself and tell just what you have seen.'

The spy went back and told, and sentries on the Wakarusa began to sift flour consigned to Lawrence to look for concealed weapons. The howitzer had arrived just that morning, thanks to a couple of Yankee tricks plus some plain Yankee luck.

The proslavery merchant in Kansas City to whom the boxes containing the 12-pounder were consigned had been suspicious when Major Bob Buffum, free-soil farmer posing as a free-soil merchant, came to collect it. 'They say you Lawrence folks are getting all manner of curious traps to wipe out our boys with and I'll jest have a squint into them goods afore they roll out of Kansas City,' the Missourian said.

'Waal, I guess Mister there ain't nothing extra in them,' said the major. 'I don't know for certain, but John Smith says he's expectin' a buggy wagon, along with some other notions, his folks are a-sendin' out from York State, and I shouldn't wonder if it wasn't them. But I guess they might have bought 'em a tarnation sight cheaper in Saint Luie and saved payin' freight, don't you?'

The merchant was not to be put off. He wanted to take a look, so Buffum called for an axe. The major guessed which box held the howitzer wheels and knocked up a corner of the lid. Spokes could be seen dimly, looking far too heavy even in the darkness of the warehouse, but the proslavery merchant must have had poor eyesight. 'Well, I just allow I was a spot too particular this time; so heist them into your wagon, boys, and roll out lively as you please,' he said. 'Jim, you infernal nigger, come here and help these gentlemen pack their plunder.' And he invited the major into his office. 'I've a powerful article of corn whisky in there,' he said.

The heavy howitzer and cases of cannister, grape, shell, and round shot were stowed in the bottom of the big Pennsylvania wagon and tin pails, wicker work, and wooden ware were spread on top. The free-soilers started for home. They knew their only chance lay in taking the little-traveled road north of the Kaw, so they ferried the river at Wyandotte City. The road out of that Indian village was steep and, on that day, it was heavy with mud. The burdened wagon bogged down and Bob Buffum and his two companions could not budge it.

'It was a fix of the darndest kind,' Major Bob told Brewerton. But he had an inspiration. 'Boys, I've hit it,' he said. 'I calculate we've played these Missouri Pukes one real Yankee trick and, tarnation seize 'em, we'll treat them to another. Just wait until some of them nigger-drivin' fellers come this way and see if we don't get all the help we want.'

Buffum picked a dry spot beside the road, squatted on his haunches, and struck up 'Yankee Doodle' to kill time. But he had got just as far as 'Yankee Doodle keep it up, Yankee Doodle dandy; when your 'lasses biles away, you can't expect much candy,' when a party of Lawrence-bound Ruffians came along.

The Yankee major knew that to help push a man's wagon out of the mud was an everyday Western courtesy, so he spotted the leader of this party and drawled, 'Waal now, Kernel, guess you'd let some of your men lend a feller in trouble a helpin' hand, wouldn't you; for I'm stalled down, don't you see?'

A couple of horses were hitched to help the tired mules, and Southern shoulders were put beside Northern shoulders to boost the heavy load out of the mudhole. 'Much obliged, gentlemen, and a good day to you,' said the free-soil major and, as the proslavery volunteers moved on, he grinned at his companions and took up where he had left off: 'Yankee Doodle is a tune Americans delight in . . .'

So the Yankees in Lawrence felt pleased with themselves on Thursday — and hopeful. They did not care for Governor Shannon. He was held in contempt by the puritanical for his reported tippling and by all free-soilers for his seeming partiality to the proslavery cause. Nonetheless, his presence in Wakarusa Camp was reassuring, as was the report that he was to confer with Law and Order Party leaders that evening and would come to Lawrence the next day to confer with Free State Party leaders.

There was hope of peace in the air — until the report came of the death of Thomas Barber.

It did not seem possible to those who had seen him leave town right after the noonday meal . . .

Thomas Barber, his brother Robert, and their brother-in-law, Thomas Pierson, had decided to go see their families in the Bloomington section, about seven miles northwest of Lawrence.

They rode west on the California Road and, just as they came to their turning-off place, a cavalcade of more than a dozen men came in sight. The Barber party guessed them to be General Richardson and his party from Lecompton Camp and they turned onto the Bloomington trail and rode on at a walk. Soon two horsemen cut across the prairie, came into the road ahead of the Barbers, and brought their horses to a stop.

There was a short, stocky man on a gray horse and a tall, slender man on a sorrel. The man on the gray asked the questions and Thomas Barber answered them. He said they had come from Lawrence and that nothing special was going on there.

'We have orders from the governor to see the laws executed in Kansas,' said the man on the gray — Major George Clarke, Indian agent.

'What laws have we disobeyed?' Thomas Barber asked.

'Then, turn your horses heads and come with us.'

Barber shook his head. 'We won't do it.'

'You won't, eh?' said Clarke as he wheeled his horse, drew his pistol, and fired.

Robert Barber drew his Navy Colt and returned fire and Thomas Pierson fumbled in his pantaloon pocket for his small Colt.

There was a quick exchange of shots and the proslavery men rode off.

Thomas said, 'Let's go, boys.' And they rode on, but they had not gone far when Thomas spoke again. 'Boys, they hit me,' he said.

Robert saw his brother hold his hand to his side and reached out a hand to support him. Then suddenly Thomas crumpled and slid from his horse. He was dead when Robert reached him, so Robert and Pierson remounted and rode on home at a fast clip, fearing pursuit.

This is the story as the free-soilers told it, and the story of the proslavery participants differed only in that they claimed the free-soilers had turned from the California Road at a gallop after they had been commanded to halt, and also that the drawing of guns and shooting had been done by both sides at the same time.

A thing that gives credence to the Southern version is that Clarke, on hearing of Barber's death, volunteered a regretful belief that the victim had been the one unarmed man in the party.

From testimony given by both Robert Barber and his brother-in-law, apparently neither Clarke nor his companion, Colonel Burns, knew that they had hit anyone when they rode off, yet the free-soil general's lady, Mrs. Robinson, said in her diary that Clarke greeted the governor when they met at Wakarusa Camp 'with horrid oaths,' saying, 'I've sent another of these damned abolitionists to his winter quarters.'

There is no evidence that Governor Shannon heard about the fatality — called murder by Northerners, war casualty by Southerners — that night. His meeting with the forty-odd leaders of the sheriff's posse was long and stormy. All the Southerners agreed with the governor's objective of 'vindicat-

ing the laws of the Territory.' But that was his second objective.
Few agreed with his first objective, which was 'to prevent the
effusion of blood.'

David Atchison was on the governor's side. 'If you attack
Lawrence now, you attack it as a mob,' he said. 'And what would
be the result? You would cause the election of an abolition president and the ruin of the Democratic Party. Wait a little. You
cannot now destroy these people without losing more than you
would gain.'

But most proslavery leaders, like their men, were so determined to demolish Lawrence that Shannon again drafted a
message to Colonel Sumner, urging him to bring federal troops.
'The absolute pressure of this crisis is such as to justify you
with the President, and the world, in moving with your force
to the scene of difficulties,' he wrote.

The governor's express was to leave at daybreak, but General Strickler — who belonged to the moderate minority which
would settle for a surrender of Eastern gift-arms — learned
that there was a plan afoot to intercept the messenger to Sumner. Proslavery extremists did not want federal interference.

Wilson Shannon gave orders for the rider to set out immediately, though it was two o'clock in the morning. Then he
went uneasily to bed as, over in Lawrence, free-soilers settled
down after an evening of rebellion against their leadership.

A tall, fierce-looking man had come to town a few days before in a wagon bristling with bayonets stuck on poles. With
him were four of his six grown sons, all walking armories, with
broadswords and navy revolvers on their belts and rifles in their
hands.

The man was John Brown, recently come to the Territory.
When he heard of the troubles in Lawrence, he came ' "to draw
a little blood," as he styled it.' He had been kept from acting,
but when the body of Thomas Barber was brought to town on
this night, John Brown almost had his way. It took all the power
'Generals' Robinson and Lane could summon to keep Lawrence's
defense army from attacking the would-be attackers.

10

Exploding Peace Pipe

A TWO-SEATED CARRIAGE drew up in front of the two-story log structure that was Bean's Hotel, and a tall man in a rusty-black frock coat and battered tile climbed into the back seat.

Wilson Shannon, Governor of the Territory of Kansas, was setting out for beleaguered Lawrence to treat of peace.

As the driver gave a flip to the ribbons, his aides — General Strickler of the Territorial Militia and Colonels Boone and Kearney of the visiting Missourians — mounted their horses and fell in behind.

The governor's carriage swayed down into the Wakarusa ravine, forded the creek, and took the road that forked north to Franklin for there, it had been arranged, His Excellency was to be met by an honor guard from Yankee Town.

With horsemen front and rear, then, the governor's equipage moved across the prairie, followed by the hostile eyes of unsatisfied Southerners and watched by the hostile eyes of dissatisfied Northerners.

First Lady of Free-soilism, Mrs. Robinson, looked out from her hillside home at the approaching cavalcade, then turned her eyes to the big Free State Hotel and the lines of soldier citizenry that stood waiting there. 'Can these men, whose murdered comrade now lies within these walls, make peace and he be unavenged?' she asked her diary.

Within those walls, laid out on a table carefully placed for display, was the body of the slain Thomas Barber.

'As the eyes of the governor fell upon his rigid limbs and the death-pallor of the young man who yesterday was so full of life, hope, and strength, he gave a perceptible shrug,' Mrs. Robinson wrote.

She was not present, but Phillips of the *Tribune* was. He was Mrs. Robinson's great friend and as extreme in his free-soil partisanship as she, but he described the governor's reaction as one of shock. 'I could see the weak, vacillating, guilty governor tremble as his eye fell on the silent figure,' he wrote.

What the governor felt or thought, no one knows. Perhaps he thought of the proslavery determination to 'run up the black flag,' and the preparations that were being made for doing it on this day, of the new camps that had been established, one within three miles of Lawrence to the south and one across the Kaw to the north, in order that troops might be thrown at the town's rear as an attack was made from its front. Perhaps he thought of the dead that might be if his peace negotiations should fail, and of how a battle between American citizens here might spark the powder trail to civil war. These may have been the things he thought of as he withdrew his eyes from the silent figure and put his foot on the unfinished stairs that led to free-state headquarters.

With Governor Shannon were 'three very gentlemanly-looking companions,' Phillips wrote, adding, 'These were fine looking Southerners, but I certainly would rather have seen the governor of the Territory come to his people in other company.'

In a long room, on the front of the third floor, these men sat down with Generals Robinson and Lane and their lieutenants at a long planked conference table and began their talks.

Shannon soon saw that the free-soilers would not relinquish their Sharp's rifles, even as a gesture under a promise of return. They claimed these guns were personal property and the governor had no way of knowing for certain that they had been donated to the Free State Militia by Bostonians. He only knew that he felt discouraged, for surrender of these arms was a minimum proslavery demand. If he lost the co-operation of even the moderates in the other camp, there would be little hope of attaining his objective of preventing bloodshed.

The conference came to a deadlock and Robinson took the governor and his party up to the hill to his home for dinner.

'The governor is a grey-haired man, tall and well-proportioned,' his hostess noted. 'He has coarse features and a hard-looking face generally. Nature must take part of the blame, but weather and bad whisky undoubtedly come in for a share. However good height of forehead and mild eyes show that naturally he is not a cruel man, his head lacks firmness, as we speak phrenologically and his course here as elsewhere is evidence that he is vacillating, weak, ill-suited to be the leader of men; that he is credulous and easily made a tool in the hands of base men; that, in brief, he is the exponent of purposes and actions of the men or party with whom he is most in contact.'

Phillips put it this way: 'The free state men wanted to use the governor in the way he had been used by others.' They wanted him to do two things: 'To strip the ruffians below of their cloak of authority' and to authorize free-soilers to defend themselves.

Governor Shannon was not among friends, nor did he return to friends in the proslavery camp. Moreover, there was a note waiting from Colonel Sumner saying he still had not received orders from Washington and would not move without them.

The solution to the crisis lay squarely on Wilson Shannon's own shoulders. He set out early the next morning for Lawrence, prepared to overlook the fact that the people of Lawrence, though they disclaimed any responsibility for the rescue of Branson, had not forced the wanted man and his rescuers to give themselves up to the sheriff, who ostensibly had surrounded their town with his huge posse for the sole purpose of making these arrests.

So Shannon met again with the free-soil leaders.

'A liberal supply of wines and liquors, supplied by the shrewd negotiators, kept the thirsty governor in temper during the proceedings,' wrote the abstemious Phillips, who a few days before had refused a drink proffered by bordermen with a stuffy, 'I never drink,' and had reported the reaction of one Ruffian, who had said, 'That's just it! This thing of temperance and abolitionism and the Emigrant Aid Society are all the same kind of thing.'

Either drink or a simple desire for peace led the governor to accept the view that the free-soil back was up only because a whole community was being held responsible for the actions of a few men. In return, free-soilers pledged themselves 'to aid in the execution of any legal process' against offending citizens. This, the governor felt, satisfied his objective of 'vindicating the laws of the Territory,' and he promised to disband the sheriff's posse.

The treaty signed, Governor Shannon spoke briefly to the people of Lawrence.

He had barely finished when somber John Brown demanded to be heard. He climbed on a dry-goods box, Phillips reported, to say that if he understood the governor's speech right something had been conceded and that the concession was that territorial laws were to be observed. 'Those laws we denounce and spit upon and will never obey!' he cried.

'No! No!'

'Down with the bogus laws!'

'Lead us down to fight first!'

The protest was loud and long. Robinson finally got the crowd's attention. He assured the people that there had been no concession. But after the outburst was quelled, he hastily conferred with the other men who had been present at the treaty table and it was agreed that the treaty should be kept secret. The terms soon leaked out and the lame explanation agreed upon was given. By 'legal process' federal process, not territorial process, was meant, the leaders said. They had no intention of recognizing the enactments of the Bogus Legislature as law.

As John Brown and his boys left town in disgust, the free-soil generals went with the governor to meet with thirteen pro-

slavery captains at Franklin. Shannon told the Southerners that
a misunderstanding had occurred, that the people of Lawrence
had violated no law, that they would not resist any properly
appointed officers in the execution of the laws. He said that their
Sharp's rifles were personal property and they, therefore, refused to surrender them. And he advised the Southerners to disband and go home.

It was not a popular speech, nor was his official order for
disbandment of the sheriff's posse, thereupon issued, a popular
document in the proslavery camp.

'Shannon has played us false!' Dr. John Stringfellow exclaimed, when the news reached Camp Lecompton. 'The Yankees
have tricked us. The Governor of Kansas has disgraced himself
and the whole proslavery party.'

Chances are the proslavery forces would have made an
all-out attack on Lawrence that very night — if it had not
been for the weather. A wind came up with the darkness, a wind
as sharp as new-honed steel. 'It came down with icy keenness,
and driving a snowy sleet,' said Phillips. 'It was a fearful night.
The wind blew almost a hurricane, as it knows how to blow in
Kansas.'

In Wakarusa Camp, men stood around campfires piled
high with logs. 'The wild gale swept the flames and sparks up
through the gnarled limbs of old oaks and walnuts in the
Wakarusa bottoms,' wrote Phillips. Wind blew the flames and
many fires had to be put out as 'cold and more bitter grew the
night.' Shots were fired in all directions, he said, 'the wild noise
being suited to the taste of these border crusaders, and being
partly intended, I suspect, as a sort of intimidation to the
"Yankees," as some fears were entertained that the free state
men would attack their camp, now that they were stripped
of all authority.'

The free-soil leaders, Robinson and Lane, left Franklin
about seven o'clock in the evening and they were forsaken by
their escort almost as soon as they started. They were in enemy
territory, in the black of night. But despite the danger and the
cutting sleet, they felt triumphant. They had outsmarted the

Southerners and the Southerners knew it. Charles Robinson probably felt a special glow when he remembered how he had stood firm against his free-soil captains who had wanted to take Dave Atchison prisoner when scouts reported that that pro-slave leader was crossing the Delaware Reserve with only twenty-five men. It was by such caution that he had forced the influential Atchison into the position of becoming a free-soil ally. For Atchison had had to take the unpopular course of persuading his fellow Southerners that an attack on Lawrence would be suicidal to their cause, since no pretext for an attack had been given.

Robinson and Lane rode homeward, in the chiseling chill of that night, warmed by the thought that they had gained their first objective. The Ruffians had been stripped of their 'cloak of legal authority.' And perhaps it was on that ride that they conceived the trick that was to gain their second objective — getting their own army authorized.

II

SUNDAY, 9 December 1855, was as cold a day as anyone who experienced it could remember.

The governor ordered the Militia generals to take their troops far from the scene of inaction to dismiss them, but this order was not needed. The proslavery men wanted to get home. Add 'to the terrible discomfort of the night, the failure of the whisky supply,' as Mrs. Robinson did, and it is easy to see why. The cold itself was enough to send anyone to cover.

The sheriff's posse straggled homeward, carrying with them their wounded and dead — the fellow who shot himself in the foot, the man killed by a falling tree, the man accidentally killed by his own sentry, and the fellow who lost a fatal barroom argument.

Prisoners on both sides were released. The free-soilers had jailed a few spies, but the bordermen had done right well in capturing suspicious wayfarers. A Dr. Cutler and a Mr. War-ren — taken prisoner at Atchison and found guilty of high treason — were brought the sixty miles to Camp Lecompton. Their prison was the draughty log cabin that served as head-quarters for Sheriff Jones' nightly two-bit poker sessions. And one night Jones, chafing under a twenty-dollar loss, forced in-formation from Warren by saying that he must 'tell or swing.' And two youthful prisoners at Camp Wakarusa told how, on the tempestuous night of 8 December, Ruffians made them hold a blanket to break the wind while they played euchre on a stone close to the fire. But the prize proslave prisoner was Samuel (Pom the Pious) Pomeroy, intercepted on his way back East to raise money, men, and munitions. He was just the sort of holier-than-thou free-soiler whom bordermen could not abide, and so many threats were made against his life that Atchison quartered him with the officers at Blue Jacket's, an inn run by an Indian. Here Pomeroy's life was safe but not his dignity. He had to take a great deal of ribbing about the way he had tried to get through the Missouri lines by posing as a Baptist preacher.

Governor Shannon apparently was much amused by this ruse. On Sunday, when he went into Lawrence to smoke the peace pipe, he was entertained by the free-soil gentry at a dinner at the Cincinnati House. 'Some who were not averse, either by nature or principle, to a social glass, had provided such entertainment for the governor,' wrote Mrs. Robinson. 'Everyone coming in who thus degraded his higher nature, "must drink with the governor." At each glass he drank, he said, "Now, here's to the Baptist preacher." '

Mrs. Robinson was not averse to invented quotations, but her husband was present for part of this party and he probably told her what went on. But when the party was at its height, he left and went to his headquarters in the Free State Hotel.

Not long afterward, Mrs. Robinson answered a knock on the door to learn that her husband, the general, had sent a carriage and a request that she come downtown. She hastily donned a heavy English shawl and furs and got in the carriage. She sent up a messenger to notify the general of her arrival, and he sent back word for her to come to the council chamber.

'I passed through a file of soldiers guarding the door and

through halls similarly guarded and up the rough staircases, until I reached the further end of the third story,' wrote Mrs. Robinson. Her escort knocked. The door opened and 'with ceremony I was ushered into the presence of and introduced to General Robinson.'

There were other ladies present and all were notified that the war was over, the hatchet buried. 'It is best to bridge over past differences by the pleasant offices of good will and friendship,' said the general, and he proposed a party next evening for the free-soil garrison, to which would be invited 'Governor Shannon and any of his friends from Missouri who will remain to a social gathering.' Then he charged the women with the responsibility of providing refreshments.

A flutter of talk broke out among the women — a day's notice to prepare refreshments for seven or eight hundred guests!

That Sunday evening, Governor Shannon and his suite were entertained at the Free State headquarters.

Good fellowship was at its height when, at about ten o'clock, Charles Robinson, who had taken a turn outside, came back to report that a mob of proslavery men was drawing in for an immediate attack on Lawrence.

There were cries from the women and men started for the door.

General Robinson held up his hand to stay them. 'The Governor of Kansas Territory is here and he will protect us,' he said. Then he turned dramatically to Wilson Shannon. 'The citizens of Lawrence claim your protection, Your Excellency. I ask you to give General Lane and myself permission to repel this invasion.'

Shannon was incensed that his orders to the sheriff's posse were being thus flaunted, heartsick that the new peace had been so short-lived. 'You require no permission from me, sir, to repel attack on your homes,' he said. 'The law of self-preservation is sufficient authority for that.'

'But, sir,' said Robinson, 'we have been represented as having arrayed ourselves against the law of this Territory.

Therefore I must request written permission to repel this invasion, in order that it might not appear hereafter, if a recounter should take place, as if we were acting against, rather than with the approbation of the territorial executive.'

The roomful of men and women, as if cued, pressed the governor for protection.

Robinson had the proper piece of paper ready and he proffered it, with an inked pen, to the governor. And this is the paper Wilson Shannon signed, without reading: 'To C. H. Robinson and James H. Lane, Commanders of the Enrolled Citizens of Lawrence: You are hereby authorized and directed to take such measures and use the enrolled forces under your command in such a manner, for the preservation of the peace and the protection of the persons and property of the people of Lawrence and its vicinity, as, in your judgment, shall best secure that end.'

Wilson Shannon had legalized, for an indefinite period, the rebel government he had so diligently worked to dissolve. When he went out into the street, saw no excitement, and learned that there had been no threatened attack, he suddenly felt very tired of Lawrence. He returned to Shawnee Mission early the next morning. He was not present when the victorious Free State Militia jammed the big hotel to eat, dance, and be merry.

11

Bloody New Year

IT WAS A WHITE CHRISTMAS in Kansas Territory. White and cold.

On Monday, the day before Christmas, it was seventeen below zero and reporter Phillips, writing his dispatch in the Robinson living room, had to keep his ink on the stove to keep it fluid. And the cold increased. It was thirty below zero on Christmas morning. Water froze in the tumblers on the breakfast table and bread had to be held to the fire to thaw between the cutting of each slice.

Seasons Greetings

'The abolitionists, or free-state men, if you please, are willing to violate the constitution of their country, which explicitly recognizes slavery, and disfranchise themselves as loyal citizens, for the purpose of stealing negroes and committing other unconstitutional and unlawful depredations. Should such men receive any compassion from an orderly, union-loving people? No! It is this class of men that had congregated at Lawrence and it is this class of men that Kansas must get rid of. And we know of no better method than for every man who loves his country, and the laws by which he is governed, to meet in Kansas and kill off this God-forsaken class of humanity as soon as they place their feet upon our soil.' — *Kansas Pioneer*, Kickapoo, 25 December 1855.

The Kansas war was a frozen threat. In towns and on home-
steads the pace slackened. Hammers and hatreds were held by
the bitter cold which went beyond anything even the Indians
could remember. Buffaloes, hunger driven, came as far east as
Council Grove, civilization's outpost on the Santa Fe Trail.
'The Delawares are daily in our streets, and, with their gay
dress, half-civilized, retaining always the Indian blanket, add a
pleasant variety,' wrote Mrs. Robinson. 'Other tribes, less
civilized, driven by the cold to winter near a settlement, have
pitched their tents on the further side of the Kansas. They also
buy provisions here, and pack them on ponies. The poor little
human is encased in a red flannel bag and carried on the backs of
the mothers.'

The Robinsons burned a cord and a half of wood a week,
most of it black walnut; and in poorly chinked cabins and
flimsy, unfloored shake huts, families that had been edgy with
nearness crowded together for warmth. 'More than once we woke
in the morning to find six inches of snow in the cabin,' Samuel
Walker was to recall.

The weather might promise to get warmer, but it always
changed its mind. Rising temperatures would fall before they
had climbed to the zero mark. The wind, whipping up or lulling,
clouding or clearing the skies, gave the only variety from day
to day.

Still, commerce went on. Sparkling sunshine ushered in the
new year and every clear day that came saw sleighs on the road,
most of them homemade. The simplest contrivance resembled
an Indian travois — a box rigged on two long, bent poles that
served both as runners and shafts. On 12 January 1856, a
weekly mail was established between Leavenworth, K.T., and
Lawrence, K.T., and wagon sleds from Missouri came regularly
into the Territory bringing food and goods.

A month after the intense cold set in, Mrs. Robinson noted
that there was no lack of provisions in garrisoned Lawrence,
whose forts were kept manned, with sentries pacing the ram-
parts day and night. Apples were plentiful, and sweet potatoes,
squash, pumpkins. Butter was scarce, but there was plenty of

pork and beef in the markets and often venison, prairie chicken,
wild turkey, rabbit, and squirrel, as well as oysters in sealed
cans. Despite 'all these gratifications for the palate,' however,
Mrs. Robinson thought it 'more than probable that some of our
people have not tasted them for want of money.' She pointed
out that many free-soilers not only had contributed freely during the siege of Lawrence, but also (though this is hard to see,
owing to the time of year) had lost their crops at home while on
guard there. 'As a people we are bankrupt,' she said, and
charged a good part of their trouble to Missouri postal clerks,
whom she accused of waylaying remittances from the East.

Food was plentiful for those who could afford to buy it, but
the cold was unrelenting. Few free-soilers braved the bitter
weather to go to the polls on 15 January 1856, to elect officers
for the spurious commonwealth they had set up in December by
voting for the Topeka Constitution.

In free-soil communities, the election — which pinned the
title of 'Governor' on 'General' Robinson — was held as
scheduled. But the outnumbered free-soilers in the Leavenworth
community set a secret voting day and place. The day, the
seventeenth; the place, the home of T. A. Minard in Easton.

The influx of sleds and sleighs into that village eight miles
from Leavenworth made it easy for local proslavery men to
guess what was going on, and they gathered in the Dawson
grocery, as a place to get warm between taunts. Taunts lead to
an exchange of threats and, finally, there was an exchange of
shots. The man who happened to be killed was a Southerner
named Cook.

When the news of his death reached Kickapoo, the Rangers,
ever ready for a fight, set out. They waylaid Reese Brown, a
free-soil captain recently returned from Lawrence. They took
him into Dawson's where Ranger Captain Martin said they
would jail him until he was given fair trial.

'Thunder, why try a guilty man?' someone asked.

'You always have to try a man before you kill him,' the
captain said, trying to control his men with lightness.

'They didn't try Cook, did they?'

'No!' and it was a chorus.

The argument went on and Captain Martin finally despaired. He went home.

'Daggone it, boys,' said another champion of justice. 'We got to try him, so we can decide how to kill him.'

A bearded giant named Gibson ran a big thumb along the edge of his hatchet. 'Arguing about how to kill a skunk!' he exclaimed in disgust. 'You can't please a buzzard,' he said, as he took a good hold on his hatchet and brought the blade down hard on Reese Brown's head.

The Kickapoo Rangers, toughest of ruffians, were shocked by the suddenness and horror of this butchery, one of them told Phillips.

'Reckon we better take him home,' someone finally said.

They loaded Reese Brown in a wagon and the men who rode in the box stiffened their spirits with a jug, so that by the time the ten rut-frozen miles to Brown's home had been traveled, they were able to dump the dying man in the dooryard and call to his wife, 'Here's Brown.'

A bloody beginning for a bloody year.

12

Hatreds Hotbedded

THE KANSAS WAR was a frozen threat, but the Kansas issue was kept alive by pen and press.

'Rally! Rally!' cried a Kickapoo *Pioneer* extra the day after the Easton slayings. 'Forebearance has now ceased to be a virtue; thereupon we call upon every proslavery man in the land to rally to the rescue. The war has again commenced, and the abolitionists have commenced it. Proslavery men, law and order men, strike for your altars! strike for your firesides! strike for your rights! Avenge the blood of your brothers who have been cowardly assailed but who have bravely fallen in defence of southern institutions. Sound the bugles of war over the length and breadth of the land, and leave not an abolitionist in the territory to relate their treacherous and contaminating deeds. Strike your piercing rifle-balls and your glittering steel to their black and poisonous hearts! Let the war cry never cease in Kansas again until our territory is wrested from the last vestige of abolitionism.'

Back East the *Springfield (Mass.) Republican* called upon the free men of New England to take up the fight. 'We have more charcoal than they have; we have more saltpetre; we have more brimstone; we have more lead; we have more bone and blood, and nerve and muscle. Will they have trial by these? Are they ready for it? Are they eager for the clinch of death? Let them beware!'

In Albany, New York, Gerit Smith, fund raiser for the New England Aid Society, said the people of Kansas Territory must not submit to their territorial government. 'They must resist, even if in so doing, they have to resist both the Congress and the President,' he said. And at a later meeting, Smith, a vice-president of the American Peace Society, cried, 'You are looking to ballots when you should be looking to bayonets!'

David Atchison wrote to friends in Georgia: 'We wish to keep ourselves right before the world, and we are provoked and aggravated beyond sufferance,' he said. 'Let your young men come forth to Missouri and Kansas. Let them come well-armed, with money enough to support them for twelve months, and determined to see this thing out! One hundred true men would be an acquisition. The more the better. I do not see how we are to avoid civil war; come it will.'

And the Lexington (Missouri) Emigrant Company wrote to Southern newspapers: 'We tell you that unless you come quickly and by the thousands, we are gone. The elections once lost, we are gone forever, then farewell to the Southern Cause, and farewell to our glorious Union.'

Major Jefferson Buford, Eufaula, Alabama, lawyer, sold forty slaves at $700 a head to finance an emigration to Kansas Territory. He advertised this fact to other slaveholders and promised to secure a bona fide settler for every $50 contributed. He also advertised for settlers. He promised every man forty acres, free passage, and means of support for a year. He wanted 300 settlers who were, he said, 'industrious, sober, discreet, reliable men, capable of bearing arms but not prone to use them wickedly or unnecessarily.'

Charles Robinson, New England Emigrant Aid Society agent, wrote to Amos Lawrence, purse-string holder: 'We are purchasing ammunition and stores of all kinds for a siege. We have telegraphed the President and members of Congress and northern governors our condition and have sent out six men to raise an army for defence of Kansas and the Union.'

The big problem for these six free-soil ambassadors was to get across Missouri. George Washington Smith solved that one.

'In Missouri, everybody carries a jug,' he said. 'Let's put our papers in jugs with corncob stoppers and they will be safe.' By this Ruffian ruse they reached the Mississippi. It was frozen solid. They walked across it, to Quincy, Illinois, with only a pause, mid-river, to take out their papers and throw their jugs away.

Amos Lawrence also got a letter from a Maine farmer, stout in speech, if weak in spelling. 'I perpose to take sixty or so good men, well-equipped and mounted and garilla as long as there is a Ruffian left in Kansas. My plan is not to show quarter and consequently take no prisoners.' The only way to handle proslavery men, he said, was 'to butcher them clean by the board.'

A Massachusetts boy was in Alabama when Buford's advertisements for money and men appeared. He sent them to Eli Thayer, who used them to raise a company of 165 men to send into the field. And 79 'rifle Christians' set out from New Haven, Connecticut. 'Like our fathers,' said their leader, C. B. Lines, 'we go with the Bible to indicate the peaceful nature of our mission and the harmless character of our company, and a weapon to teach those who may be disposed to molest us, if any such there be, that while we are determined to do that which is right, we will not submit tamely to that which is wrong.' The weapons were donated by Henry Ward Beecher, Brooklyn preacher, whose collections to equip free-soil volunteers with Sharp's rifles had given them the nickname of Beecher's Bibles. 'We shall not forget you!' he cried from his pulpit as the 79 set out. 'Every morning breeze shall catch the blessings of our prayers and roll them westward to your prairie home.'

Agitation over what was called the Kansas Question reached such heights that, on 11 February 1856, the President of the United States, Franklin Pierce, issued a proclamation. He called upon all citizens of states close to Kansas Territory, and distant from it, to stop meddling in her territorial affairs.

The proclamation reached Alabama on the eve of the departure of Jefferson Buford and the 350 men who had responded to his advertisements. It caused Buford to change his plan to arm his expedition with guns, according to an Alabama historian, Walter Fleming. 'Since ministers in the North are raising money to equip settlers with Sharp's rifles, let us equip our settlers with a more powerful weapon, the Bible,' Reverend I. T. Tichenor told a gathering of Montgomery citizens. Money was quickly subscribed. When it was found that there were not enough Bibles in town to supply all the men, Buford was presented with a large token Bible. 'Providence may change our relations to the inferior race, but the principle is eternal — the supremacy of the white race,' Henry Hillard said as he handed the Bible to Buford. The 5000 citizens gathered to see the expedition board the *Messenger* for Mobile cheered. And the battalion went aboard carrying banners, one of which read, 'Alabama for Kansas, north of 36-30 — Bibles not Rifles.' This banner was carried in Mobile as the men marched to a bookstore to collect their Bibles, before embarking on the *Florida* for New Orleans. And it was to be carried three months later at the first sack of Lawrence.

Mrs. Robinson wrote in her diary on 23 January that 'a half ton of lead and nearly as much powder arrived today.'

There was much talk and some action, North and South. In Kansas Territory itself, hatreds lay dormant. It was a bitter winter, with everyone elsewhere more concerned about the Kansas Issue than were the people who lived there. They were concerned with keeping alive. Judge Rush Elmore of Tecumseh, the chief resident slaveholder, frankly questioned the feasibility of slave labor in this harsh new land. The extreme cold, he wrote friends in the South, had rendered his nineteen slaves useless. Mrs. Elmore, who never before had cooked a meal, spent the winter feeding their slaves while the judge was kept busy cutting wood to keep them warm.

II

SPRING MADE FALSE promises, finally arrived, revealing the changes the long hard winter had wrought. Weaklings were gone. They stood with branches dead to budding or lay as carcasses on the prairies. Matted clods of virgin soil, frost cracked and turned skyward, softened as the melting snow soaked in and were ready then to take the plow and seed.

Spring came and there was the clop of horses' hooves sucking in the rain-soft earth in the country. There was that and the heavy breathing of men who, legs straining, gripped sodbuster handles and added their push to the pull of the cattle. These sounds, then the sodden rip as grass roots, endlessly undisturbed, gave way to man's impatience.

Spring came and there was a sound of hammers in the towns, the sound of chisels shaping, of hoes wedding sand to cement. You could hear the clinking thud as brick met brick in the hod, the scrape of trowels, the shouts of men.

These were the sounds heard along the eastern rim of the disputed land, when the spring thaws came and the spring influx of squatters began. They came by the boatload to Kansas City, and they came in their own wagons, bumping and swaying over the gumbo-bog corduroy roads of mid-Missouri.

The New England Emigrant Aid Society was not the only northern organization drumming for settlers. The Kansas Emigrant Aid Society of Oberlin, Ohio, was active and the German Kansas Settlement Society of Cincinnati. Two upstate New York corporations had come and gone, leaving a light residue of squatters. A combination of ague and unkept promises had defeated both the anti-liquor Vegetarian Kansas Emigrant Company and the anti-liquor Octagon Kansas Settlement Company. Both were of a communal pattern, with settlers as shareholders. But the squatter-investors who went to Kansas under the aegis of the Octagon Company — which had the original notion of laying out its lands in triangular farms centered about the community of schoolhouse and homes — had much the same experience as a family named Colt which had joined the Vegetarian Company. This family arrived at Neosho, down near Fort Scott, to find that sawmills and gristmills they had bought shares in had not been built. Miriam Colt found the country lovely, but harsh. She lost her husband in the great shakes plague of 1855 and went back to York State, as did most of the other survivors.

There was one emigrant society in Missouri, but the South, for the most part, relied on the individual efforts of men of wealth such as Buford to build citizen strength in the disputed land. His was the only sizable migration, though a number of prominent Southerners — such men as Colonel Zachabod Jackson of Georgia and Warren Wilkes of South Carolina — came to Missouri to lead Missourians into the fray. And Colonel H. T. Titus of Florida actually settled in Kansas about the time the men of 'the noble Buford,' as he was hailed by the border press, shouldered their Bibles.

For the most part, people simply went to Kansas on their own. As the second birthday of K.T. approached, she could boast of 58 post offices, though mail service was largely an if-you're-riding-that-way affair.

Governor Shannon moved that spring to Lecompton, the new territorial capital. A large stone hotel and a brick capitol were under construction there, and a log jail stood ready to receive political prisoners when the spring arrest season opened. Cabins were being built among the trees and Dr. Aristides Roderique, physician and postmaster, lived in the town's big house, a two-story frame house prefabricated in St. Louis.

At Lawrence, the Kansas River takes a turn to the north and it was at the bend where the river heads west again, some ten miles distant, that the new capital stood. There were two roads to it from the south — a cut-off, across high country, from the California Road and a river road that branched from the Big Road at the Wakarusa and went down through Franklin and Lawrence, then followed the bottom to Lecompton.

A trail running southwest out of Lecompton met and merged with the California Road at the old trading post of Big Springs. It was on this trail, not far southwest of Lecompton, that Titus of Florida built a stout blockhouse for his family that spring. A mile west of Big Springs was Washington, where travelers could eat excellent meals in a pleasant room with a huge stone fireplace, a brocatelle-covered lounge, and damask-curtained windows.

The next town west was Tecumseh, where the finishing touches were being put on a brick courthouse with pillars — the pillars perhaps because the town could boast not only of the courthouse, a large brick store, and a capacious wooden hotel, but also of Southern residents who actually had slaves. This was the place where the Rush Elmores had worked so hard to keep their slaves alive the winter past. And a Mr. Stinson, though he owned only three slaves, was the largest landholder in those parts. He had had the sagacity to marry a Shawnee wife and was therefore entitled to 200 acres of land for each member of his household, including his slaves.

Five miles farther west, at Pappan's Crossing, where the California Road crossed the Kaw to head northward, a town was booming. It was a town of unknown parentage that went by the name of Topeka.

Most towns were formed by town companies, whose shareholders were easily detected by their loud-voiced conviction that no town could touch their town as a location for anything, particularly a seat of government. No one ever seemed to ballyhoo Topeka, yet the fathers of the Territory's largest free-soil city, Lawrence, accepted Topeka as the capital of their 'government' with a singular readiness. Its Constitution Hall was one of the first buildings erected there and now in the spring of 1856, its leading hostelry, Commercial Head Quarters, was building a large addition. 'Dwelling houses of brick, wood, and stone, show clearly their Yankee origin, and that in coming West they had not forgotten thrift and enterprise,' noted Mrs. Robinson.

Topeka, some 70 miles from the border, was the westernmost town of importance, though there were villages along the north of the Kaw as far west as Fort Riley — St. Mary's Mission, Wabousa, St. George, Manhattan, and the already extinct first capital, Pawnee. This was a predominantly free-soil section, though Manhattan, at the confluence of the Big Blue and the Kaw, had a number of Southern residents, including at least one slaveholder.

To the south and west of Lawrence, on or near the Santa Fe Trail, were Hickory Point, Palmyra, Union Junction, communities which the free-soilers were taking over, and the New York Settlement Company's Council City. Lawrence itself was growing fast. Four religious organizations were planning to build churches that summer. A bookstore had been opened and also a circulating library where, according to Mrs. Robinson, members could find "standard works, new books, and publications, as soon as issued.' And the Robinson home — 'amid a confusion of lathers, plasterers, paperers, and varnishers, with company all the time' — was finished that spring. It was built entirely of black walnut, with a high finish on doors, window casings, and mantels.

Three miles to the east of Lawrence, at Franklin, the proslavery country began. Along the south of the river, there were Blue Jacket's, Donaldson's, Shawnee Mission.

Most of these post offices have already been heard from and most of them will be heard from again, as will the towns along the proslavery west bank of the Missouri — Troy, Atchison, Oak Mills, Kickapoo, Easton, and the Leavenworths, city and fort. Inland, in this northeast section, there was another Hickory Point, and Charley's Trading Post, Johnny Cake, Strawberry Hill, Osaweka. Town lots were on sale for Grasshopper Falls.

Along the border south of the Kaw were a number of post offices not yet mentioned that were to be a part of the drama before this seven-year curtain-raiser to civil war had run its serio-comic course. Down on the Marais des Cygnes, with its Pottawatomie and Bull Creek branches, and on the Neosho, there will be action. There were settlements as far south as Fort Scott. Trading Post, Dutch Henry's Crossing, Sugar Mound City, Raysville were some of the names.

This was a section of strong proslavery leanings, but its free-soil residents made up for in intensity what they lacked in numbers. Osawatomie was the only abolitionist stronghold in the Territory, though 'abolitionist' was the Border Ruffian's generic term for all Northerners. This town had been colonized by the six Brown boys, who had been sent by their father to fight to free the black man. This one-man emigrant aid society had also sent his daughter and her husband, Henry Thompson, and was himself to make quite a name on his few visits to his colony. In fact, later reviewers were to give John Brown star billing in the Kansas drama, though he had only a walk-on part.

These were the towns in Kansas Territory when the spring thaws came in 1856 and brought near the day on which hatreds hotbedded by pen, press, and personal proselyting were to be transplanted to the field of action.

13

How Territories Became States

A TECHNIQUE had been established for making states of territories.

When a new land got beyond the wilderness stage, its territorial government could present a memorial to Congress praying for admission to the sisterhood of the United States of America. Chances are Congress would then pass an enabling act authorizing the citizens of the territory to frame the constitution by which they wished to govern themselves. The territorial legislature could then set up a constitutional convention and if Congress approved the instrument it framed, the territory would become a state.

There were circumstances peculiar to every case, but every case, up to now, had met the basic requirements of having attained the specified population to put them 'beyond the wilderness stage' and of proceeding through authoritative territorial channels.

Now, in 1856, President Pierce was eager to see an end to the difficulties in Kansas Territory. They were killing him politically, but that was not his only concern. His Secretary of War, Jefferson Davis, to whom he was greatly attached, had convinced him that the hope of Union lay in a legislative resolution of the issues that threatened it. So the President wanted the South to have its equal voice in the Senate. He wanted her to have Kansas. Action toward admission, then, should come while the South still had the political advantage in Kansas Territory.

On 24 January 1856, President Pierce asked Congress to authorize the people of Kansas to frame a constitution. And in his special message, he endorsed the proslave Territorial Legislature and condemned the free-soil Topeka government, calling it revolutionary. Its formation without a congressional enabling act and in defiance of the elected government was, he said, 'an act of treason.'

This did not deter the Free State Party. The legislature it had elected, in defiance of the duly constituted authorities, convened in Topeka on 4 March and drafted a memorial to Congress praying for the admission of Kansas to the Union under the Topeka Constitution. And it commissioned James H. Lane — named with Andrew H. Reeder to be U.S. Senators, if the Territory became a state — to take the memorial to Congress and present it there.

Meantime, the President's message on Kansas Territory was referred to the Committee on Territories with a Senate request for a transcript on certain papers relating to affairs in the Territory. Senator Douglas presented the report and what to do about Kansas became the question of the day. Toombs of Georgia made the fairest proposal. His bill would set up a nonpartisan commission of five men to take an accurate census of the Territory, apportion it into districts, and cause an election to be held for delegates to a constitutional convention. But the bill was defeated by Northern congressmen who distrusted President Pierce and the men he might appoint as commissioners.

Of the dozens of bills introduced and killed either by the House or the Senate, only one passed and it simply sent a House committee out to investigate the goings on in Kansas Territory. William Howard of Michigan, John Sherman of Ohio, and Mordecai Oliver of Missouri set out for K.T. about the time that James Lane arrived in the national capital to present the Topeka Constitution to Congress.

On 7 April 1856, General Lewis Cass presented the Topeka memorial to the Senate. It was a messy looking document, full of interlineations and erasures. 'It looks as if some person who had it in charge had watched the progress of discussion in this body, and had stricken out propositions to accommodate it to the present stage of discussion,' said Senator Pugh. Senator Douglas pointed out that the signatures were all in one handwriting, and Benjamin of Louisiana sneered, 'Are we not aware that the men whose signatures purport to be attached to this paper are fugitives from justice?'

General Cass, embarrassed, asked leave to withdraw the memorial 'with a view to return it to the gentleman who handed it to me.'

Jim Lane, undaunted, drew up an affidavit of explanation. The Topeka Legislature, he said, had asked him to revise the phraseology of the document. He had left this editorial job to do in Washington and when it was done he found that 'the sets of signatures' had been lost, so his private secretary had written the names of the original signers.

Lane persuaded Harlan of Iowa to present this affidavit to the Senate, but it found no champions there. Douglas expressed the general scorn for this document 'without signatures, authentication, or date,' and also pointed out that the copy which Lane was trying to palm off on the Senate was an imperfect one. 'You withheld what you dare not defend!' Douglas cried, for this time Lane had stricken out the legislative instructions that would exclude all people of Negro blood, free or slave, from the state of Kansas. 'In every line of your expurgated and recast memorial, evidences of fraud appear.'

Still undaunted, Lane got the memorial introduced in the House, which finally voted to admit Kansas under the Topeka Constitution. But the Senate would have none of it.

This first Kansas bid for statehood was doomed from the beginning. The Free State men had acted in defiance of all precedent. State governments had come into existence before without enabling acts, but never before had one been formed in defiance of the territorial authorities. Bayard of Delaware tagged the conduct of the Kansas Free State Party 'incipient treason.'

14

Harrowing Time

A LARGE FORCE was marching on Lawrence . . .

That was the persistent rumor.

It kept free-soil sentries on day and night patrol on the walls of Lawrence's forts throughout the bitter winter and into the spring, though vigilance was relaxed somewhat after the Topeka Legislature met without interference. The Sheriff of Douglas County did pay it a brief visit, but he was, someone said, 'dreadful quiet.' He just listened, made notes, and took down the names of those present in his memorandum book.

Mrs. Robinson remarked how quiet things were as she made ready to turn the page of her diary from March to April, though she did say, 'Rumors fly as fast as autumn leaves and we scarcely know what to believe.' Latest one was that a box of Sharp's rifles consigned to a Lawrence citizen had been taken off a boat at Lexington, Missouri. But this rumor amused rather than alarmed the free-soil first lady. The rifles would be useless to the Missourians, she said, 'for the slides are understood to be in another place, and it will puzzle them quite as much to use a rifle open at both ends, as it did the one they threw away in December as useless, because there was no ramrod!'

The bordermen had got around to doing a bit of river patrolling, though a couple of months were to pass before they would go so far as to board steamers to seize cargo. When they did get around to that, they made a real haul of Sharp's rifles —

a shipment worth $4000. When news of this loss reached Amos Lawrence in Boston, he passed it on to Dr. Samuel Cabot with this comment: 'If we were not officers of the Emigrant Aid Society, we could recover them by suit, but whether or not we can recover them by proxy remains to be seen.' They were not recovered.

Several things happened in the two months between the time Mrs. Robinson heard the rumor about the loss of a box of Sharp's rifles and the day Mr. Lawrence learned the news about the loss of the $4000 shipment.

April had been a month of coming and going. Wilson Shannon returned from an official visit to the capital of the United States. The Congressional Investigation Committee arrived in Lawrence on 17 April and established headquarters in the New England Emigrant Aid Society's Free State Hotel, which stood finished now, a sturdy symbol of free-soilism's determination to dig in its roots and stay. The next day, Samuel N. Wood of Branson rescue fame returned to Lawrence from a combined business and pleasure trip to Ohio. And the day after that, Samuel J. Jones, the Sheriff of Douglas County, K.T., paid his first official visit of the 1856 open season to the free-soil stronghold. Object: The arrest of the returned Mr. Wood.

Sheriff Jones walked up to Sam Wood on the street, as he stood near the office of Dr. J. N. O. P. (Alphabet) Wood. 'You are my prisoner,' the sheriff said.

'By what authority?' Wood asked.

'As Sheriff of Douglas County.'

'I do not recognize such authority,' Wood said, and coolly turned to walk away.

Sheriff Jones reached out and caught Wood by the wrist but he, with a sudden twist, jerked loose.

By this time, several free-soilers had gathered and the sheriff's deputies had moved closer. As Sam Jones jumped for Sam Wood, John Speer caught the sheriff by the collar. Wood grabbed the sheriff's revolver. Jones's deputies leapt to the rescue but free-soil bystanders moved, too. Jim Abbott knocked one deputy down, Charles Garrett swung another off of the office porch by his coattails, and Sam Tappan throttled the third.

'Put 'em in the river!' someone cried, but John Speer said to let them go.

Jones went to untie his horse, sputtering something about resisting officers of the law.

The next day was Sunday. Reverend S. Y. Lum was preaching to an armed delegation when who should come riding into town but Sheriff Sam Jones, this time with a posse of ten. They dismounted in front of the Free State Hotel and tied their horses to the hitching rail.

Sam Tappan, one of the offenders of the day before and on the arrest list as a Branson rescuer, came sauntering down the street. He was a decoy, as it turned out. Jones no sooner made a grab at Tappan than the menfolks of Reverend Lum's congregation came pouring out of the church. Tappan gave Jones a staggering punch.

The sheriff glared at Tappan, then looked pleased. He walked over to his horse. 'Come on, boys, let's go,' he said.

An hour later, the tall, handsome, and not-too-brave sheriff strode into the barroom of Lecompton's Brooke Hotel. He went straight to the table where the governor was conferring on territorial affairs. 'I have been assaulted, sir, in the discharge of my duties.' And he told the story as it had grown in his mind, ending with a demand for military escort.

The governor was just back from Washington. Congress and the President were agreed that the free-state government was a defiance of the legal government of Kansas Territory and therefore federal troops could be used, if needed, to control the free-soil rebels.

Wilson Shannon now walked to the window, where he stood a long time — a large, untidy, but impressive figure of a man.

Nothing was said. Men had been chatting with the governor on many things, about Indian lands and other problems of settlement. Now their eyes were on the chief executive's back, on his broad shoulders, drooping under the weight of his thankless office.

At last he turned and came back. 'The President of the United States has authorized me to use federal troops in cases of emergency,' he said. 'This, I believe, is what he meant by emergency.'

By Wednesday arrangements had been made with the Army. Sheriff Jones and his deputy, Sam Salters, escorted by Lieutenant McIntosh and ten federal dragoons, rode into Lawrence to play hide-and-seek with the men on the sheriff's list of offenders.

The free-soilers sneaked from house to house or took to the ravines. One of the men who stopped at the Robinson home that day 'had scarcely seated himself before the dragoons, their sabres flashing in the sunlight, came prancing out of town' — and he had to take to his horse again.

One free-soil wife had hoped to have her house made fast against the rains that day. But her husband had just got the lumber cut when he was warned to hide out. This so annoyed her that she placed a loaded rifle in a window and told her daughter to keep watch. 'Call me if you see that Sam Salters coming,' she said, 'and I will shoot him.'

And Mrs. John Speer got sick and tired of having her house searched for Sam Wood. The third time Sam Salters and his dragoon escort came to her house, the dragoons refused to go near, so Sam Salters said he would go by himself. The youngest Speer boy took a shot at the deputy with a squirt gun and this so enraged Sam Salters that he opened the door without knocking. He let out a yelp and stepped back. Mrs. Speer had thrown a dipperful of water in his face. 'I have respect for the United States troops,' she said. 'You can search the house but as for this puke of a Missourian, he shall not come in.'

The hide-and-seek game was called when rain came late in the afternoon. The sheriff and his escort retired to the camp they had pitched under the trees along the river. Only six arrests had been made, none of them top grade. When a fellow named Hunt was arrested, bystanders urged him to shoot Jones, using, according to O. N. Merrill, one of the few proslavery recorders, 'expressions of wrath and the deepest revenge ever indulged in.'

And that evening, a young free-soiler translated that wrathful language into action.

A crowd of free-soilers gathered in the woods near the sheriff's camp. The murmur of their voices could be heard beyond the circle of light thrown by the campfire and now and then a shot was fired into the air.

The sheriff and Lieutenant McIntosh, who were tenting together, went for a drink at the water barrel, and just as they passed the fire, another shot rang out.

'That shot was meant for me,' Sam Jones said.

'Just another threat,' said the lieutenant.

'That was intended for me,' the sheriff said, and he showed the lieutenant a hole in his pants.

That gave the lieutenant pause. How, under the circumstances, should a federal officer act? There had been no course in civil war at West Point. He told Jones to go to the tent, while he investigated the affair. 'I joined the crowd,' he later reported, 'and while speaking to them heard another shot, then some of my men exclaimed, "Lieutenant, the sheriff is dead." '

A murmur of shock went through the free-soil fringe, as it quickly dispersed to tell the news.

And because it was just a rumor lacking substantiation it spread the more rapidly. Stringfellow's *Squatter Sovereign* screamed it as news and editorialized: 'His murder shall be avenged, if at the sacrifice of every abolitionist in the Territory. We are now in favor of levelling Lawrence and chastising the traitors there congregated, should it result in the total destruction of the Union.'

The newspapers of Leavenworth, Kickapoo, and Missouri border towns took up the cry for revenge, before fact overtook rumor — and afterward. The sheriff was badly wounded, but not dead — nor dying. But this 'noble patriot' had, as one paper put it, 'been shot down by the thieving paupers of the North.'

Free-soilers themselves were shocked. It was a bad thing to have happen, and Lawrence citizens met to pass a resolution which began, 'Resolved, that the attempt made in our town last evening, upon the life of S. J. Jones, Esq., while claiming to act as sheriff of the county, was the isolated act of some malicious and evil-disposed citizen, unexpected and unlooked for by our community and unsustained by any portion of them.' A committee was appointed to seek out 'the guilty author' and surrender him to justice. But a few days later Mrs. Robinson wrote, without qualm, 'Many feared at first that the act was committed by some free state man.' And all free-soilers — except young J. P. Filer and the friends who kept his secret for many years — came to accept the handy view that the sheriff had been shot by a Southerner to cast blame on the North.

II

THE SHERIFF WAS wounded, but his deputy Sam Salters carried on, building a saga of ineptitude to lighten the growing intensity of the drama. The Territory was full of bands of roving Southerners, Missourians, and the patrols of Buford and Titus. 'As citizens were often stopped by these persons,' wrote Phillips of the *Tribune*, 'the following pass was given by the redoubtable Sam Salters to a Law and Order man who found it necessary to travel: "Let this man pass i no him two be a Law and abidin Sittisen." '

Then early in May, the federal judiciary appeared on the scene. The grand jury of Douglas County went into session at Lecompton before Samuel D. Lecompte, chief justice of the Territorial Supreme Court. The Court took up the question of whether treason could be committed against the United States by levying war upon a territorial government. Nearly thirty years later, Lecompte wrote, 'I then held and still hold such hostility to be treason . . . Under the provocation of unprincipled leaders, the laws of the Territory had been denounced as "bogus," their authority defied, and an opposing legislature, without semblance of authority set up, and insurgent military forces were organizing, equipping, drilling.' He defended his instruction and the jury that indicted as traitors such promi-

nent free-soilers as Reeder, Lane, and Robinson, and found bills
of indictment against Lawrence's *Herald of Freedom* and *Kansas Free State* for their 'inflammatory and seditious language,'
and against the Free State Hotel for being 'regularly parapeted and port-holed for use of small cannon and arms.'

While the grand jury was arriving at these conclusions,
and the Congressional Investigation Committee was interviewing for its report, the small fry of the Territory's two factions
pestered each other. Stealing horses was the chief occupation of
the proslavery bands, though they called it 'pressing,' since the
horses were being taken, they said, in the interest of preserving
law and order. Getting the horses back, or substitutes for them,
occupied the time of many free-soil gangs.

Reverend Pardee Butler, undaunted by his cottonwood-raft ride of the year before, returned to Atchison, K.T. He was
immediately spotted by the *Squatter Sovereign's* fiery junior
editor, Robert S. Kelley. A crowd gathered around and one of
the men asked Butler whether he had a revolver. When the
preacher shook his head, the man handed him a pistol. 'There
take that and stand off ten steps and, goddam you, I'll blow you
through in an instant,' he said. The others protested. They
wanted to hang the preacher.

The noose was around Pardee Butler's neck when an old
Missourian, General Tut of Buchanan County, demanded to be
heard. 'I am a slaveholder and I desire to make Kansas a slave
state, if it can be done by honorable means,' he said. 'If this man
has violated a law, let him be punished according to the law;
but for the sake of Missouri, for the sake of Kansas, for the
sake of the proslavery cause, do not act in this way.' He was
persuasive. The mob contented itself with giving Reverend Butler a good tarring and feathering.

Such personal encounters happened too often for them to
be enumerated here, though there seems to have been only two
killings in those first weeks of May. A young free-soiler named
Jones got in a fight with a couple of proslavery men at Blanton's
Bridge on the Wakarusa, and was mortally wounded. When the
news of the shooting reached Lawrence, three men set out to

avenge their friend, but it was one of them, a fellow named Stewart, who was killed in the exchange of shots.

At about this time, the grand jury summoned Andrew Reeder to appear before it. He was attending the session of the Congressional Investigating Committee and refused to go with U.S. Marshal Israel B. Donelson, claiming congressional immunity, though Congress had refused to recognize him as delegate to Congress. The free-soil majority of this congressional committee, however, backed Reeder's resistance to territorial authority. The committee 'allied themselves with the party that resisted the law and, by that act, sent forth to Kansas and to the nation a declaration of war,' wrote O. N. Merrill, Southern chronicler.

The marshal sent his deputy, W. P. Fain, with an attachment against Reeder for contempt of court. Reeder, cheered on by the spectators, again defied the law, but that evening he decided May would be a fine time to further Free State interests in the East. At Kansas City, he was frightened into hiding. It was two weeks before he dared to slip out of the American House in disguise. Dressed in blue jeans, with a battered straw hat, a clay pipe, and an axe, he was rowed down the Missouri to an out-of-the-way landing where a river captain, in on the secret, shouted, 'Get aboard, you old scallywag; I won't wait for you.'

Detained at Lexington, by that time, was Charles Robinson, who also had decided that he could do more for the Territory from the outside than from the inside. Indicted on two counts by the Grand Jury — treason and usurpation of office — he was held under arrest as a fugitive from justice, but Mrs. Robinson had been permitted to go on her way. Jim Lane had escaped by way of Iowa.

The grand jury announced its findings. Next day, the eleventh of May, Marshal Donelson issued a proclamation calling for a 'large posse of law-abiding citizens' to help serve the grand jury papers and to carry out its mandates.

Bordermen had been waiting for this invitation all spring and large forces were soon assembled under such leaders as the Honorable David Atchison, Colonel Zachabod Jackson, and 'the noble Buford.' And Governor Wilson Shannon, filled with foreboding, wrote wistfully to President Pierce: 'Had the Marshal called upon me for a posse, I should have felt bound to furnish him with one comprised entirely of United States troops.'

15

First Sack of Lawrence

THE TWENTY-FIRST DAY of May 1856, was a perfect day, sunny and clear. The countryside was a garden of fragrant color — wild roses and verbenas and pinks. The air was warm and light to the lungs after the heavy rains.

High waters had slowed down Law and Order operations. Such proslave leaders as Dr. John Stringfellow of Atchison, his brother, General Ben of Weston, and Colonel Boone of Westport had reached Lecompton and joined Marshal Donelson's posse. But 'Old Dave' Atchison was bringing a complement of men and traveling heavy, with wagons carrying ammunition, provisions, and two brass six-pound howitzers. He was held up two days by the Big Stranger, but by the twentieth he could ford that creek, cross the rest of the Delaware Reserve, and ferry to the capital to join forces with Richardson's militia. By midmorning of the twenty-first, a posse 800-strong stood ready for action on the high prairies west of Lawrence. The unoccupied Robinson home, on Mt. Oread's side, was taken over for headquarters.

On the valley floor below lay Lawrence, ringed by unmanned forts and breastworks. Lawrence had men and guns, stores of ammunition and food, but Lawrence had no leaders. They had fled eastward. More importantly, Lawrence had been soundly spanked by the President, by Congress, and by the Territorial Grand Jury. She had no legal ground on which to give resistance.

The Southerners needed no pretext to move upon the town. The United States Marshal carried the pretext right in his pocket — warrants of arrest and writs of indictment. A jury sitting under a federal judge had ordered the arrest of prominent free-soil citizens as traitors and the destruction of Lawrence's newspapers and hotel.

The Committee of Safety, of which Samuel Pomeroy was chairman, sent a note to the marshal saying that the citizens of Lawrence had no intention of resisting the laws 'national or territorial.' (Committee members Lyman Allen, C. W. Babcock, A. H. Mallory, Joel Grover, and Dr. S. N. Prentiss later denied that they had ever signed a paper thus recognizing the enactments of the Bogus Legislature.)

Marshal Donelson and the Southern leaders came into town and while the marshal picked up as many men on his list as he could find, Atchison, Buford, and the others strolled about town and were invited by the Eldridge brothers, proprietors of the Free State Hotel, to dine.

Up on the rim, the privates of the marshal's posse were getting restless. They had taken care of most of the whisky that the thoughtful marshal had provided, and they were itching for action.

A crier came riding. He shouted for attention, then said, 'I am authorized to say that the federal marshal has no further use for you.' He had to wave his hands to silence the protest. 'The marshal thanks you for the manner in which you have discharged your duties and asks you to make out an affidavit with the number of days service, and you shall be paid.' Then quickly, above the grumble: 'Now, gentlemen, I summons you as a posse for Sheriff Samuel Jones. He is a law and order man and acts under the same authority as the marshal. All those who care to — '

He got no further. The men joined the sheriff's posse by acclamation. And at that moment the now-recovered leader, Samuel J. Jones himself, appeared.

He received an ovation.

It was three o'clock in the afternoon. The May sun was bright. The air was still. In marching formation the great posse moved down the slope to the base of broad Massachusetts, warily until no shot was fired, then with great bravado. The five artillery pieces seemed to take on a momentum of their own. They rolled out smartly and banners that had drooped forlornly asked for a breeze and got it. Their proud legends rippled out for all to see: 'Southern Rights!'; 'The Superiority of the White Race!'; 'Alabama for Kansas north of 36-30; Bibles not Rifles!' There were other state banners from all over the South — and out in front, alongside the Stars and Stripes, was a black-and-white-striped flag, with a crouched tiger in the corner.

The pace of march quickened; then, without apparent command, the ranks broke and the army became a mob.

Josiah Miller, standing at the window of his *Kansas Free State*, saw it happen. 'Well, boys, we're in for it,' he said. A brick crashed through the window of the store below, then another came up into the *Kansas Free State* shop. Then, men swarmed in, destroying as they moved. A case of type was dumped on the floor, a press smashed. 'To the river!' someone cried, and others made it a chorus as they picked locked forms and went shouting down the stairs. And on the streets, they met up with a gang going their way, carrying locked forms from the *Herald of Freedom* office.

Mrs. Robinson, who was in the East, told her diary that this mob had been incited by a speech by ex-Vice-President Atchison. She quoted him at great length, and with many blanks to denote cuss words. She said he said, among other things, 'And now, boys, we will go in again, with our highly honorable Jones, and test the strength of that damned Free State Hotel.'

Free-soil eyewitnesses gave a different account. They told of Atchison riding about trying to restore order when Jones's army became a mob. 'It was not my wish that the hotel be destroyed,' Atchison said later. 'I urged Jones to spare it. I told him it would satisfy the ends of justice if he should throw a cannonball through it.'

But Sheriff Sam Jones had many a free-soil indignity to avenge. He warned the Eldridges to get their families out of the hotel, then trained his five cannon on it.

As cannoneers stood with slow matches burning, Zachabod Jackson and Jefferson Buford added their appeals to Atchison's.

Jones did not listen. 'Fire!' he cried. He shrugged off a restraining hand. 'Reload!'

Five times the five cannon roared and, though free-soilers then denied that they had built their hotel with an eye to defense, she withstood the salvos with scarcely a tremor. Her scarred walls showed no signs of crumbling. Men carried powder kegs inside, came out trailing damask drapes, their arms loaded with bottles of liquor. The exploding powder kegs carried the boom of destruction, but their effect on the structure was remarkably feeble. (Aid Society men were to brag in later years how cleverly they had built this fortress.) A few windows blew out and that was all.

Finally, the torch was applied and Law and Order men cheered as fire broke out in the big hotel.

'And the eyes of the nation are on Kansas!' Atchison was heard to exclaim.

Back in Washington the day before, Senator Charles Sumner of Massachusetts had brought to a close his lengthy harangue, 'The Crime Against Kansas,' a piece of oratory that gave his name lasting fame and brought upon his head a rain of blows from the cane of Preston S. Brooks of South Carolina.

In K.T., Border Ruffians were having the time of their lives. Pinch-shouldered dresscoats stretched near to bursting over a select number of red shirts and one fellow had unearthed a satin waistcoat in a ransacked home. Drinks were on the house and probably no building would have been left standing had not someone, quite early, remembered the man who dared to call himself Governor of Kansas. Charles Robinson's house, high on the hillside, was the only home destroyed but it was a prize bonfire, and therefore the climax. Men sang and drank as it went up in flames, little dreaming that they were laying the cornerstone of a handsome fortune, for the astute owner of the small frame house was to collect damages, when his faction got control of the Territory, based on such inflated claims as $4500 for his library and $3500 for a manuscript history of California.

No one was killed, except the Southerner who was hit by a falling piece of hotel wall. That was about all that could be said for the debacle next morning.

16

Bit Player, John Brown

SAY 'KANSAS' and many people will say 'John Brown,' for a legend has grown up about this man. It is a legend that has made a fiction of history and a saint of a madman.

John Brown was in Kansas three times during its territorial period. His first stay was the longest and bloodiest, and it might have been of great historical importance had its brutal climax been handled honestly by the Northern press.

John Brown was one of those rare things in Kansas, an abolitionist. He wanted the black man freed, and at any cost.

He was a tall man with a face as stern and full of righteousness as that of an Old Testament prophet. His apologist, William Phillips of the *New York Tribune*, called him 'a strange, resolute, repulsive, iron-willed, inexorable old man,' though 'one of those Christians who have not quite vanished from the face of the earth — that is, he asks the blessings of God when he breaks his bread and does not, even in camp, forget his devotions in his zeal against the border ruffians.'

And the zeal of Old Brown, as he was called by the Kansans who knew of him, was great. He had no patience with anyone who did not believe exactly as he believed. He considered the men who ran Lawrence and the Free State Party a lily-livered bunch. He could not abide their policy of non-resistance. There was only one way to make Kansas free to his mind and that was by ridding the Territory of proslave settlers. At the time of the sack of Lawrence, he and his boys were busy doing just that. His namesake son, with some fifty or sixty men, was conducting a successful campaign of intimidation. His chief weapon was threat, but he had had to burn out a couple of stubborn settlers on Bull Creek. The other four Brown boys and their brother-in-law were, with Old Brown, intimidating the scattered Southerners along the Marais des Cygnes.

News came of the sack of Lawrence and Old Brown was beside himself with anger at the spinelessness of the Free State men. They would get nowhere until they fought back.

Some free-soil gangs were operating as Old Brown thought they should. Eight free-soil guerrillas out hunting Missourians, spotted a gang of them on the Santa Fe Trail. When these men saw that there were eighteen in the Southern party, 'they did not deem it advisable to attack them,' Phillips said, so, 'They lay in wait for them where the road passes some thickets and, as the proslavery men passed, fired at them. Several Southerners were killed and the rest, thinking the ambush party larger than it was, galloped off.'

Another free-soil gang looted Joab Bernhard's store at the junction of the California and Fort Scott Roads, took $4000 worth of goods. A young woman into whose apartment the free-soilers broke described them as 'desperate and vicious looking men, more like barbarians than civilized beings' — but that was the stock description of the women of one side for the men of the other side.

There were too few free-soilers engaged in such activities, to John Brown's way of thinking. They should all be in arms to drive out the remnants of the Southern posse who were roaming the countryside helping themselves to free-soil horses and the fruits of free-soil labor. And the limits of Old Brown's patience were reached when Hank Williams rode into his camp on Bull Creek to report that Southerners had threatened Old Man Morse, who kept store at Dutch Henry's Crossing and refused to sell ammunition to anyone but free-soilers. 'It's time to put a stop to that sort of thing,' he said.

John Brown set his boys and his son-in-law and the other

men to work sharpening cutlasses. 'I'll attend to those fellows,' he said.

No one dared question Old Brown's orders, except Hank Williams. As the broadswords, which resembled Scotch hackmores, were given a razor edge, Williams asked Old Brown, 'What's up?'

'We are going down to make an example,' Brown said. 'Are you coming with us?'

Williams did not like the way John Brown looked at that moment, nor did most of the other men. Only James Townsley and Theodore Weiner could be bullied into going along.

When the cutlasses were in the wagon, Old Brown called his sons Jason and John, Jr., aside. 'You'd better go home to your families,' he said.

They did not argue.

James Townsley and Theodore Weiner mounted their horses. Old Brown got into his wagon. His boys, Watson, Oliver, and Frederick, and his son-in-law Henry Thompson climbed into the wagon.

A fellow named Bondi stood by the wagon, hesitant.

Old Brown looked down at him. 'You had better have proof of where you have been the next few nights,' he said. Then he flicked the reins and the wagon, with its death-dealing cargo, began to roll.

They headed for Pottawatomie Creek, and that afternoon they met up with James Blood on his way from Westport to his home in Lawrence, by circuitous route. He declined Brown's invitation to join the expedition. 'Don't tell anyone you met us,' John Brown told him. 'We're on a secret mission.' And that evening after they made camp in a gulch, John Brown told the others what he planned to do. With their help, he was going to sweep off all the proslavery men up and down Pottawatomie Creek, he said.

'How?' asked Townsley, who was to recount this scene many years later.

'With those,' said Brown, pointing to the cutlasses.

Townsley shook his head. 'Not me,' he said.

Brown needed Townsley to act as guide and he went into a long, persuasive discourse, using God as his authority.

'If God is such a powerful man as you say, why don't he attend to this business himself?' Townsley asked.

Brown explained that God was acting through him.

'But it's killing men in cold blood,' Townsley protested.

John Brown drew himself up to his full height. 'I have no choice,' he said. 'It has been ordained by the Almighty God, ordained from eternity, that I should make an example of these men.'

Townsley, impressed, still felt that killing just one man would both satisfy God and scare off the other proslave settlers. He held out all that night and all the next day. They finally came to a compromise. John Brown agreed not to go to Townsley's own neighborhood and to strike all but about half a dozen names off his list. And that night, his bloody work was done.

It was about eleven o'clock when the Doyle household, just getting ready to go to bed, was startled by a knock on the door. The head of the house answered the knock and his wife, Mahala, heard a man ask where Allen Wilkinson lived, a question that seemed natural enough since young Wilkinson was a member of the Territorial Legislature. James Doyle gave directions on how to get there. Then he was ordered back into his house.

Eight men followed him in. They pressed into the room where his family of eight lived. Then the tall, grizzled leader ordered James Doyle to surrender 'in the name of the Army of the North.'

James Doyle was unarmed and half-dressed. And though his oldest sons, William, 22, Drury, 20, and John, 16, stepped to his side, they could be of no assistance for they, too, were unarmed and half-dressed. The eight men all had pistols in their belts and carried broadswords. James Doyle did the only thing he could do. He obeyed orders. He stepped outside to meet whatever was in store for him, as two men of the 'Army of the North' stood guard over his family.

After a few minutes of dead silence, the leader came back and ordered the boys to step outside. William and Drury went and John would have gone had not his mother 'asked them in tears to spare him.'

There was more silence, then two pistol shots, then moans — and at daybreak Mahala Doyle and her son John found, in scattered places but all a hundred yards or so from the house, James Doyle, husband and father, shot dead and pierced in the side, and the two boys. William and Drury had not been on Old Brown's revised list but they were as dead as if they had been. The heads of both of them had been split open. Their sides were pierced, and William's body, inexplicably, had had its fingers chopped off.

About an hour later, Allen Wilkinson, up late because his wife Louisa was sick with the measles, went to answer a thunderous knock at the door. 'In the name of the Northern Army, open your door,' a deep voice commanded.

Eight men came into the room where Louisa lay on one bed and the two small Wilkinson children slept in another. They ordered the young legislator to come outside. 'I begged them to let Mr. Wilkinson stay with me,' Louisa testified. 'My husband also asked them to let him stay until he could get someone to stay with me, told them he would be around next day.' But the old man, tall and stern, who was the leader, said, 'You have neighbors.' Louisa said they could not get them that late at night. 'It matters not,' said the old man. And he ordered Wilkinson out of the house, and would not even give him time to put on his boots.

Death came with a silent and brutal suddenness to young Allen Wilkinson that night. His wife heard no commotion and thought he had been taken somewhere as a prisoner, until the next morning when a shocked neighborhood found his body — bearing the John Brown brand of hacked skull and pierced side — a hundred yards from the house where his sick wife lay.

The last call made that night was at the home of James Harris. But his name was not on John Brown's revised list of the doomed, even though he was the only first-hand witness that night who knew for certain the identity of the grizzled leader of the murderous band. The man taken outside to meet his God was William Sherman, brother of Dutch Henry and one of the overnight guests at the Harris home. Sherman and his friend, John Whiteman, had stopped there on their way home from buying a cow. The third guest was a stranger who had asked for shelter.

Harris was in bed with his wife and child when John Brown's knock came. Old Brown questioned Harris, then told him if he would keep his mouth shut and get out of the Territory, he would not be harmed. Brown asked Sherman to step outside and Harris stood at the door, under guard, as William Sherman disappeared into the darkness.

There was no sound until a pistol cap popped, apparently a signal, for the two guards left then. Harris had heard no shot, but he was uneasy about his friend and at dawn he went out to look for Bill Sherman. He finally found him. His skull was split, with the brains spilled out but still holding in the waters of Mosquito Creek. There was the rest of the John Brown brand, too, the pierced side — and the hands lay severed from the body, as if in gruesome testimony that savagery is an unquenchable thirst.

Minerva Shelby, proslave Amazon who farmed near by, testified that James Harris was in a dazed condition when he and his family stopped by that afternoon. They sat in a wagon piled high with household goods and they were on their way to Missouri. The heaven-ordained example John Brown had made of William Sherman had worked on James Harris.

The whole community was shocked by the brutal massacre. Free-soiler Samuel Walker, sent by Governor Shannon on a fact-finding mission, thoroughly agreed with local squatters, free-soil and proslave, who met to pronounce the killings 'an outrage of the darkest and foulest nature.' Walker reported that the slaughter had been unprovoked and unwarranted.

The cold-blooded ferocity of these dark deeds committed on that night of 24 May was to be unsurpassed in all the bloody years that were to write Bleeding Kansas into history books, yet the free-soil propagandists of the day were so clever that the Pottawatomie Creek massacre gave no pause to the building

belief that all Northerners were right and good, all Southerners
wrong and evil.

The sack of Lawrence had come at a time when majority
thought, even in the North, was that the Kansas Free State
Party had taken a rash, and perhaps treasonable, course in
forming its own government in defiance of the established territorial government. To free-soil propagandists, then, the destruction of the free-soil center came as a burst of sun on a
gloom-bogged land. The free-soil leaders who had fled eastward
— Reeder, Lane, and Mrs. Robinson — had new fuel for their
platform fires. And there were tales of the depredations of the
Missouri gangs who roamed the Territory after the sack to keep
indignation at white heat — and money and munitions rolling
in.

It was not a good time for a Northerner to behave as John
Brown had behaved, so the free-soil chroniclers of the day, who
were writing to stimulate an influx of free-soil settlers and Eastern aid to the Territory, virtually ignored the Pottawatomie
massacre.

The New York papers were still devoting columns to the
sack of Lawrence when the massacre took place. *The New York
Times* had headlined its first stories of the sack with wholesale
slaughter. There was a discreet admission later that there had
been no bloodshed, but the impression of brutality still carried
in the eyewitness accounts featured in the same issue with the
item about the Pottawatomie Creek massacre. This item was a
very brief dispatch, buried inside. Of the eleven lines, four were
devoted to making it plain that the source of the information
that a few proslavery men had been killed by free-soilers was the
proslave *St. Louis Republican*. 'A story quite as improbable as
many others that have appeared in that journal,' said *The
Times*, in its one-sentence editorial reference to the matter.

It is little wonder that Mrs. Robinson missed the item in
the Eastern press. The proslavery border press was still scream-
ing about the massacre when she arrived in Kansas City on
4 June, however, so she did mention it in her diary, which was
scheduled for fall publication. She dismissed it in a sentence

with three things known to be rumors: 'The extras stated the
murder of eight proslavery men by the abolitionists, and the
cruel mutilation of their bodies; the death of the United States
Marshal, of H. C. Pate, and J. McGee.' That was all she said
about John Brown's murder march in the 1856 edition of her
Kansas: Its Interior and Exterior Life. But many years later,
in a revised edition published at the time when such free-soil
names as Charles Robinson and Eli Thayer were being put into
eclipse by the growing brilliancy of the name John Brown, she
devoted considerable shocked space to what Old Brown himself
always referred to as 'the Dutch Henry business.'

In 1856, William Phillips was also piecing together a book
for fall publication from his dispatches to the *Tribune.* In a
nine-page chapter entitled 'Guerilla War,' he relates a number
of happenings, such as the time 'the two waggish free-state
guerillas,' who, in retaliation for the way proslavery men were
pressing horses, stole two belonging to Governor Shannon,
dubbed them Shannon and Pierce, and went guerillaing on
them.' Then he says:

'It was about this time that the Pottawatomie affair happened. It was one of those stern and remorseless acts in civil war
which make the delicate and sensitive shrink.' He took some space
to paint a black character for each of the murdered men, then
said, 'Terrible stories have floated through the newspapers, distorted and misrepresented by those whose interest it was to mis-
represent them. From all I can learn, five of these proslavery men
had assembled in one of their houses to arrange their plans for
an attack on one man, whose life they had threatened that night,
when a party of seven or eight guerillas attacked them and in the
scuffle every proslavery man was killed.' Phillips throws the
blame on 'corrupt government and perverted official authority,'
and goes on to say, 'A Mr. Sherman, who was killed at that time
by the Comanches, he having gone out on the plains to hunt
buffalo. The Indians not only killed him, but mutilated his body;
and his friends, when they found the body, brought it home to
Pottawatomie. The proslavery men in the neighborhood took
advantage of this circumstance to confound this affair with the

others and charge it upon the "abolitionists" and it afforded a fine theme for war extras along the Missouri frontier.'

Mr. Phillips chose to ignore the Walker findings and to dismiss the charge against John Brown, as perpetrator, by a passing acknowledgment that such was the charge.

T. H. Gladstone, correspondent of the London *Times*, who credits Phillips for his background misinformation, arrived in Kansas Territory soon after the sack of Lawrence. This he reviewed at length in his book on Kansas, calling it 'the severest blow that Kansas has yet received,' but the day 'that turned the tide of popular feeling.' He was in Leavenworth the day news of the Pottawatomie massacre reached there, but this incident he does not mention, except for a few lines in a round-up chapter at the end of his book. Then he makes it a mysterious fight between matched forces, a fearsome struggle in which all the proslavery men were killed and three of the Free State men.

The Congressional Investigation Committee, winding up its fact-finding inquiry, called in James Harris at Westport, Missouri, but quickly cut him off when he started to talk about the massacre. The minutes say, in parenthesis, that the Committee decided 'that no testimony in regard to acts of violence committed since the resolutions organizing this commission will be received.' But the majority report did refer to the sack of Lawrence and to the tarring and feathering of Pardee Butler, both 'acts of violence' committed (but by Southerners) not only after the committee was commissioned but when it had virtually completed its work.

The minority member, Mordecai Oliver, and the committee clerk did listen to James Harris. They heard him name 'the man called Old Man Brown' as leader of the butcher band. They listened to the accounts of the widows of James Doyle and Allen Wilkinson, heard young John Doyle tell of finding the bodies of his father and two brothers.

The whole story of the Pottawatomie Creek massacre was printed in 1856, against the will of the Committee majority. But Mr. Howard and Mr. Sherman need not have worried. The Northern press made great capital of the Howard Report, but

ignored Mordecai Oliver's minority report. The true story of
John Brown's murder march might have been buried forever in
the congressional archives had not James Townsley, more than
twenty years later, eased his conscience by telling the same story
that the massacre survivors had told at the time. And two other
men, Townsley said — William Sherman's brother, Dutch
Henry, and Judge George Wilson — missed immortality at
John Brown's hand that May night by not being at home when
he called.

John Brown never had to deny his authorship of the brutal
saga until the last days of his life, because no one dared ask him.
But as his assurance of himself as God's Handyman grew, he
often spoke approvingly of 'the Dutch Henry business.' More
examples like that, he said, were what Kansas Territory and the
country needed.

17

Battle of Black Jack

FREE-SOILERS chose to ignore the Pottawatomie Creek massacre, but proslavery men did not. First in the field was H. C. Pate, Kansas correspondent of the *Missouri Republican* and a captain in the Territorial Militia. When news of the butchery reached Lecompton, Pate and his Sharp Shooters set out. Before their departure, Pate's Lieutenant Brock was interviewed by the *Lecompton Union.* 'We are going down to the southern part of the territory, expecting to see rattlesnakes and abolitionists, and we are taking our guns along,' the lieutenant said.

They went to look for Old Brown but found him hard to find. In scouring the Osawatomie neighborhood, the only Browns they turned up were two of the old man's sons, Jason and John, Jr., the only two of the clan who had not been involved in the dark deeds of 24 May.

Pate's company burned young John's house and the store of the German, Theodore Weiner, suspected of having been with Old Brown on his murder spree. The company headed north then, with the Brown boys as prisoners — 'chained like beasts,' according to Phillips, 'and made to walk in the hot sun.' Pate met up with a patrol of federal dragoons and turned the prisoners over to them. The Brown boys stayed in chains. 'For twenty-five miles they thus suffered this outrageous inhumanity,' wrote Phillips. 'Nor was this all. John Brown, Jun., who had been excited by the wild stories of murder told against his father, by their enemies, and who was of a sensitive mind, was unable to hold up against this and his treatment during the march, and afterwards, while confined in camp, startled his remorseless captors by the wild ravings of a maniac, while he lashed his chains in fury till the dull iron shone like polished steel.'

George W. Brown, editor of the *Herald of Freedom,* was one of the Aid Society leaders who was to smart under the post-war canonization of John Brown. In his *False Claims Corrected,* he devotes considerable space to evidence that John Brown's background was one of hereditary insanity. And he tells how John Brown once killed a dog because it preferred a man named Perkins to himself.

But, in 1856, George Brown, had his paper not been destroyed, would probably have taken William Phillips' view of Junior's insanity. And he would probably have written in the same sympathetic vein as Phillips did about the captured boys' father who 'like a wolf robbed of his young, stealthily, but resolutely, watched for his foes while he skirted through the thickets of the Meroderin and Ottawa Creeks . . .'

John Brown's foes were looking for him, too. The dragoons headed for Lecompton with their prisoners, but Pate kept looking. On Saturday, the last day of May and a week to the day after the massacre, Pate's Sharp Shooters made camp at the head of Black Jack ravine in the Hickory Point section. Some of the boys rode into Palmyra to do a bit of plundering, came back with a few stolen arms and two prisoners, Dr. Graham of Prairie City and a Baptist preacher named Moore. The latter was known to be a free-soiler from Missouri and his captors tormented him with what Phillips calls 'a wicked refinement of cruelty.' They knew Moore 'was opposed to drinking, so they seized his person and, putting a tin funnel in his mouth, poured liquor down his throat — the scoundrels swearing they would "make the old preacher drunk." '

That made a pleasant evening, but by Sunday afternoon the boys were bored again. Against their captain's protest, half a dozen of them rode into Prairie City to see what excitement they could stir up. Two of them never came back.

The townspeople had gathered in the captured Dr. Graham's cabin to hear preaching, but they had gone prepared for visitors.

The congregation was singing the closing hymn, when its sentry rushed in to cry, 'The Missourians! They are coming!'

Twenty men grabbed their guns and rushed out to greet the surprised bordermen, who quickly wheeled their horses to dash away. Shots rang out. And two Southerners fell from their horses, mortally wounded.

When John Brown heard of this shooting, he knew that Pate was somewhere around. And at dawn the next morning, scouts brought news that his camp had been located. Brown, who had already joined forces with Captain Shore's Prairie City Company, sent couriers to Palmyra and to Abbott's Blue Mound Infantry, camped on the Wakarusa. But he did not wait for reinforcements. He attacked the camp at Black Jack at dawn Tuesday.

'Who goes there?' cried Captain Pate. 'What do you want?'

'When I get my line formed, I'll show you!' cried Captain Shore.

A moment later a volley poured in on the Southerners, who returned the volley, then scrambled for the protection of their wagon barricade.

The firing lasted two or three hours. The Northerners, who were fewer in number, shot from concealed positions and made things very hot for the fifty men in Pate's camp. And when Old Brown's son Frederick — described by Phillips as 'a half-witted lad' — appeared on a land rise brandishing a sword and yelled, 'Come on,' as if he had a regiment behind him, the Missourians began to decamp, slipping down the ravine and over the ridge to their horses.

There were just twenty-three men left when Pate finally surrendered, eight of them wounded in battle and the prisoner, Dr. Graham, winged while trying to escape.

Captain Jim Abbott arrived on the scene with fifty men just after the surrender, and other free-soilers who had heard of the battle began to appear. By Wednesday, 4 June, there was a good-sized army gathered at Black Jack. The companies already mentioned had been joined by Captain Samuel Walker and his Bloomington Rifles, Captain Joseph Cracklin and his Lawrence Stubbs, and Captain McWhinney's Wakarusa Boys.

These companies, however, had not mobilized to aid John Brown. News of the battle of Black Jack simply had concentrated forces already under arms to repel a reported new invasion from Missouri. About the time these free-soil companies, organized under an informal command, moved eastward, some 300 Missourians under Whitfield and Coffey encamped on Bull Creek.

At dawn on Wednesday, 5 June, the two armies were within battle distance — but there was no attack. All was quiet, with each side awaiting the sound of a shot to signal them to action. It was as if two dogs of more bark than bite had broken leash and found themselves, to their dismay, face to face and free to lunge.

These were armies, well equipped and organized. One command would make war between brothers a reality. Relief, then, underlay the growls that went up next day when Colonel Edwin Sumner and his federal dragoons came riding into no man's land with a proclamation from Governor Shannon.

All armed forces in the Territory were commanded to disperse. And with only one skirmish in the never-ending battle of words, they did.

Captain John Brown, at the command of Colonel Sumner, released his prisoner, Captain Pate. Then Deputy Marshal Fain stepped forward to arrest John Brown, only to find that he had lost his warrant. Colonel Sumner ruled that, under the circumstances, no arrest could be made.

Old Brown's recent captive, handsome Captain Pate, became very angry. He took the stump in protest, but he had only begun to talk when the federal colonel commanded him to be quiet.

'I don't want to hear a word from you, sir,' said the colonel.

'Not a word, sir. You have no business here. The governor told me so.'

The skirmish was over. John Brown went free. The armies dispersed — and gang rule took over again.

18

At Home and Abroad

'HE'S A FLUNG UP, pilfering, blue-bellied Yankee, that's what he is.'

'The hanging bone villain may say his prayers mighty smart now. I'll be daggoned if we don't string him up afore this day is out.'

'Hangin's a nation sight too good for him, the mean cuss.'

The place, Leavenworth, K.T. The time, the last day of the blood-red May. The 'mean cuss,' Charles Robinson, free-soil pretender to the gubernatorial throne, who had been brought upriver from Kansas City and was being held, under guard, in the small wooden structure known as McCarty's Hotel. The reporter, Thomas Gladstone of the *London Times*.

The talk had commenced a week before, on the day Robinson was landed on the broad levee with its half-mile stretch of saloons and warehouses.

Gladstone had arrived on the same boat as Robinson, without knowing it. He had followed the prisoner and his guard around piles of merchandise on the pier and in and out among the long wagons that blocked the quay with their loads of goods and their ten-yoke oxen teams.

He learned the identity of the prisoner when he heard a man ask, 'Who's that they got there?'

'It's Governor Robinson,' another man answered.

'*Governor* Robinson! Who taught you to call that infernal nigger-stealer "governor," I should like to know?'

Robinson was in town! The word spread. Gladstone could feel the swell of animosity as he followed the 'governor's party' up the steep road to McCarty's. He could hear the rising tide of threats through the open windows of the hotel's front room as the prisoner was questioned by Chief Justice Lecompte and other officials.

Gladstone, sick of hearing the revilements, went into the office and sat down 'to meditate and observe.' The clerk was visiting with everyone who came that way about the state of the Territory; and, on the counter, papers screamed 'War to the Knife!'

There was a stack of firearms in one corner and a man came in and said, 'Hand me a pair out of them hundred pistols I left with you, captain.' Then, as he buckled on the pistols, he said, 'I just had a turn down with a damned free-soiler. I didn't ought to have left these here tools behind this morning, I allow.' He had to take care of that one with his fists, he explained. 'I brought him down kinda smart, I reckon; expect he felt chawed up some.' He patted his pistols. 'I calculate they won't be so saucy now,' he said, and left.

The talk, inside and out, went on all that day and 'As night advanced, the ceaseless whisky drinking showed its fruits. Pistols went off sometimes unguardedly; knots of people collected at each street corner. The barrooms in the hotels, which were all political clubs, became crowded with noisy debaters.'

Armed intruders kept coming into Gladstone's room at night, and by day he had to listen to the 'painfully revolting talk,' which, though he failed to mention the incident, had been given its intensity of pitch by news of the Pottawatomie massacre. Robinson just happened to be the free-soiler at hand on whom revenge might be wreaked.

'He ought to have a shot through his head; that's the way I'd serve the old polecat abolitionist out.'

'Yessir, lead's the best argument for them infernal rascals.'

'Tall times these, gentleman. Knife to the hilt, I say.'

'Knife to the hilt! Just let me get a-holt of him and I'll make wolfmeat out of him.'

But talk, like a daydream, can go so far that it pales any conceivable deed. There was no way to kill a man that the bordermen had not used on Charles Robinson, so suddenly, toward midnight on the last day of May, they quitted their guard on McCarty's to repair to the groceries ('an emendation of groggeries' to Gladstone). Supreme Court Justice Sterling Cato and an escort of federal dragoons under Colonel Preston were able to slip Charles Robinson out of town, in the early hours of Sunday, 1 June, and take him to join other free-soilers in the tent prison camp the U.S. Army had set up a mile and a half south of Lecompton.

He was the fifth of eight major political prisoners. Reeder, Lane, and Sam Wood were now the only major offenders still at large, though there were several lesser lights in 'The Pavilion,' as the prisoners called the row of tents which they had joined together with a cloth roofing, to provide pleasant shade against the hot Kansas sun.

The next Wednesday, Mrs. Robinson, after a successful trip back East, arrived in Kansas City. But it took more than two weeks for her to reach her husband's side. Free-soil traffic westward through Westport had been rumored to a standstill. Highways were blockaded by such tall tales as the one about free-soil bodies hanging from trees — five of them along the Santa Fe Trail between Westport and Palmyra. The only safe way to get to Lawrence, everybody said, was to go by boat thirty miles upriver to Leavenworth, K.T., then take the weekly stage across the Delaware lands.

The problem then was to get passage on a boat. 'One came in heavily loaded with Mormons,' Mrs. Robinson wrote. 'Every place on the upper deck was crowded with large emigrant waggons and the living freight packed in at every corner. Dirt and filth were visible and the looks of the women "sealed" to the Mormon faith and their tyrannical husbands was one of utter misery.'

After more than a week of trying, she got space for the overnight run on the *Keystone*. It ran into a bank in the dawn fog and she missed the Saturday morning stage to Lawrence.

But, fortunately, Mrs. Robinson had friends in the K.T. metropolis; and on Monday, a Lawrence citizen, in Leavenworth on business, gave her a lift in his buggy. The next day, 17 June, she and Mrs. Jenkins, wife of Gaius, arrived at Lecompton Camp, where they were permitted to stay with their husbands. And they lived a jolly, luxurious camp life, until it was brought to an abrupt end by rumors of a free-soil attack to free them. The prisoners were moved to an airless log cabin in the capital. All were packed, Mrs. Robinson reported, in a greasy wagon. 'Some bluecoats rode on each side of us and the main body of this portion of the President's army of subjugation brought up the rear.'

That was the attitude Northerners in Kansas Territory had toward the blues of the United States Army in June, 1856, the month when the two-year congressional debate about Kansas came to a head.

II

THE YEAR 1856 was election year and June was the month of planks, platforms, and presidential nominees.

Democrats convened at Cincinnati on 2 June 1856. They reaffirmed the party stand on slavery as stated in the Kansas-Nebraska Bill. The national government should not interfere with slavery. Settlers of territories had a right to establish whatever domestic institutions they wished. They could have slavery or not have slavery, as they saw fit.

The Democratic Party staked its chances on the merits of the Kansas-Nebraska Bill, but snubbed the bill's father. Stephen A. Douglas fully expected to be rewarded by being chosen as the Democratic standard-bearer, but he was thrown out on the first ballot. Douglas was rejected, but so was the President himself. Franklin Pierce's administration was endorsed, but James Buchanan of Pennsylvania, who had been Ambassador to England, safely away from the Kansas-Nebraska controversy, was selected as the party's presidential candidate, with John Breckinridge of Kentucky as his running mate.

The Republican Party, holding its first national convention under that name, built its whole platform on a 'Free Kansas' slogan. Declaring it 'both the right and duty of Congress to prohibit in the Territories those twin relics of barbarism, polygamy and slavery,' the convention resolved: 'That Kansas should be immediately admitted as a State of the Union with her present free constitution, as at once the most effectual way of securing to her citizens the enjoyment of the right and privileges to which they are entitled, and of ending the civil strife now raging in the Territory.'

The new party wanted its most illustrious spokesman, William H. Seward, to carry this standard, but he refused. His friend Thurlow Weed advised him to wait another four years, until the party grew stronger. So General John C. Frémont was nominated. And a man named Dayton nosed out a man named Lincoln for the dubious honor of being the vice-presidential candidate.

Left-over Whigs met with Know-Nothings in Philadelphia in May and united under the name of the American Party, with the slogan, 'Americans must rule America.' Millard Fillmore was nominated its candidate on a platform that was against the interference of Congress with questions 'pertaining solely to the individual states, and non-intervention by each State with the affairs of any other State.'

It is interesting to keep these candidates and their platforms in mind as the show goes on — in the Territory of Kansas.

19

Heat Lightning

HEAT CAME and with an air of having come to stay. It lay
heavily upon the land, as the sun sucked the moisture of the
earth into the still air and June sweltered its way toward July.

Women worked in the fields, trying to save crops their
husbands had planted and then left for the less back-breaking
fields of glory. Southerners built two more forts — Saunders
on Washington Creek and Fort Franklin at Franklin, which
was first attacked by free-soilers when it was only half-built. A
proslave man named Tischmaker was killed and a wagonload of
ammunition and alligator guns was captured.

Roads were filled with wagons carrying families from the
North and from the South, either into the Territory or out of
it. Free-soil Major David Starr Hoyt, who earlier had been
detained in Missouri for smuggling Sharp's rifles, was killed
from ambush. Another free-soiler by the name of Cantral was
taken prisoner in the Black Jack section and given the final
lesson of lead. And Captain Samuel Walker of the Free State
Militia, hearing that Major Henry Titus of the Law and Order
Militia planned to pay a call at his home at the fork of the
California and Lecompton roads, invited some thirty free-soil
friends in to help him welcome the rumored visitors.

It was such a large reception committee that the Walker
log cabin could not accommodate all of it. A dozen or so members
took their places with Walker in his house and the others under a

Colonel Topliff, whom Charles Robinson had hired to drill the Free State military companies, repaired to a deserted log cabin near by. Chinking was knocked out of the walls of both cabins, in order that the committee might extend its welcoming arms and, along about midnight, the expected guests arrived.

The fifteen or so horsemen who came riding up the Lecompton Road had quietly filed through the gate in Sam Walker's picket fence, when their host gave the order to fire. A dozen guns barked through the walls of the two cabins and the Southerners topped the timbers. Some of them remounted as their steeds went over the fence. Only a dead horse and a coat pocket caught on a paling with its bottle of whisky intact were left to attest the visit. Next day, Titus offered three hundred dollars for Sam Walker's head, on or off his shoulders.

These were some of the goings on as summer built its head of steam.

The President of the United States issued a proclamation against the Kansas Free State government, gave orders that its legislature was not to meet on the Fourth of July, as scheduled. But the Fourth found Topeka filled with legislators and their families.

The day dawned bright and hot. As midday drew near, it was a blistering hundred degrees Fahrenheit in the shade. A gala array of townspeople and other free-soilers gathered for a morning of parades and speeches, their hearts high with excitement. The legislature planned to convene at high noon, despite the President's proclamation, and despite the warning that had come from Colonel Edwin Sumner of the United States Army.

Just before noon the band struck up a martial air. Half a dozen companies of Free State Militia, some members dressed in their newly adopted gray uniform, fell in line in front of Constitution Hall to receive a banner from the ladies, who were out in full force, carrying parasols gay with streamers.

A sentry came riding to say that the bluecoats were coming.

The band played on, blew and beat harder as the dragoons, riding at a brisk trot, swung into Kansas Avenue some hundred yards above the hall.

'The Bull of the Woods,' as Sumner's men called him, rode
at the head of a column of two hundred dragoons, in three
squadrons, including one of light artillery.

He rode right up to where the free-soil band was playing
and he held up a gloved hand to silence the musicmakers. 'First
squadron, fall in!' he cried. Other orders quickly followed and
were quickly executed. Two cannons were posted on a rise up
the street. An army surgeon dismounted and opened his case
on a bench, ready for business. The cannons were loaded and
cannoneers stood with slow matches burning as Colonel Sumner
dismounted and walked into the assembly hall.

It was high noon. Members of the House of Representatives took their seats as the assistant clerk, Samuel Tappan, in
the absence of Speaker T. Minard and Chief Clerk Joel Goodwin, stood behind the presiding table. As Tappan lifted the gavel,
Colonel Sumner appeared in the doorway. Tappan motioned
him to a chair up front. 'Do you want to make a speaker of me?'
Sumner asked as he took the proffered chair (laughter).

Tappan called the roll. There was not a quorum present.
Sergeant at arms J. Mitchell was sent to bring in absentees.
More men came in, but though there were thirty-three members
in the room when the next roll was called, only seventeen answered.

Colonel Sumner got to his feet. 'Gentlemen, I am called
upon this day to perform the most painful duty of my whole
life,' he said. 'Under the authority of the President's proclamation, I am here to disperse this legislature and therefore inform
you that you cannot meet. I, therefore, order you to disperse.'

Judge Phillip Schuyler was recognized by the colonel. 'Are
we to understand, Colonel Sumner, that the legislature are
driven out at the point of a bayonet?'

'I shall use all the forces in my command to carry out my
orders,' said the Colonel. He walked from the room and went
upstairs to disperse the upper chamber. Out in front again, he
assured the gathered crowds that he had no wish to interfere
with their Fourth of July celebration, that he had come only to
disperse the legislature.

There were three cheers for the colonel, as he and his dragoons mounted their horses. There were three cheers for the Republican presidential candidate, John Frémont, and, as the dragoons fell into formation, three groans for Franklin Pierce.

The Kansas Free State was 'politically prostrate,' Phillips wrote. 'Her legislature was dispersed by federal troops; her leading men were languishing in prison. The Missouri River was closed to emigrants from the free states, and the tedious uncertain route through Iowa was menaced and the only security by that route was by companies sufficiently determined to take care of themselves.'

That closed the last Kansas-written chapter of his book, *Conquest of Kansas.* He brought the book to an end with this wisdom: 'It is a grave fact that must never be forgotten by the American people, military power is and must ever be inimical to popular institutions.'

It was a thought shared by many. Four days after Sumner and his federal dragoons dispersed the Free State legislature, an aroused Northern majority in the national House of Representatives held up the Army appropriation bill. They would not pass it, they said, unless it carried a proviso that the Army should not be used in putting down free-soil men in the Territory of Kansas.

The House was deadlocked on this question when it adjourned ten days later. However, when Pierce called it back on 21 August to act on the appropriation bill, it passed the bill without the proviso. Secretary of War Jefferson Davis' sound spanking of Sumner for using military force to disperse a meeting simply 'in anticipation of serious difficulties' probably swung the vote.

Out in Kansas Territory there was such confusion that it was difficult, even for the people who lived there, to know who were the offenders and who the offended.

20

Two Governors Down and Four To Go

KANSAS WAS the inescapable word that summer. It was sounded again and again by the presidential candidates and by those who were campaigning for them. Churches rang with it and headlines screamed it.

Atchison and other border slaveholders sent hard dollar-and-cents appeals southward. *DeBow's Review*, New Orleans, carried a letter from a Kansas squatter. 'Slaves now yield a greater profit in Kansas than in any state,' the letter said. 'Planters are making twice as much money per hand as in any other part of the Union. One hand will raise six tons of hemp and this don't interfere with the corn, wheat, and oat crop. A near neighbor with fourteen hands — men, women, and children — last year averaged $836 a hand.'

The appeal trend in the north was toward the emotional. Free-soilers in Kansas Territory were pictured as fighting the cause of humanity at great cost of life and personal property. 'Settlers have raised issues, not crops,' one pamphleteer wrote. Kansas Relief became a great project in the North. Milwaukee raised $3,000; Chicago, $20,000; the Grand Kansas Aid Society of Buffalo, $120,000; The Boston Committee, $20,000; and the New England Aid Society, $78,000. These were gifts in cold cash, sent in addition to large supplies of food, clothing, and ammunition.

Vigilance was the watchword in Missouri. The river was

policed. Steamers were raided and Free State consignments confiscated. Men recruited by Jim Lane in Chicago lost their rifles and were sent back down the river. 'We are of the opinion that if the citizens of Leavenworth would hang one or two boat-loads of Abolitionists, it would do more toward establishing peace in Kansas than all the speeches delivered in Congress,' said the *Squatter Sovereign*, crying, 'Let the experiment be tried!'

That experiment was not tried, but Captain Emory's Regulators of Leavenworth did swear to expel every abolition-ist in that vicinity. They rounded up free-soilers and sent them down the river by the boatload.

Free-soil communications were established through Iowa and Nebraska. Late in July nearly four hundred emigrants enlisted by Lane, and called 'Lane's Army,' were encamped near Nebraska City. Governor Shannon urged General Persifer Smith, who had just succeeded Colonel Sumner as commandant of Fort Leavenworth, to 'take to the field with the whole disposable force in the Territory.' Smith refused on the basis that Shannon was misinformed. The governor then sent two free-state men whom he trusted, Dr. S. G. Howe and Thaddaeus Hyatt, to find out the nature of 'Lane's Army.' They found it unmilitary enough. In fact, the immigrants were in such a forlorn condition that the investigators demanded that Lane sever his connection with them.

Jim Lane, ever the actor in search of an audience, said, 'If the people of Kansas don't want me, I'll cut my throat today.' And he rode off. He was chased around for a while by federal dragoons but was never caught, and he arrived in Lawrence on 11 August, disguised as Captain Jo Cook. As his immigrant party crossed the border to establish the towns of Plymouth and Holton, he was made welcome in provisionless, leaderless Lawrence and he began to round up a real army and to plan his campaigns.

Two days after his return he marched with eighty-nine men against Fort Franklin, now completed, which consisted of a blockhouse flanked by a post office and a hotel. The free-soilers

crept up in the darkness, fired a token round to announce their
presence, and commanded the garrison to surrender. The answer
was a round of shots from the defenders. After three hours of
firing, Lane's men wheeled a wagonload of hay against the post
office and set it afire. It, the blockhouse, and the hotel were
quickly emptied.

The fort had fallen, but there were no dead — a poor
showing for three hours of gunfire. General Lane decided that
to make the engagement pay, he must make an example of one
of the Southerners.

He announced his intention. The period of non-resistance
was over, he said. He was launching an offensive to drive the
proslave armies out of the Territory. Now he was going to show
the bordermen that he meant business. He asked Sam Crane,
Sr., Franklin postmaster, to step forward.

Crane stepped forward, but so did his wife. She stood
before the conquering general. 'Oh, don't shoot my husband,'
she said. 'Don't shoot him.'

'He deserves to die, madam,' said Lane. 'He is a great
villain.'

'I know it,' said the marked man's wife. 'That's the reason
I don't want you to shoot him.'

Laughter exploded from the depths of a hundred bellies,
erasing, for this crucial moment, the Mason-Dixie Line. Lane
ordered a detail to load the garrison's cannon into the free-soil
loot wagon and returned to Lawrence.

Postmaster Crane's life was spared, but Jim Lane was in
the saddle now and he convinced a sizeable group of men in and
about Lawrence that the time for turning the other cheek was
past. Free-soil men must take the offensive.

And on 15 August, the general set out to capture Fort
Saunders on Washington Creek with a fine show of horse and
artillery.

The attack was well planned and well executed. It fell flat
only because the fort had been abandoned, and the ravine, when
charged, had no one in it.

This empty victory may have been what sent Lane off, without apparent purpose, to the Nebraska border.

Half a dozen companies went with Lane. Samuel Walker, left in command of the others, thought of his neglected crops and ordered the troops to disperse. But the men were not in the mood to be dispersed. They had been itching for a fight and they were determined to have one. They would camp right there on Rock Creek and wait until Jim Lane came back.

Sam Walker said that he was going home. Then a scout came in with the rumor that the free-state prisoners at Lecompton were about to be hung. Walker sent a runner to Lawrence to rally reinforcements and he headed north with his command.

About eight miles from Lecompton, Walker's forces met Titus and his band. There was a skirmish that amounted to little in the deep dark of that starless night, except as it acted to discourage free-soilers from trying to reach Lecompton.

The skirmish was close to Sam Walker's home so he went there. He was at breakfast next morning when there was a knock on his cabin door. The driver of the Lecompton-Westport stage had stopped on the pretext of asking about the road and for the purpose of saying, hurriedly, 'I've got Titus' wife and two children on the stage. If you want to get that damned scoundrel, now is the time.'

Titus had just raised his bounty on Sam Walker's head from $300 to $500.

Sam Walker thought of that and of the encampment of federal dragoons which stood almost in sight of Fort Titus. Well, Major John Sedgwick had as much as said that if he, Sam Walker, ever wanted to nab Titus he would probably be able to do it before the dragoons could get there. Walker decided to take a chance. He sent a runner to Lawrence for the captured six-pounder. Then, with the fifty horsemen camped on Rock Creek, he made a daylight attack.

The garrison was surprised but quickly returned fire. One free-soiler had been killed by the heated rifle volleys when footmen came from Lawrence with the cannon. With balls made from *Herald of Freedom* type salvaged from the Kaw, a hole was hammered through the blockhouse wall.

Before long, the white flag went up and Titus appeared in the doorway covered with blood, wounded in hand, face, and shoulder. He slumped on a bench against the wall, right under the handbill offering $500 for the head of Samuel Walker, 'on or off the shoulders.'

Titus was the most hated of all Southerners and when he appeared there was a general cry to kill him.

'Well, Titus, I beat you to it,' Sam Walker said. 'And I reckon I might as well finish the job.' He cocked his pistol but, as he told it later, 'The cuss got me in the right place. He saw the devil was to pay and he made a personal appeal to me. "You have children, so have I," he pleaded. "For God's sake, save my life." '

When a near-by free-soiler saw that Walker was not going to shoot, he cursed and raised his rifle.

Walker commanded him not to shoot.

The man was not to be stopped. He looked down the sights at Titus and was about to pull the trigger when Sam Walker's fist came hard against his jaw and sent him to the ground.

When this fellow got to his feet again, Walker said, 'There Titus sits. If any one of you is brute enough to shoot, shoot.'

No one shot.

As Walker attended his six wounded men, a detail went into the blockhouse to bring out the proslave casualties, the two dead, two wounded. Then Titus and eighteen other prisoners were taken to Lawrence.

A mob tried to get hold of Titus but was thwarted. The next day, 17 August, Governor Shannon, accompanied by Major Sedgwick of the dragoons and Dr. Aristides Roderique, Lecompton postmaster, came to Lawrence in the interest of peace. After a day's conference with Captain James Blood and William Hutchinson, of *The New York Times*, the only Safety Committee members in town at the time, a treaty was signed. The United States, in the person of Governor Shannon, agreed that the cannon captured at the sack of Lawrence would be returned and that the five or six men who had been arrested for participation in the attack on Fort Franklin would be liberated. In exchange, free-soilers released Titus and his men.

There was a round of handshaking, then the peacemakers went out into the street. The governor attempted to address the mob that was gathered there. Men pulled their revolvers as they sent up a great yell against Wilson Shannon.

Sam Walker leaped on his horse and pulled his pistols. 'The first man who insults the governor does it over my dead body!' he cried. 'He shan't be insulted. Boys, I am with you, but he shan't be insulted.'

When Wilson Shannon got back to the capital that night, he sat down and wrote to General Persifer Smith. 'We are threatened with utter extermination by a large force of free-state men,' he said. 'I have just returned from Lawrence, where I have been this day with a view to procuring the release of nineteen prisoners that were taken. I saw in that place at least 800 men who manifested a fixed purpose of destroying this town.'

And the next day, on Monday, 18 August 1856, Wilson Shannon resigned. He wrote to President Pierce, 'I am unwilling to perform the duties of governor of this Territory any longer.' And years later, he said, 'Govern Kansas in 1855 and '56! You might as well attempt to govern the devil in hell.'

Three days after the governor wrote to the President, he received notification of his removal. Meanwhile, the midsummer madness went on. Free-soilers from Lawrence pillaged pro-slavery homes in Tecumseh, took wagonloads of plunder to Topeka, where they dumped it in the street and told people to help themselves to the tables, chairs, dresses, suits, beds, and kitchenware. And in Leavenworth, a border bully by the name of Fugit bet six dollars against a pair of boots that he would scalp an abolitionist within two hours. He won his bet.

21

'Reign of Terror'

Top jobs in territorial government were held by men appointed by the President of the United States and confirmed by the Senate. Appointees held these jobs as long as they stayed in federal favor, or could take the gaff.

Next highest office to the governorship was that of secretary of state, an office resembling the vice-presidency of the United States in its impotence and potential power. This officer had nothing of real importance to do except when the governor was out of the territory, or, when there was a lapse between governors, then he became the acting-governor. When Andrew Reeder was made the first governor of the Territory of Kansas, a handsome, thirty-year-old Marylander, Daniel Woodson, was named secretary of state. He still had that office when Wilson Shannon resigned.

Residents of a territory had no say in the selection of the men who governed them. They were citizens of the United States living outside her limits. Their only contact with the federal government was through their delegate to Congress, who was simply a lobbyist, a man without the right to vote. It is doubtful whether many squatters would have liked to have had Daniel Woodson appointed governor, but Missouri leaders strongly favored his appointment, or preferably, that of John Calhoun, sound-on-the-goose surveyor general. They were sharply disappointed when President Pierce named John W. Geary of Pennsylvania instead.

Missourians were disappointed in the news, but they were prepared for it. An army more than a thousand strong, under Dave Atchison, stood camped at Little Santa Fe on the border, ready to take advantage of a time when Daniel Woodson would be in power. And the day Shannon left the Territory, they got the invitation they had been waiting for. Woodson declared Kansas Territory in a state of insurrection and rebellion and asked 'all patriotic citizens' to rally in defense of the law.

Among those present in Atchison's camp was a hot-headed man of the cloth, the Reverend Martin White, recently a citizen of Dutch Henry's Crossing, K.T. An ardent proslavery man, he had time and again been threatened by free-soil patrols. When a gang under J. C. Holmes helped themselves to his property and told his son, 'When we've killed old Martin, we will have all the proslavery men in the neighborhood,' Martin White had gone back to Missouri. Now he was set to get revenge.

The parson's objective was the abolitionist stronghold of Osawatomie, which would have been an early objective of the Missourians in any case, since it was the home of the hated Browns. With Reverend White as guide, a detail under General John Reid set out to wipe Osawatomie off the map.

Citizens of that town were forewarned by free-soil scouts, but not in time to call in the men who were out harassing pro-slave settlers who had stubbornly stayed on their land, despite the 'example' John Brown had made of Pottawatomie Creek Southerners. There were only forty men in town and Reid had a force of two hundred and fifty.

Indian warfare was called for. When Reid arrived at dawn on 30 August, he was greeted by a volley of shots from the trees skirting the Marais des Cygnes.

Reid was surprised, but he quickly set up his field piece and sent patrols into the woods. There was a brief skirmish. Five free-soilers were killed and three wounded to two killed, three wounded on the proslavery side. The free-soilers disappeared and General Reid and his force could proceed on their mission. As they neared town, they met a late-comer to the field of action — John Brown's deficient son, Frederick.

The outraged parson had the pleasure of killing him. 'The ball passed clean through his body,' Martin White used to say, with pride.

With this last line of defense out of the way, the Missourians swarmed into Osawatomie, helped themselves to whatever articles appealed to them, then applied the torch. When flames had run their course only four houses still stood.

Meantime, Free State General James H. Lane had heard of Woodson's proclamation and had returned from Nebraska. He was marching toward Atchison's camp with some 300 men.

This march followed the formal warfare pattern of the Territory. Again it was all bark and no bite. This time shots were fired. Lane's army shot a volley and Atchison's army answered, then both armies retired from the field. Atchison for some reason returned to Missouri, but Lane decided it was time to get down to business.

Acting-Governor Woodson had ordered the Fort Riley commandant, Colonel P. St. George Cooke, to go to Topeka to disarm free-soil insurrectionists there and to level their fortifications. The colonel ignored this order. But Lecompton citizens, under the leadership of Sheriff Sam Jones, took care of their local free-soil situation. They burned the cabins of the seven Northern families who lived in the territorial capital.

This made Lecompton Lane's first objective. He ordered Colonel J. A. Harvey to station his regiment north of the Kaw, across from the capital, to cut off retreat in that direction as he marched from Lawrence to attack from the south.

Lecompton citizens lived in dread of an attack. Women and children had been evacuated. 'Nearly every home I passed within five or six miles of Lecompton is deserted,' Dragoon Captain D. B. Sacket commented in a dispatch. And Colonel Cooke himself took command of the dragoon garrison in the capital.

Mid-afternoon of 5 September, citizens came running into camp to report 'a large force approaching Lecompton from below.' The colonel sounded 'boots and saddles.' A courier came from Woodson, asking protection for the town. 'Some minutes after,' the colonel reported, 'I marched in person at the head of a squadron of Second Dragoons, ordering the First Cavalry and artillery to follow.'

When free-soil scouts sighted the federal dragoons, General Lane, long wanted by the Territorial government as an offender against it, grabbed a musket from one of his men and stepped into the infantry ranks. Colonel Samuel Walker was in command of the free-soilers when the dragoons appeared.

'What have you come for?' asked Colonel Cooke.

'We have come to release the prisoners and to get our rights,' Sam Walker said.

Cooke told him that the army of Missourians was dispersing and that the free-soil prisoners in Lecompton were going to be set free.

At that point, Deputy U.S. Marshal Crane rode up. He had reliable information, he said, that James Lane was present in the ranks. He commanded Lane to step forward in the name of the law.

Jim Lane was never a man to step in any direction unless he figured it as a step to his advantage. If Crane had been given time to look for Lane in the ranks, he would have passed over him as the perfect example of a man in the ranks.

Samuel Walker ordered an about face, and so did Colonel Cooke.

As the free-soilers marched back to Lawrence in the cold, drizzling rain that came down, and Colonel Harvey's men shivered around sputtering campfires, awaiting shots that never came to signal them to action, Colonel P. St. George Cooke sat down to write his report of the day. 'Lecompton and its defenders were outnumbered and apparently in the power of a determined force,' he wrote. 'Americans thus stood face to face in hostile array and most earnest of purpose. As I marched back over these beautiful hills, all crowned with moving troops and marching men, I rejoiced that I had stayed the madness of the hour and prevented, on almost any terms, the fratricidal onslaught of countrymen and fellow citizens.'

A letter was on its way from Secretary of War Jefferson

Davis to Cooke's boss, General Persifer Smith, commander of the Department of the West, authorizing him to call upon the governors of Illinois and Kentucky if aid was needed 'to suppress insurrection against the government of the Territory of Kansas.' Jeff Davis said, 'Patriotism and humanity alike require that the rebellion should be promptly crushed.' He added that he realized that to the general, 'as to every soldier, whose habitual feeling is to protect the citizens of his own country, and only to use his arms against a public enemy, it cannot be otherwise than deeply painful to be brought into conflict with any portion of his fellow-countrymen.'

General Smith made no call upon the militia. He was not going to give Woodson another chance to call in the Missourians. As it was, the Territory was alive with roving bands of them and another march on Lawrence was said to be planned.

William Hutchinson of the Lawrence Committee of Safety wrote an appeal to Woodson.

'Your troubles,' answered the acting-governor, 'are the natural and inevitable result of the present lawless and revolutionary position in which you have, of your own accord, placed yourselves.'

The committee was ready with its retort: 'You have left us no alternative but to perish or fight. You have called into the field, under the name of militia, a set of thieves, robbers, home-burners and murderers to prey upon the people you have sworn to protect. This is the position you occupy before the country, and a just God, and on you, not on us, must rest the responsibility.'

Members of the Free State Party were good strategists. They always moved with an eye to public opinion. This formal exchange of documents was to establish their rightness in the all-out campaign Jim Lane was planning.

But a new governor was soon to arrive and bring to an end Woodson's 'Reign of Terror.'

This three-week period was actually no different from any other three weeks of that free-booting, murderous summer of

1856 — a summer to which Kansas natives today are indebted for their nickname, 'Jayhawkers.'

The story goes that soon after daybreak of one of those summer days, an Irish free-soil guerrilla, Pat Delvin, was met on the road by an early-rising neighbor.

'Where have you been, Pat?' the neighbor asked.

'Jayhawking,' said Pat.

'Jayhawking? What's that?'

'Well,' said Pat, 'in the old country, we have a bird called the jayhawk, which kind of worries its prey. It seems to me, as I ride home, that that's what I've been doing.'

Jayhawking was the order of the day for both sides that summer.

II

THE NEW GOVERNOR, John Geary, landed at Fort Leavenworth early in the morning on 9 September 1856. He had arrived well briefed on what to expect in Kansas Territory, but unbelieving.

He had met up with eastbound ex-Governor Shannon quite by accident on the Sabbath morning of 7 September as his boat, the *Keystone*, was docked at Glasgow, Missouri.

The *Keystone* had been welcomed to this river town by a salute of cannon, almost lost in the cheers of the people who lined the bluff. Men, women, and children, white and black, dressed in their Sunday clothes, shouted and swooped down as the packet docked. Then, out of the melee merged a certain order, as troops recruited by Captain Claiborne Jackson fell into ranks. The cannon was wheeled forward smartly, and kinfolk and friends looked on as their heroes, 'from smooth-faced boys to gray-haired old men,' made a formation of sorts, reported John Geary's secretary, John W. Gihon, M.D., who watched with interest from the packet rail. 'Each man carried some description of fire-arm, not any two of which were alike. There were muskets, carbines, rifles, shotguns, and pistols of every size, quality, shape, and style, some of them in good condition, but others never intended for use, and still others unfit to shoot robins or tomtits.'

As Jackson's cannon and ammunition wagons were put aboard the *Keystone*, Wilson Shannon, on the downriver steamer, learned that his successor was on the other packet and he paid a call.

The ex-governor, Gihon said, 'had fled in haste from the Territory and still seemed to be laboring under an apprehension for his personal safety.' His description of Kansas 'was suggestive of everything frightful. The whole Territory was in a state of insurrection and destructive civil war was devastating the whole country. Murder was rampant and the roads everywhere were strewn with the bodies of slaughtered men.'

The incoming governor was interested in his predecessor's account but seemed to feel confident that he, John Geary, could bring order out of chaos. Already he had settled one sore spot. At Jefferson City he had conferred with Missouri's governor, Sterling Price, and it had been agreed that all obstructions to the passage of free-soil settlers up the Missouri were to be removed.

Wilson Shannon refrained from commenting on his successor's move. He simply wished the new governor luck and went on his way.

Jackson's recruits had come aboard and, to the sound of cheers from the bank and shouted farewells from the decks, the *Keystone* moved upriver. Few of the recruits 'had any definite idea of the nature of the enterprise on which they were embarked,' Gihon found. 'The most they seemed to understand was that they were to receive so much per diem for going to Kansas to hunt and kill abolitionists.'

At all the river towns 'active preparations for war were discernible.' At Kansas City the omnibus to Westport stood waiting, its sides proudly proclaiming 'in flaming capitals' its name, *Border Ruffian*. Standing in groups on the levee were a number of men 'who claim for themselves that gentle appellation,' Gihon said, and he described the species:

'Imagine a man standing in a pair of long boots, covered

with dust and mud and drawn over his trousers, the latter made of coarse, fancy-colored cloth, well soiled; the handle of a large Bowie knife projecting from one or both boottops; a leathern belt buckled around his waist, on each side of which is fastened a large revolver; a red or blue shirt, with a heart, anchor, eagle, or some other favorite device braided on the breast and back, over which is swung a rifle or carbine; a sword dangling by his side; an old slouched hat, with a cockade or brass star on the front or side, and a chicken, turkey, or goose feather sticking in the top; hair uncut and uncombed, covering his neck and shoulders; an unshaven face and unwashed hands. Imagine such a picture of humanity, who can swear any given number of oaths in any specified time, drink any quantity of bad whiskey without getting drunk, and boast of having stole half a dozen horses and killed one or more abolitionists, and you will have a pretty fair conception of the border ruffian, as he appears in Missouri and Kansas.

'He has, however, the happy faculty of assuming a very different aspect. Like other animals, he can shed his coat and change his colors. In the city of Washington, he is quite another person. You will see him in the corridors of first-class hotels — upon Pennsylvania avenue — in the rotunda of the capitol, or the spacious halls of the White House, dressed in the finest broadcloths and in the extreme of fashion; his hair trimmed, his face smoothed and his hands cleansed; his manner gentle, kind, and courteous; his whole deportment that of innocence, and his speech so smooth, studied and oily as to convince even the sagacious president himself that he is a veritable and polished gentleman, and obtain from the wise heads that form the cabinet the most important posts of trust, honor and emolument in the gift of the nation.'

Half a dozen of these creatures boarded the *Keystone* when she was docked. They dashed through the cabins and over the decks to make sure there were no abolitionists aboard. Claiborne Jackson disembarked his troops and the packet moved on again upriver, to dock at Leavenworth City soon after daybreak on 9 September.

Gihon was up to see it. 'In front of the grog shops and these comprised nearly every house on the river front; on piles of lumber and stone, upon the heads of whisky barrels; at the corners of the streets and up on the river bank — lounged, strolled and idled, singly or in squads, men and boys clad in ruffian attire. Armed horsemen were dashing about in every direction, the horses' feet striking fire from the stones beneath and the sabres of the riders rattling at their sides. The drum and fife disturbed the stillness of the morning, and volunteer companies were on parade and drill, with all the habiliments and panoply of war. The town was evidently under a complete military rule, and on every side were visible indications of a destructive civil strife.'

The town lived, Gihon reported, under constant fear of attack by Jim Lane, a man 'whose very name was a terror.'

Three miles upriver, at Fort Leavenworth, the governor's party disembarked. The fort, in contrast to the straggling, clamorous town of the same name, was a picture of orderliness and stability, with its well-arranged buildings of brick and gleaming white, its commanding site and spacious parade grounds. But there was something strange there, too. Groups of civilians were everywhere; free-soil families had sought refuge from Emory's Regulators inside the fort's walls.

This supposedly secret band did do some of its dirty work in disguise, but most members proudly proclaimed their membership and avowed purpose of cleansing the Territory of all abolitionists. Several times a day a crier rode through the streets of Leavenworth City warning free-soil families to get out, if they did not want to be driven out.

Many a boatload had been 'sent down the river' and Fort Leavenworth had become so crowded an asylum that steps had to be taken. Everywhere John Gihon looked he saw posted handbills warning all civilians that they must leave the post the next day.

As the governor's party drew up at the quarters of the commanding general, Persifer Smith, a prominent Regulator, John D. (Jack) Henderson, editor of the *Leavenworth Journal*, who had probably come to size up the morrow's cargo, was riding by.

One of the governor's party greeted him and said, 'That's a fine horse you are riding, sir.'

'Yes, he's a splendid animal,' Henderson agreed. 'He's a pressed horse. All of these are pressed horses.'

'Pressed? What does that mean?'

'Oh, pressed into the service.'

'I suppose you mean the horses are stolen. Who are the owners?'

'Those damned abolitionists over there,' Henderson said. 'We don't call it stealing to take their property.'

Free-soilers who defended their property were sometimes killed. The week before, William Phillips, the lawyer who had once been tarred and feathered and auctioned off by a slave, had attempted to defend his home. He and his brother-in-law saw the Regulators approaching, so they grabbed guns and fired. Both shots counted. Two Regulators fell dead. The others stormed the house and killed William Phillips, right before his wife's eyes. Still enraged, the Regulators rounded up fifty free-soilers and drove them aboard the *Polar Star*. Next day, they loaded another hundred on the *Emma*.

'A Major Hackett of the U.S. Army reported finding several slain men on a road near town,' Gihon wrote. Perhaps he meant Captain D. B. Sacket who heard that there were three murdered bodies near Singa-rock-sies west of the Stranger. 'I could find but one,' he reported. 'I had him intered.'

Such reports caused the new governor to write a long letter to William Marcy, Secretary of State. He said he found 'the existing difficulties of a far more complicated character' than he had expected. As chief executive, he had not only to contend with armed bands of brigands but also with men in authority who were using 'all the destructive agents around them to promote their own personal interests as the sacrifice of every just, honorable, and lawful consideration.' He described the situation in Leavenworth and laid the blame on 'infatuated adherents of conflicting political sentiments' and outside influences. 'The actual proslavery settlers of the territory are generally as well-disposed citizens as are to be found in most communities,' he said. 'It is also true that among the freesoil residents are many peaceable and useful citizens, who if uninfluenced by aspiring demagogues would commit no unlawful act. But many of these, too, have been rendered turbulent by officious meddlers from abroad.'

Early next morning, when Governor Geary set out for his capital, he passed a barricade of wagons which frightened citizens had set up against feared attack by Jim Lane, said to be on his way with 1500 men.

The governor rode in a carriage with his secretary and a Lieutenant Drum of the United States Army. A dragoon sergeant rode as an outrider and an Army wagon filled with infantrymen followed.

All along the road were 'fearful evidences of violence,' reported Gihon. 'Almost every house had been destroyed and the sites they had occupied were marked only by solitary chimneys standing in the midst of ashes.' At Alexandria, on the Stranger, 'about one hundred and fifty of Lane's men' had just pillaged the town's two buildings and strewn the road with whisky barrels, heads broken in. And not long afterward six horsemen rode down upon the governor's carriage. When they saw the Army wagon, they turned tail and fled.

'Such is the condition of Kansas, faintly pictured,' the new governor had written Secretary Marcy. 'It can be no worse.' But still he felt he would 'be able ere long to establish peace and quiet.'

It was to look for a while as if he could.

22

Harvest Time

ACROSS THE RIVER lay Lecompton, capital of the Territory of
Kansas. The new governor could see that a town of sorts lay
hidden by the trees at the foot of the river bluff, as he paced
the bank opposite, eying the river for signs of a rise in water
level that might float the ferry off of its midstream sandbar
mooring.

A two-story building was nearing completion, a raw-wood
temporary capitol, but the city's more impressive structures
were still in the foundation stage. Largest was the block-long
excavation for a hotel projected as 'the finest west of the Mississippi.' Most expensive, by far, was that of the capitol. On a
stone base and a few feet of wall had already been expended the
whole of the $50,000 Congress had appropriated to erect a
capitol building. Governor Geary's secretary came to blame
this waste of funds on the fact that the building's contractors
were also the town's incorporators.

The incorporators were a number of prominent proslavery
men. They had bought an Indian 'floating claim' a mile square.
Though it was well off of the Territory's two great thorough-
fares — the California Road south of the Kaw, and the Military
Road north of the Kaw — the incorporators had persuaded the
Territorial Legislature to designate that site for the capital.
Promised gifts of town lots may have influenced the vote, as
some claimed, but looking at the town as it appeared as a year-

ling it could be held that the legislators had been swindled rather than bribed.

Floating populations are characteristic of capitals, but Lecompton's population was virtually all floating. Families, foundation of any stable society, had not taken root there. Northern families had been burned out by their neighbors, and Southern families had been frightened out by constant threat of attack from their Northern cousins. There were few homes in town. More than half of the capital's twenty-odd buildings were commercial grocery stores of the border type, or just plain saloons. Some of the latter served as homes for men. Jack Thompson's, for example, devoted its ground floor to such comforts as are provided by a commodious barroom and to accommodations for playing faro and poker, while an extensive basement took care of the other necessities of border life. There was a kitchen there and a number of tables upon which men could eat, and sleep.

Nobody was buying anybody's town lots in Lecompton.

The general air of impermanence that always characterized the place was at its height that Wednesday evening of 10 September 1856, when the new governor, after hours of waiting, finally got ferriage to his capital. Threat of attack by Jim Lane's army had been a daily fear for the month past. Here, as in Leavenworth, apprehension increased at each new rumor of his approach. And on this day, it was a known fact that Lane and his 1500, also expected at Leavenworth, were preparing to march from Lawrence.

The sentinel at the ferry was mounted, ready to ride off to sound an alarm at the least suspicious sign, so that even though he knew that the new governor was being awaited at the Brooke Hotel by a welcoming committee, it took the United States Army in the person of Lieutenant Drum to convince him that this man who called himself governor was indeed that.

The thirty-six hours John W. Geary had been in Kansas Territory had given him a headache, but they had also given him a course of action. Both sides were wrong, he had decided, so he would build his course between them.

He listened politely to the helpful hints given that first night by the top men of the territorial government, federal and local. 'To insure his own comfort and safety, and accomplish any good whatever in the Territory,' he was told he must identify himself with the proslavery party. He must use his influence and power to help that party 'wipe out the damned abolitionists.' It was a command backed with persuasion. Countless tales were told in which free-soilers were always the villains and proslavery men always, as Dr. Gihon put it, 'peace-loving and law and order citizens, who with Christian forbearance and Job-like patience had meekly submitted to outrages that no pencil could portray nor language properly depict.'

Governor Geary listened, but what he heard simply strengthened his conviction. The next day he wrote an address in which he announced a firm middle-way stand.

He expressed a strong belief in popular sovereignty but scored the men outside the Territory, in various sections of the Union, who had 'endeavored to stir up internal strife and to array brother against brother.' He asked the citizens of the Territory to banish these outside influences. 'The territory of the United States is the common property of the several states, or of the people thereof,' he said. 'No obstacle should be interposed to the free settlement of this common property while in a territorial condition.' His administration would strive to remove any restrictions to the free settlement of Kansas Territory, but it would also uphold the territorial laws. Citizens aggrieved by legislation that had been passed had a right to ask the next legislature to revise any or all laws. But, he pleaded, 'as you value the peace of the Territory and the maintenance of future laws, I would earnestly ask you to refrain from all violations of the present statutes.'

He also issued two proclamations. One ordered the disbandment of the volunteer militia now in the field, and the other called on 'all free male citizens qualified to bear arms' to enlist in the regular militia of the Territory.

Geary got a rush job of printing done on these documents and sent them by emissary to leaders of both sides. Secretary

Woodson took them to General Strickler, encamped with gathering proslavery forces at Franklin, and the governor's personal messenger, Theodore Adams, took them to Lawrence.

The people of Lawrence welcomed the governor's papers, Adams reported. General Lane had left town with most of his strength at the very time that the forces recruited at Acting-Governor Woodson's invitation threatened to descend on the Yankee stronghold. Adams quickly relayed free-soil fears to Governor Geary. A thousand Missourians stood ready to attack, Adams said.

It was after midnight when Geary got the message. An hour later he was on his way to the scene, accompanied by Colonel Cooke and 300 troops, including a battery of light artillery.

The governor found that the immediacy of the situation had been exaggerated and he returned to the capital. He spent that Saturday evening in his office. A procession of citizens called upon him. They represented all shades of political sentiment, but they had a common complaint. All had lost property to the marauding bands, proslave or free-soil, that infested the Territory. 'Many of these grievances needed immediate redress, but unfortunately the law is a dead letter, no magistrate or judge being at hand to take an affidavit or issue a process,' Geary wrote to Washington, before going late to bed.

He was awakened early. Lane's army had by-passed Lecompton but was harassing proslavery settlers north of the river. News came of devastation at Osawkee and at the northern Hickory Point, sometimes called Hardteville.

Geary asked Colonel Cooke to send a detachment to the scene of disturbance and explained to his chief in Washington that he had had to act quickly, on his own responsibility.

Late that night, the federals came across a detail of Harvey's men. They arrested the free-soilers and took them to Lecompton.

Harvey had made a six-hour siege on Hardteville, using the brass four-pounder that Colonel Doniphan had captured at the Battle of Sacramento and that free-soilers had captured in their raid on Fort Franklin. The town finally surrendered.

One defender had been killed, but the conquered joined the victors in celebrating the peace.

As a treaty was negotiated, a whisky demijohn passed from man to man. 'The drinking was not general, but the consequences were serious,' John Swift, free-state captain, reported. 'We had been without sleep for thirty-six hours, without drinking through the hot afternoon skirmish, so that the whisky was too much for those who drank.' They camped where they were and were easy to find.

But Governor Geary could not give the prisoners much thought when they were brought to Lecompton. He was puzzling over a communique from one William Heiskill, who signed himself, 'Brigadier General Commanding First Brigade, Southern Division, Kansas Militia.' Writing from his headquarters on Mission Creek, Heiskill said, 'In obedience to the call of Acting-Governor Woodson, I have organized a militia force of about eight hundred men, who are now in the field, ready for duty and impatient to act. Hearing of your arrival, I beg leave to report to you for orders.'

The new governor was bewildered. Heiskill obviously had not heard his proclamations, and this was the first the governor had heard of Woodson's call to arms. He began to suspect that Woodson had not delivered his papers to General Strickler, a suspicion soon confirmed by a dispatch from Special Agent Adams. Strickler had not received the governor's orders and his army was being augmented daily by companies of Missourians, such as the one Geary had seen Claiborne Jackson bring aboard the *Keystone*. Adams estimated that 2700 men were encamped at Franklin and in the more than 300 tents a mile away on the Wakarusa. An attack on Lawrence was imminent.

Geary sent the Adams message to Colonel Cooke, with a request for federal troops. The response was immediate.

At sunset Sunday, a proslave scouting party clashed with a free-soil outpost. It was a brief encounter, but one man was killed and several were wounded.

Soon after sunset, Governor Geary arrived. Colonel Cooke stationed his dragoons in a commanding position on Mt. Oread and Geary went down into Lawrence to find that there was no organized command. Charles Robinson, general of the Free State Militia, had been released from prison at President Pierce's insistence and was back in town but not in charge. All his captains — Walker, Blood, Abbott, Cracklin — seemed to be acting independently, though there were no more than 300 men under arms and only twenty rounds of ammunition in town. The old broadswordsman, John Brown, had appeared, but he was just going here and there urging his favorite maxim, 'Keep cool and fire low.'

Geary got the leaders together and assured them that Lawrence would be protected, 'Go to your homes in confidence,' he said. He told them they could take their arms but warned them to use them 'only as the last resort, to protect your lives and property and the chastity of your females.'

When scouts came early next morning with the news that the Southerners were forming to attack, Governor Geary set out for the proslavery camp.

He had not gone far when he met an advanced guard of some 300 men. When he was challenged, he counter-challenged. 'Who are you?' he asked.

'We are the territorial militia, called into service by His Excellency, the Governor of Kansas,' said the officer in command. 'We are marching to wipe out Lawrence and every damned abolitionist in the country.'

'I am Governor of Kansas and Commander-in-Chief of the Territorial Militia,' said Geary. 'Countermarch your troops and conduct me to your commanding general.'

'You're not Woodson.'

'I'm Geary, and I am Governor. Do as I order.'

The officer reluctantly obeyed and Geary soon came into view of the Southern army, drawn up in battle array.

'The militia had taken a position upon an extensive and beautiful plain near the juncture of the Wakarusa with the Kansas River,' Gihon wrote. 'On one side towered a lofty hill, known as Blue Mound, and on the other Mount Oread showed its fortified summit. The town of Franklin, from its elevated site, looked down upon the active scene, while beyond, in a quiet vale, the more flourishing city of Lawrence reposed as though unconscious of its threatened doom. The waters of the Kansas River might be seen gliding rapidly toward the Missouri, and the tall forest trees that line its banks plainly indicated the course of the Wakarusa. The red face of the rising sun was just peering over the top of the Blue Mound, as the governor with his strange escort of three hundred mounted men, with red shirts and odd-shaped hats, descended upon the Wakarusa Plain. There, in battle array, were ranged at least three thousand armed and desperate men.'

These men 'drawn up, horse and foot, and a strong six-pound battery' were well supplied with generals. John Reid, member of the Missouri Legislature, was in command, ably assisted by Dave Atchison, B. F. Stringfellow, L. A. MacLean, J. W. Whitfield, George W. Clarke, William Heiskell, William Richardson, and F. A. Marshall. They were present at the conference Geary called, as was the ever-present Sheriff Jones, and, to the governor's surprise, his own Supreme Court Justice, Sterling Cato.

'Though held in a board house, the present is the most important meeting since the days of the Revolution, as its issues involve the fate of the Union then formed,' Geary said. Then he looked squarely at David Atchison. 'When I saw you last, you were acting as vice-president of the nation and president of the most dignified body of men in the world, the Senate of the United States,' he said. 'It is with sorrow and pain that I see you now, leading on to a civil and disastrous war an army of men, with uncontrollable passions and determined upon wholesale slaughter and destruction.'

He reaffirmed the position he had taken in his inaugural address and his proclamations and ordered this volunteer militia disbanded. He would, he said, manage the Northern rebels himself. General Clarke protested. He would pitch into the United States troops rather than abandon the objectives of the expedition, he said. General MacLean and Sheriff Jones heartily applauded Clarke, but in the end, the governor's orders were obeyed. 'He promised us all we wanted,' was Atchison's only comment.

Free-state men suspected as much. When Geary returned to Lawrence and reported that the threatened attack had been thwarted and that the invaders were dispersing, free-soilers were relieved but leery of what the governor might have promised the other side. Why, they asked, had he not arrested any Southerners when he was holding 100 men of Harvey's command at Lecompton?

Geary explained that the forces on the Wakarusa had been called into service by Woodson, as acting-governor, and had been given authority as the duly constituted militia of the Territory. As such, he had been forced to recognize them. The men who had attacked Hardteville, on the other hand, were in arms not only without sanction of the law but in open violation of it.

It was a matter, he said, not of moral right but of legal authority. And again he assured the free-staters that their right to change the laws of the Territory would be protected. His was to be an impartial administration.

'Well, Your Excellency,' said Sam Walker, 'what you say suits us first rate, but mark my word, you'll take the underground out of Kansas in six months.'

The governor had been in the saddle a week and he felt he had accomplished a great deal — as he had. 'I'll show you and all the damned rascals that I am Governor of Kansas,' he said.

23

Geary Tries To Govern

PROSPECTS FOR PEACE seemed bright. The Missourians pressed their way homeward, stealing a few horses but killing only one man, lame David Buffum. Rabble-rouser Jim Lane had again disappeared into Nebraska, and God's Handyman, Old John Brown, had taken off for the East where he would next be heard from as he appeared before the Massachusetts Legislature to give a wrathful recital of proslave offenses.

John Geary felt he could turn his attention now to the thing he felt to be the Territory's crying need — a reform of the judiciary.

His suspicion of legal laxity had been aroused on his first day in Kansas. Shocked by things that were going on in Leavenworth, he had summoned the United States District Attorney, A. J. Isaacs, out of the turmoil of the city to the quiet of the fort. He tried to impress the federal officer, according to Gihon, 'with the importance of resurrecting the courts, holding more frequent terms, and arresting, bringing to trial, and legally punishing the numerous criminals who were committing with impunity atrocious outrages.' But Mr. Isaacs, rumored to be one of Emory's Regulators, did not agree. 'Like other prominent proslavery men, he was fully imbued with the idea that no person had a right in Kansas who was not favorable to making it a slave state,' Gihon said.

Governor Geary soon found that the D.A.'s attitude was

shared by the other members of the federal judiciary, particularly by Sterling Cato, associate justice, and in a measure by Chief Justice Lecompte, though his interest lay elsewhere. The chief justice was devoted to his fine plantation near Leavenworth and found it more convenient, Gihon said, 'to discharge prisoners on straw-bail, than travel twenty or more miles to hold court and go through the troublesome forms of trial.' Kansans were fond of saying that the chief justice adjourned the spring term of his court to plant potatoes, the summer term to hoe potatoes, the fall term to dig potatoes, and the winter term because he had to be at home to sell potatoes.

Geary called a conference of Justices Lecompte and Cato (a third justice was forever being appointed and forever resigning). He called to their attention the many prisoners who were being held awaiting trial. He said the courts should be opened to dispose of their cases and to issue processes so that other offenders might be put under immediate arrest.

He reminded Justice Cato that no action had been taken on the murder of David Buffum, though they had both been at the dying man's bedside and the justice had taken an affidavit.

The Kickapoo Rangers had returned home from Camp Franklin by way of Lecompton. And down in the Bloomington neighborhood a party of six Rangers had ridden off on a little 'pressing' expedition. They came upon lame Dave Buffum at work in his fields. They demanded his horses and when he implored them not to take them, one of the men, as David Buffum told it on his deathbed, called him a goddamned abolitionist and shot him in the abdomen.

A quick arrest of Buffum's murderer, Geary told the justices, would give heart to the citizens of the Territory. It would be a clear sign that justice had taken root and 'would hereafter serve malefactors with severity, protect the rights of all with impartiality.'

Geary asked Lecompte and Cato to dispose of the prisoners at hand, and, feeling that he had set the machinery of justice in motion, he went off to Topeka on official business. When he returned, he found that the chief justice had returned to Leavenworth without making arrangements for the immediate examination of prisoners. Instead, he had appointed a court for that purpose to be held three weeks later at Leavenworth, forty miles away. Gihon pointed out that Lecompte knew it would be impossible, both from a financial and judicial point of view, to convey so many prisoners and witnesses so far from the scene of the alleged crimes.

There were about 125 prisoners in the tent compound near the capital, most of them the men of Harvey's command who had been arrested while sleeping off their peace-treaty drunk.

Geary finally persuaded Justice Cato to give Harvey's men a hearing. Joseph Anderson, a member of the Territorial Legislature, was so persuasive a prosecuting attorney that Justice Cato committed the whole party for trial on the charge of murder in the first degree. One hundred and one men stood accused of killing the one proslave man who had fallen in the attack on Hardteville. And neither Cato nor Lecompte, when he was appealed to, would release any of the accused men on bail.

Colonel Cooke of the United States Army found this discouraging. He had housed, fed, and guarded the prisoners, but now he felt that the federal government had done more than its share. He announced that he would no longer take care of the prisoners, so they were brought to the capital and crowded into a dilapidated cabin. Some escaped. Others were so overrun with vermin, so underfed and exposed that one died and many became ill.

Days passed and weeks and nothing was done about them, nor was the murderer of David Buffum brought in, though his identity was well known to the marshal and though Governor Geary personally offered a $500 reward for his capture. It was not until Geary's special agent, Adams, picked up the murderer's name through grocery store boasts in Kickapoo that the marshal reluctantly brought in Charles Hays of Atchison.

The evidence against Hays was so overwhelming that the grand jury, though comprised entirely of proslave men, found a true bill of murder in the first degree against him.

This good news came to Governor Geary as he was hearing

a deputation of free-soilers who had come to charge his government, particularly the judiciary, of partiality to Southern interests. Geary now happily announced that the grand jury had
just indicted Hays as murderer of Buffum.

The free-soilers were impressed by this proof of Geary's
determination to establish a truly impartial government. They
were bidding a friendly farewell, when a party of proslavery
men came into the governor's office in the unceremonious way
of the West. They were jubilant, and they became even more
joyous when they saw that free-soilers were present. They told
the governor, with great public show, that Justice Lecompte,
who happened to be in town, had admitted Hays to bail with
Sheriff Jones standing bail-bond. The great joke was, of course,
that the sheriff would be hard put to it to raise a ready dollar —
and everybody knew it.

For the first time Geary fully realized his position. He
stood alone. Not another officer sent by the federal government
intended to support him in his efforts to do justice to the people
and to secure the peace he had effected. He was surrounded
by men resolved to defeat his impartial policy.

'You see how it is, Your Excellency,' one of the free-state
men said. 'All our statements are confirmed. We can no longer
expect even-handed justice. Our only hope must be in physical
force.'

To Geary it seemed that civil war hung in balance. He
boldly denounced Lecompte's action in dismissing Buffum's indicted murderer as 'a judicial outrage, without precedent.' He
declared he would treat the chief justice's action as a nullity. He
would order Hays re-arrested, as though he had merely escaped,
and he would submit the matter to the President of the United
States.

John Geary had organized and was keeping mobilized two
companies of territorial militia, a Southern one commanded by
H. T. Titus and a Northern one commanded by Samuel Walker.
He now hastened to put a warrant for the arrest of Hays into
the hands of Colonel Titus, who, despite his own strong proslave
bias, immediately made the arrest.

When Chief Justice Lecompte then secured the prisoner on a writ of habeas corpus and again released him, the governor did not attempt to interfere further. He had convinced free-soilers that he would do them justice to the full extent of his power.

The scales of justice appeared to be badly out of balance, weighted on the southside, but it might be argued, from a look at court records in that fall of 1856, that the scales were in balance and had never been otherwise. They were as good as new because they had scarcely been used. For twenty-seven months Northerners and Southerners had been committing murder, arson, and manslaughter, yet territorial court records showed only a dozen convictions. There had been one conviction for horse stealing, three for assumption of office, and eight for the unlicensed selling of liquor.

II

THE COURT SQUABBLE lasted through the autumn, a season so comparatively free of warlike moves and guerrilla activity that the Territory held, for the first time in its history, a promise of peace.

There was a threat of outbreak, however — a persistent rumor that Jim Lane and his Army of the North were about to invade Kansas Territory from Nebraska Territory.

When Governor Geary learned that Lane had contracted with ferrymen at Nebraska City to transport some 700 men across the Missouri, he ordered the border patrolled by United States troops.

A company of 130 Northerners under Captain James Redpath, correspondent of the strongly free-soil *St. Louis Democrat*, was arrested and brought before Geary. Though they were well armed and unencumbered by the implements of agriculture and industry, Geary chose to take their word for it that they were not an advance guard of Lane's army but rather peaceable immigrants. He let them go on their way.

Not many days later, a deputation came to Geary with a

request from Samuel Pomeroy and Shaler Eldridge. They stood at the Nebraska border, they said, with 300 emigrants. They asked the governor's permission to bring these 'bona fide settlers, with agricultural implements and some guns to protect themselves and shoot game' into Kansas Territory.

Geary looked William Hutchinson, *New York Times* correspondent and Pomeroy's chief emissary, in the eye. 'Is this party in any way connected with Lane's Army of the North?' he asked.

'Decidedly not!' said Hutchinson. 'These are, as General Pomeroy has said, bona fide settlers.'

'I am determined that no armed bodies of men, equipped for war and of a hostile attitude shall enter this Territory,' Geary said. 'On the other hand, I will welcome with all my heart all immigrants who come for peaceful and lawful purposes.' And assured again that the Pomeroy-Eldridge party was of a peaceful nature, he gave Hutchinson a letter directing any military commanders whom it might concern to give this party safe conduct 'should its members be as represented, a party of immigrants of peaceable intent.'

The letter, with its implied command to search, was not given to Colonel Cooke when his guard halted the Pomeroy party. In fact, when Samuel Pomeroy and Shaler Eldridge were told that the wagons must be searched for arms, there was 'much temper shown and some show of a disposition to resist,' according to Colonel Cooke.

Colonel Cooke had not known about Hutchinson's trip to see Governor Geary, so he told Pomeroy and Eldridge of the governor's proclamation outlawing armed immigrations. They said that they were bona fide settlers and that their wagons were filled with implements of peaceful pursuits, of homemaking and agriculture. The reluctance of the leaders to have the twenty wagons searched and the fact that there were only 'about five women' in this party of nearly 300 prompted Colonel Cooke to authorize a search. The wagons carried 'none of the ordinary baggage of immigrants, not a chair or other furniture, but one tool chest, no agricultural implements,' Colonel Cooke reported.

'There were, however, boxed, many new saddles and 242 percussion muskets, Hall's muskets, and Sharpe's carbines, two officers' and 61 common sabres, about 50 Colt's revolvers *boxed*, four boxes ball cartridges, &c, &c.' It looked as if the immigrants had robbed an armory — which, indeed, they had. With the connivance of authorities, they had raided the government stores at Iowa City.

So the Pomeroy-Eldridge party that William Hutchinson had vouched for was put under arrest and taken to Lecompton.

Governor Geary was becoming inured to duplicity. He had thwarted a free-soil scheme for entry into the Territory without challenge to find himself with nearly 300 armed immigrants on his hands. Twenty wagons filled with arms — yet he had to accept the story that they had come to Kansas Territory for the sole purpose of establishing homes. He did not want to arouse Missouri again by making a public issue of their entry. He let them go with a lecture. He told them that since the Army had taken over their surplus war matériel, they could go free on the promise that they would break up as an organization and would disperse themselves over the Territory. He wanted only one thing, and that was peace.

By mid-October, it seemed as if he had gained it.

He had even managed to arouse in most municipal authorities, through promise of strong support, a determination to enforce the law. The outstanding holdout was the mayor of his own town, Lecompton. Mayor Stewart ignored Geary's memorandum pointing out the over-preponderence of tippling houses in the capital. The fact that 'United States troops in the vicinity are almost unfitted for duty in consequence of the facilities by which they obtain the means of intoxication,' did not bother the mayor. He ignored the governor's order to close the open-all-night groceries and other unlicensed places, so the governor sent a file of soldiers to close them and to destroy their liquor if they persisted 'in selling contrary to the law and to the detriment of the public peace.'

It did seem in the light, bright sunlight of mid-October as though territorial affairs were coming into focus and John

Geary, with pardonable pride, set out on a triumphal tour of his province.

III

On 17 October 1856, Governor Geary rode south from Lecompton, accompanied by his admiring secretary and others. A man could travel now without fear of sudden death, Gihon commented. Near Lawrence, 'females rode alone on horseback from house to house.' And one morning, as the governor rode toward Prairie City, his horse stepped on the head of a large rattlesnake which lay coiled in the road. The snake's head was crushed, and the governor's secretary, reporting, asked, 'May this not have been a happy omen?'

Time would answer this question, but as the days that made autumn flowed on, it looked as though the answer might be, Yes.

Everywhere, John Geary was greeted with warmth and gratitude. John (Ottawa) Jones expressed the sentiment of many when he told the governor it was a pity he had not come to the Territory sooner. This Indian graduate of Hamilton Institute in New York and his Maine wife, who had come to the Ottawa lands as a missionary in 1842, had kept one of the really decent hotels in the Territory until the bloody summer of 1856, when a proslavery band had burned it to the ground.

At Osawatomie people were grateful, but still apprehensive. Geary visited one sick family — parents and five children all in bed — and learned that the eldest boy, on whom they depended for support, had fled the country because of threats against his life by proslavery men. Geary assured them that such threats were a thing of the past.

A ride eastward 'over a rich and beautiful country, occasionally enlivened by the flight of an immense number of prairie fowl,' brought the party to Paola. There the governor stayed at a good hotel run by another educated Indian, Baptiste, a Peoria and an interpreter for his tribe and for the Kaskaskias, Weas, and Piankeshaws — all recently united under the Wea name.

The governor's party crossed the Pottawatomie Creek country where 'woods abounded with wild turkeys, the creeks with geese and ducks, and the prairies with grouse.' Riding through a day of drenching rain, they crossed South Middle Creek and encamped on Big Sugar Creek. Next day, with the usual halts to address settlers, they arrived at Sugar Mound and camped on Little Sugar Creek, well-timbered with oak, hickory, walnut, and sugar maple. 'The settlers in this section are prosperous and well-content,' Gihon reported. 'They value their claims, upon which the improvements are of little value, from eight hundred to twelve hundred dollars.' Maple sugar, extensively manufactured, 'sold readily at twenty cents a pound.' Temple Wayne had sold 600 pounds at that price.

Tents were struck at an early hour. The next camp was made at Centropolis on Eight Mile Creek. Then a twenty-mile ride over a rolling, treeless plain brought the party to One Hundred and Ten, celebrated stopping place on the Santa Fe Trail.

The next day was enlivened by several coyote chases and the southward flight of great flocks of wild geese and brant, and camp was made on the headwaters of the Wakarusa. The country between there and Fort Riley was described as 'barren and desolate, with great quarries of white limestone.' In this Flint Hills region there was virtually no settlement, only a cluster of families on Clark's Creek. A freshet from the Smoky made fording the Kaw difficult, but the governor's party finally made it and arrived at Fort Riley wet but unharmed.

His Excellency was greeted with a fifteen-gun salute, and he found it good to be under a roof again. The fort was only three years old, but it had substantial limestone buildings and a spirit of hospitality. A ball was given in the governor's honor, to which the countryside was invited. 'This was a brilliant affair,' Gihon reported. 'Although gotten up in a region almost beyond the bounds of civilization, it would have done credit for the education, intelligence, refinement and, it may be added, delicacy and beauty of its female participants, to any community in the world.'

After three days of festivity and business the gubernatorial suite headed back east.

Sunday, the second of November, was a thoroughly disagreeable day, cold and rainy. Wild turkeys were so dulled by cold that they could be shot with pistols. The river was crossed at Manhattan — a town of 150 population, boasting three stores, a hotel, and a gristmill. In the limestone hills behind the town, deer and game fowl abounded.

A snowstorm, the season's first, kept the company in camp on Monday, but Tuesday they rode on east, through the fertile Pottawatomie reserve. Crystal-clear Mill Creek was crossed, then Mission Creek, and on to Topeka, where eighty new buildings were under construction.

Back in the capital on the seventh, Governor Geary took up official business. He fired Owen Stewart, town mayor, as superintendent of capitol construction. The $50,000 appropriated by Congress for erection of public buildings in the capital of the Territory of Kansas would have been sufficient 'if properly expended,' Gihon wrote and commented that if the capitol were to be completed on 'the same liberal scale as commenced,' it might 'be ready for roofing in by the use of another appropriation of two or three hundred thousand dollars.'

Then the governor reported on his trip to Washington. 'The general peace of the Territory remains unimpaired,' he wrote Secretary Marcy. 'Confidence is gradually and surely being restored; business is resuming its ordinary channels; citizens are preparing for the winter; and there is a readiness among the good people of all parties to sustain my administration.'

And he issued a proclamation 'in consonance with general custom and my own feelings,' setting apart November twentieth as a day of general thanksgiving.

'I am perfectly enthusiastic about my mission,' he wrote to Amos Lawrence.

The effects of the national election were yet to be felt.

24

The National Election

NOVEMBER FOURTH was the day after the first snow in the Territory of Kansas, but back in the States, it was the first Tuesday after the first Monday of that month — election day.

Americans went to the polls to choose their fifteenth president, after a spirited but unusually dignified campaign. There was virtually no name-calling. 'Never before did a presidential campaign turn so largely on questions of statesmanship, ethics, and the higher law,' the historian, Leverett Spring, was to say. He credited this 'temporary lustration of national politics' to the chief issue involved — the extension of slavery.

The campaign was based on the Constitution of the United States. Citizens were asked to reflect upon their organic law as thoughtfully and judiciously as if they were Supreme Court justices. Did the Constitution give territories, as potential states, the right to choose and regulate their own institutions, as the Democrats held, or were the Republicans right in saying that it was not only 'the right but the duty' of the central government to abolish 'those twin relics of barbarism, polygamy and slavery'? Did an American lose the sovereignty he had enjoyed as a citizen of a state when he became a squatter on land owned by all the people?

It was a matter of interpretation and had been debated in Congress for months preceding the passage of the Kansas-Nebraska Bill. The passage of the bill had established 'squatter sovereignty.' Now, in this election, the people were given their first referendum on the question.

The issue was clear-cut and it cut clearly across old party lines to establish new ones. Such traditional Democrats as Bennett of the *New York Herald* shifted to the standard of the new Republican party, and many an old-line Whig who had once taken everything Greeley of the *Tribune* said as gospel voted Democratic. Most Whigs and Know-Nothings below the Mason-Dixon Line became Democrats, while the Northern members of these parties who had not united under the new American Party became Republicans.

The issue was clear-cut, but that did not mean it could not be beclouded for popular consumption.

Focal word of the whole campaign was 'Kansas.' Its brief but violent history was voluminously reviewed and, by omission here and emphasis there, was made to send great billows of emotional vapors into the air.

Republicans harped on the word that means the most to every American — Freedom. It was Freedom against slavery in Kansas, with those who loved freedom suffering every wrong at the hands of those who favored human bondage. No mention was made of Lane's Black Law, which branded the black man as unworthy of living on the new soil. The word was Freedom and it was played upon in all keys. For the intellectual there was the appeal of the basic democratic principle of the equality of man, and for the emotional there was the appeal of the inhumanity of slavery, as dramatized in *Uncle Tom's Cabin*. For those not too much concerned with slavery as an offense against humanity, the economic disadvantages to free labor of competition from slave labor were stressed. Whatever the appeal, the impression given was that the Republicans were in favor of freedom and the Democrats were not.

Freedom was not a word to be disavowed. The Democrats could point out that freedom was the right of choice and that they were fighting for the right of Kansas squatters to choose their own institutions, but they needed a word of their own. And soon they hit upon it. The word was Union.

At just the right time, the Democrats remembered what their standard-bearer had said in his letter accepting the nomination. Buchanan had stressed the Unionism of the Democratic Party in contrast to the sectionalism of the Republican Party. The Democrats had chosen himself, a Pennsylvanian, he said, as their candidate for the highest office in the land, while both members of the Republican team were from Northern states. Not only that, the whole Republican campaign was being directed toward arousing the North against the South. Republicans were citing the crimes that had been committed in Kansas Territory as though they had all been committed by Southerners. And they were ignoring the peace that now reigned in Kansas — thanks to her Democratic governor, John Geary.

The Republicans, the Democrats said, were challenging the South to secede from the Union and, as the campaign neared its climax, the Democrats intimated that the South would be forced to do just that — if the Republicans won.

Election day came and when the votes were counted, the word Union won. The Democrats were in again, even though the newly consolidated 'Solid South' controlled only 121 electoral college votes to the 176 controlled by the North. Pennsylvania, New Jersey, Indiana, Illinois, and California helped to give James Buchanan a popular vote of 1,927,995 as compared to John Frémont's 1,391,555 and Millard Fillmore's 864,523 — and the number of electoral votes needed to win.

The tempest in Kansas Territory could fix to blow again.

25

Out Like a Lamb

THE BLUSTERING, bloody year of 1856 drew to a peaceful close. On the last day of the year, John Geary wrote to Secretary Marcy to 'congratulate the Administration and the country' upon the change of conditions in Kansas Territory in the four months since he had become governor. 'Crime so rife and daring, at the period of my arrival, is almost entirely banished,' he said. 'I can truthfully assure you that, in proportion to her population and extent, less crime is being committed in Kansas than in any other portion of the United States.'

And there had been virtually no violence for nearly two months. The governor could devote time to territorial affairs.

He took up the matter of postal service. He complained to the postmaster general that every package he received had been opened along the way, and he asked for more regular and prompt mail facilities. 'It requires eleven days for a letter to reach this place from Washington city, when a person traveling with an expedition can accomplish the same distance in six days,' he said.

He took up the matter of prison facilities and asked for an appropriation for a penitentiary as well as for funds to complete the capitol building.

But most of his time, during the last months of 1856, were taken up with Indian affairs, though he had no jurisdiction over them, as he rather petulantly pointed out to Washington.

Settlers from near Council Grove came to him because they had been given a three-day dispossess notice by the same Kaw Indian agent who, two years before, had assured them that the land they were claiming was open for settlement. Shawnee agent Maxwell McClasin and Pottawatomie agent George Clarke asked for federal troops to be on hand when the United States paid its annual dole to the original Americans. And the governor was twice called to Leavenworth because of anticipated difficulties over the public auction of the Delaware trust lands, on which the city had been illegally founded.

The Delawares — as well as the Weas, the Piankeshaws, Peorias, Kaskaskias, and the Iowas — ceded their lands in 1854 on the condition that they were to be trust lands. That is, they were to be sold to the highest bidder, the proceeds to go to the Indians. The land on which Leavenworth was founded was not subject to pre-emption. The Indians, of course, had made no trouble about it. Through the generations, they had learned never to expect the white man to keep his word. The anticipated troubles at the Leavenworth public sales, then, were those that might arise between the settlers and the outside purchasers invited by presidential proclamation to the public auction.

Everything went off all right — thanks, we gather, to Governor Geary's efforts — and the Delawares realized more than $450,000. Gihon, overlooking the fact that this sum was divided among more than 900 Indians, said the sale made this nation 'perhaps the wealthiest community in the world.'

All this activity pleased John Geary. He was busily engaged in work he liked and he felt he was doing a great job. He was a man of decision. He was quick to act and willing to shoulder responsibility for his actions — a rare quality which often tends to make its possessors assume more credit than is their due and ignore other forces that have operated in their favor.

Certainly the fact that 1856 was a presidential year, with nothing so important to the South as having a Democrat elected, aided John Geary in establishing peace in Kansas Territory during the closing months of the campaign. Yet he never seemed to realize that Southern leaders such as Atchison and Reid had been relieved when he appeared with United States troops to prevent an attack by Missouri Democrats upon Lawrence in September.

These men honestly felt that the Union, as well as the South, had been insulted by Free State Party activities. They had marched into Kansas Territory with a serious intent of bringing the rebels to time, but they were quick to see the political advantage of having a Democratic governor bring peace to Kansas at a time when Republicans were basing their presidential campaign on the turbulence there.

In answer to criticism in Missouri of this quick capitulation, Reid wrote an explanation to the *Independence (Mo.) Occidental Register*. It appeared in the 20 September 1856 issue. 'The arrival of the new governor was most opportune for us, for Kansas, and for the whole country in suspending the strife which had been forced upon us, in such a manner as regarding our honor and our rights we could not decline it, and which threatened to involve the whole country in a civil and sectional war,' Reid wrote. It was, he said, 'Providential that Governor Geary interposed between us and our purpose.'

If Geary read Reid's statement, he missed the fine irony of the phrase 'suspending the strife.' He believed that he had licked the grave crisis single-handed and forever and apparently never did know just what hit him later.

He closed his end-of-the-year report to Washington on a note of high optimism, but its earlier passages did reveal a certain uneasiness. He reiterated his impartial policy. 'Its happy results have produced considerable agitation among some ultra men,' he admitted, warning that 'various rumors, as unfounded as they are desperate, have been put in circulation here.' He wanted Washington to know in advance that these rumors were without foundation. 'Because I will not co-operate with certain efforts to establish a state government, and lend myself to carry out the views which are outside the constitution and the laws, I am misrepresented by a few ultra men of one party,' he said. 'Because I will not enter upon a crusade in support of one idea, making but a single issue in Kansas, to wit the introduction of slavery, I am equally the subject of misrepresentation by a few violent men on the other side.'

It has been claimed that Geary did enter into a plot with Charles Robinson, in a secret meeting in a Lecompton garret, to make Kansas a free state. The alleged bargain was that if Geary would get the Territory admitted to the Union under the Topeka Constitution, Robinson would hand over the governorship of the new state to him. There is nothing recorded by Geary or Gihon to support this contention. Years later, Robinson intimated that Geary proposed some such solution to him, but all evidence points to Geary's complete agreement with the Administration on the whole Topeka movement. Early in January 1857, Secretary of State Marcy wrote expressing concern over the slated meeting of 'a body calling themselves a legislature' at Topeka. And Geary was pleased to report later that less than a quorum of Free State Party legislators had appeared in Topeka on January sixth.

Chances are that Robinson, in an attempt to turn the defeat of the Free State cause at the national polls into a victory, did make some sort of a proposal to Geary, and that Geary turned it down, just as he intimated in the report to Washington. Gihon reports the proposition made by the proslave side in detail. The Law and Order Party, encouraged by Buchanan's election, decided to change itself to the National Democratic Party of Kansas. Jack Henderson, of Leavenworth, chairman of the central committee, called upon Governor Geary to ask him to identify himself with this party which recognized only one issue — slavery. The reward would be a United States senatorship.

'The devil has as many kingdoms to bestow as you have senatorships, or ever will have, by honest means,' Geary retorted to this proposal. 'I despise your promises of reward as much as I did your infamous threats of injury . . .'

Northern leaders showed no love for the governor, but they lacked the means Southern leaders had to show their animosity.

II

Six days after the Free State Legislature failed to convene, the Territorial Legislature met in Lecompton, prefacing its formal opening with a secret meeting at which it was agreed that any act passed by both the House and the Council and vetoed by the governor would automatically be passed over his veto.

But little time was spent in legislating, as it turned out. Legislators were too busy denouncing the governor. It became a popular pastime among the idlers of the capital to go listen to the legislators abuse Geary. 'It is a great loss to the world that their speeches were not phonographed and preserved for future generations,' wrote Gihon. 'Never again will a similar amount of that peculiar style of eloquence emanate from any legislative body.'

'On one occasion, Jenkins, who was the most violent of the violent, had advocated a certain measure with great vehemence, and supposing it would meet with the governor's disapprobation, caused a vote to be passed asking information of his excellency on the subject. It so happened the governor agreed precisely with Mr. Jenkins, and sent in a brief message to that effect.

'Jenkins, however, despised listening to anything from the governor's pen and therefore crammed his fingers into his ears until the message was read, when suddenly he sprang to his feet and for the hundredth time repeated his tirades of abuse. He was proceeding in one of his most eloquent strains. He stamped violently on the floor — struck a table with his fist, knocking over the inkstand, pronounced his anathemas with a violence that fairly shook the roof overhead — when he was arrested by a loud and universal burst of laughter. He stopped and looked as though inquiring the cause of such an unusual interruption, when the speaker informed him that he had mistaken the tenor of the governor's message, his excellency having agreed with his views in every particular. "Then," said the orator, striking the table another violent blow, "had I known, I would have taken the other side of the question!" '

The honeymoon was over. Geary, like a man married on the rebound, found himself the middleman.

26

Three Governors Down and Three To Go

RESPECTABLE MEMBERS of the Territorial Legislature who could not obtain lodging either in Brooke's Hotel or in the private homes of Lecompton, slept on the floors of the legislative halls. But the legislative majority, according to Gihon, patronized the establishment of their fellow solon, Jack Thompson. There were not enough tables in his basement to accommodate such an influx of sleeping guests, so late at night the barroom floor was covered with a few inches of sawdust to provide bedding for the honorables who had not passed out on ten-cent whisky.

One night a stage driver hit the sawdust with the legislators and the next morning, as he was brushing off his pantaloons, one of the lawmakers tried to gain his influence and vote for a certain measure. This made the stage driver fighting mad. 'It's bad enough to get drunk and make a fool of myself,' he said, 'but no man shall insult me by mistaking me for a member of the Kansas Legislature!'

A look at the record:

The first enactment of the Legislature was designed to show disapproval of the governor's attempt to interfere in judicial matters. It gave the judges power to admit prisoners to bail 'whether such an offence has been heretofore bailable or not.'

The governor returned the bill unsigned, pointing out that

the impunity that had been given to crime in Kansas Territory had caused many of the offenses that had been committed. One of the tendencies of the act, he said, 'was to corrupt the judiciary,' and case after case of unjustifiable bail would, he predicted, cause 'an offended people to arise in their majesty and take the law into their own hands.'

The governor's veto message was carefully thought out, but no one listened to it. The bill was passed over his objection by as casual a signal as it takes for a veteran auction-buyer to raise a bid — a brief interruption to the business at hand. Legislators were busy, at the time, drawing up a venomous resolution demanding that the governor explain why he had not issued a commission to William Sherrard, who had been named to succeed the resigned Sam Jones as Sheriff of Douglas County.

The resolution was calculated to inveigle the governor into a quarrel.

Sherrard, a well-born and embittered young man, had been heckling Geary for weeks, paying frequent and insolent calls to his office.

On the first visit, Geary had not issued the commission simply because it was not his job. The secretary of state issued such papers and he was out of town. Sherrard came back several times, and his defiance took such a threatening form that the governor would have hesitated to put the guardianship of the law in such rash hands, even if the county commissioners themselves had not told him they repented their choice of this young man who was constantly getting into scrapes. Sherrard tangled with Doctor Brooke and got a couple of shiners and a lumpish-looking jaw for his insults. He challenged Brooke to a duel, and when Brooke refused he posted huge handbills branding Brooke as a liar, a scoundrel, and a coward. Sherrard also became annoyed at a man named Locklane, who boarded where he boarded, at the Virginia House. When a poorly aimed plate failed to bring Locklane around to Sherrard's point of view, the sheriff-candidate drew and fired. The pistol-ball carried away a piece of Mr. Locklane's eyebrow.

The sheriffship of Douglas County was none of the Terri-

torial Legislature's business, but since Geary was against having Sherrard in the office, the legislators were for it and they
used the matter as a goad until it came to its fatal conclusion.

Geary, determined to act as a chief executive should in
dealing with the legislative branch, answered the resolution demanding a commission for Sherrard with a carefully respectful
statement. Its very clarity and reason threw the legislators into
a fury. Jenkins said Geary should be 'strung, quartered, and
burned, body and soul.' Johnson called him a 'damned despot'
who had assumed 'an arbitrary power from which the autocrat
of Russia would have shrunk dismayed.' And O. H. Brown,
hands thrust in pockets and pacing, said he had studied heathen
mythology until he was familiar with it to his very finger tips.
He had wondered at the atrocities of Nero and Caligula, but he
had never heard or read anything so abominable as this conduct
of Geary in withholding Mr. Sherrard's commission.

'After these and other distinguished gentlemen,' says
Gihon, 'had exhausted the English vocabulary of abusive epi-
thets, well interlarded with Latin, French, and Spanish male-
dictions, and sprinkled with specimens of various Indian
dialects, a resolution was almost unanimously passed appoint-
ing Sherrard to the office of county sheriff.'

This happened in the lower house. When the upper house,
the Council, failed to concur, young Sherrard was thrown into
a real frenzy. He went down the street flailing his arms.

The next morning, Governor Geary visited the legislative
session and when he got up to leave, Sherrard, who was also in
the room, a pistol on each thigh, got up, too. As the governor
stepped from the House chamber into the anteroom, he came
face to face with Sherrard, who stood with pistols drawn. Geary
coolly walked out of the anteroom into the hall. Sherrard followed, his pistols cocked and trained on Geary's back. He followed him through the hall and stood at the top of the stairs
as the governor walked down.

Geary never looked back and Sherrard never fired.

The Council quickly passed a resolution condemning Sherrard's action, but when a representative introduced a similar

measure in the House, it simply loosed another round of Geary abuse.

The governor's few friends in the Territory were determined to punish Sherrard and his backers. They were determined, among other things, to dump the type of the *Lecompton Union* into the Kaw, but the governor persuaded them to do nothing rash. In the end, they simply called a protest meeting.

Sherrard's friends declared in the streets and in the grog-shops that the meeting — set for Wednesday, 14 February — would never be held. Such promise of excitement drew a good crowd from the country surrounding. Brooke's Hotel could not begin to hold the assemblage, so it adjourned to Capitol Hill.

Proslavery Mayor Stewart was elected chairman of the conclave. He appointed a committee to draw up resolutions and while it argued things out, the citizenry was given a chance to have its say. Proslavery Captain C. J. Hampton made a mild address; then Bob Bennett, junior editor of *The Union*, staggered onto the speakers stand and demanded to be heard.

'This meetin's not a meetin of gentlemen,' he said. 'I say is — I tell you this meetin's the ragtail and bobtail of the ab'lishunists — '

He was very drunk and the highly amused crowd encouraged him with shouts:

'Go to it, Bennett!'

'You're one of the orators, you are!'

'Have another drink, Bennett!'

He was still entertaining the crowd when the committee brought in its report. It expressed approval of Governor Geary's 'impartial and vigorous administration,' and pledged him 'the support of all the actual settlers of Kansas, without distinction of party,' so long as he continued to administer the government as he had been doing.

James Legate had no sooner finished reading these resolutions than Sherrard jumped to his feet. 'Any man who will dare to endorse these resolutions is a liar, a scoundrel, and a coward!' he cried.

A Mr. Sheppard stood up in the midst of the crowd and said, in a quiet, firm tone, 'I endorse them, and I am neither a liar, a scoundrel, nor a coward.'

Sherrard drew a revolver and fired all the loads as fast as he could pull the trigger.

Three balls hit Sheppard and one hit a bystander.

The wounded Sheppard took off his gloves, drew his pistol, and attempted to return the shots, but his caps were wet and burst without discharging the balls. He moved toward his assailant, then, with his pistol clubbed. Sherrard pulled his other revolver but could not fire before the bleeding Sheppard moved in to strike with the butt of his pistol. Sherrard clubbed his own revolver and struck back. The two men kept hitting each other until they were pulled apart and Sheppard, thought to be mortally wounded, was carried away.

The air was a-pop with random shots.

When seventy-year-old Tom Porterfield saw Sheriff Jones draw his pistol, he, who had once been a Jones prisoner, took off his spectacles, wiped them carefully, and adjusted them on his nose. Then he drew a Navy revolver, examined the caps, and placed the barrel on his left arm. He kept his gun trained on Jones as he moved about, waiting. If Sam Jones had fired that day, he would have been killed.

Things happened fast.

With Sheppard taken out of range, Sherrard looked about for other game. He spotted Geary's young aide, John A. W. Jones. He twirled his pistol into position as a shooting iron and advanced, finger on trigger.

Young Jones saw him just in time. He quickly drew his own revolver and fired.

Sherrard fell with a bullet in his head and on Saturday he died.

When someone offered $500 to the man who would kill John Jones, he sought the protection of the law. He gave himself up to Justice Cato, who pronounced a decision against him before any testimony was taken. So the young man posted a $5000 bail and decamped. With the aid of a guide, he evaded pursuers and reached Nebraska and safety.

Sherrard was no longer available for the sheriffship. The Legislature could turn to matters more within its jurisdiction. It set to work on a crafty census bill.

A census was to be taken preparatory to an election scheduled for June to elect delegates to a convention that would meet to frame a state constitution. The joker in the bill was that all the census takers and election judges were to be proslavery men.

Governor Geary learned the nature of the bill and sent word that he would approve it, if a clause of referendum were included, so that any constitution framed by the convention would have to have the approval of the citizens of the Territory when it was submitted to Congress. He was told frankly that the principle had been discussed and rejected since its adoption 'would defeat the object of the act, which was to secure, beyond any possibility of doubt, the Territory of Kansas to the South as a slave state.'

When Geary received the bill, he based his veto on the fact that no provision for a referendum had been made. 'The fundamental law of a commonwealth, so inseparably connected with the happiness and prosperity of the citizens, cannot be too well discussed, and cannot pass through too many ordeals of popular scrutiny,' he said, in his message. 'The great principle upon which our free institutions rest is the unqualified and absolute sovereignty of the people; and constituting, as that principle does, the most positive and essential feature in the great charter of our liberties, it is better calculated than any other to give elevation to our hope and dignity to our actions. So long as the people feel that the powers to alter the form or change the character of the government abides in them, so long will they be impressed with that sense of security and dignity which must ever spring from the consciousness that they hold within their own hands a remedy for every political evil — a corrective for every government abuse and usurpation.'

No one ever reminded Americans more clearly of their

constitutional right to shape America into the dream of true democracy than John Geary. But he had no audience. No one listened to his message. By the gesture of sticking their fingers in their ears, the legislators passed the Census Bill over Geary's veto.

The governor's enthusiasm for his job was waning. 'How much longer I shall be required to sacrifice pecuniary interests, comfort, and health in what appears to be almost a thankless work remains to be determined,' he wrote to Amos Lawrence.

Armies no longer marched against each other. Marauding bands had disappeared from the land, at least for the winter, which, though not as severe as the winter before, was bitter enough. Even person-to-person combat was at low ebb. Only one recent near-killing had occurred in Tecumseh. John Speer had printed a diatribe against Judge Rush Elmore in his *Kansas Tribune*. The author was J. H. Kagi, correspondent of the *New York Post* destined to die at Harpers Ferry. Kagi's pen-assault was fresh in the judge's mind the day they came face to face in front of the court house in Tecumseh. Elmore raised his cane to strike his defamer. Kagi drew and fired, inflicting a severe flesh wound on the judge's thigh. Then Kagi ran, as Elmore whipped out his revolver to fire and fire again. The fleeing man was wounded, but only slightly.

Things seemed peaceful, but it was only a surface quiet and the man most aware of that was John W. Geary. The growing tension in Lecompton caused His Excellency to request two companies of dragoons to supplement the two companies detailed to the capital for the winter. The request was denied. John Geary's authorization to call upon federal troops had been rescinded. The President had been influenced, it turned out, not only by proslavery leaders in the Territory but also by General Persifer Smith himself. Smith, writing to Washington for more money, reported that federal troops had restored peace to Kansas. 'Being no longer occupied with the affairs of the Territory, undivided attention can be paid to punishing the Cheyenne Indians,' he said. 'In pursuing them in the spring, the great want will be forage and transportation of supplies . . .'

Things seemed peaceful, but there was a mounting tension in the man who had as much as been told that he no longer had the support of the party that had appointed him to office.

On 3 March 1857, the prisoners at Tecumseh petitioned the governor to better their condition. They had subsisted on coffee for four days, they said. The person under contract to furnish provisions had stopped deliveries because he had not been paid by the marshal.

The next day, the day Buchanan was inaugurated, John Geary secretly wrote his resignation to the new President.

On March sixth, a freshet caused by several days of heavy rain broke ice on the long-frozen surface of the Kaw.

On March tenth, Governor Geary wrote a note to Secretary Woodson saying he had had several hemorrhages of the lungs and would be absent from Lecompton for a few days.

At midnight that night, Samuel Walker cautiously opened his door to a heavy knock. In the light his candle threw he saw Governor John Geary, who looked to him as Shannon had looked to Gihon on the *Keystone*, 'as if laboring under an apprehension for his personal safety.'

The governor wore two guns and was breathing heavily. 'I'm going to Washington and I'll straighten things out,' he said. Then he disappeared into the darkness.

On 10 March 1857, John Geary left Kansas Territory, never to return. It was just as Sam Walker, a moderate man himself, had predicted — six months to a day.

27

The Dred Scott Decision

EVERYBODY HAS HEARD of the Dred Scott decision, but likely few remember that it became one of those historical phrases to heckle the memory chiefly because of its effects on doings in Kansas Territory.

The decision was handed down by Roger Taney, Chief Justice of the Supreme Court, on 6 March 1857, two days after James Buchanan was inaugurated as President of the United States.

Dred Scott was the slave of an army surgeon, Dr. John Emerson, who bought him from Captain Peter Blow and took him, in 1834, from the slave soil of Missouri to the free soil of Illinois. He was held in servitude there for two years, then taken to Fort Snelling in what was then Upper Louisiana Territory, made free by the Missouri Compromise. Dred married Harriett, whom Dr. Emerson bought from Major Talliaferro in 1836, and two years later they were both taken to Jefferson Barracks in Missouri. Their first daughter, Eliza, was born on the boat coming down.

Emerson died in 1843 and Mrs. Emerson's brother, John F. A. Sanford, became administrator of his estate. In 1846, Dred Scott, at the behest of the son of his former owner, Captain Blow, went to court to try to secure freedom for himself and his family on the grounds that the years he and his wife had spent on free soil had made them free. Sanford based Mrs. Emerson's

defense on Scott's inability to sue. Scott was not a citizen of
Missouri since he was of African descent; he was also a slave,
and slaves could not bring suit against their masters.

The Missouri Circuit Court granted Scott a judgment,
however, since Missouri courts had repeatedly ruled that slaves
residing on free soil for any length of time automatically became
free. In the most recent case, *Charlotte vs. Chouteau*, the judge,
finding for Charlotte, had said, 'When any of the negro race
who were reduced to slavery, acquired their freedom under the
laws of the country in which they live, we are aware of no law
by which they, except for crime, can again be reduced to
slavery.'

But the Missouri Supreme Court did not uphold the lower
court's decision. In 1852, the high court said that laws of other
states and territories had no extra-territorial effect in Missouri.
Dred Scott was and must remain a slave.

Meantime, the widowed Mrs. Emerson, having become the
wife of an ardent anti-slavery congressman, Dr. C. C. Chaffee,
had made a fictitious sale of Dred Scott to her brother, John
Sanford, who had moved to New York, leaving Dred Scott to
shift for himself in Missouri. He was persuaded to sue for his
freedom in the federal circuit court. Sanford charged that Scott
was not a citizen of Missouri and therefore could not sue in a
federal court. When the case was taken to the Supreme Court
of the United States on a writ of error, the Supreme Court decided that the jurisdiction of the lower court was not subject
to review. The Court majority concurred in the opinion of
Justice Nelson that when a slave returned to a slave state, his
condition was determined by the courts of that state. Dred
Scott was a slave because the Missouri Supreme Court said he
was a slave.

Dissents by Justices McLean and Curtis, unfortunately,
caused Taney to decide that the Court had a right to review the
merits of the case. And, in the end, Taney decided that the power
of Congress to make rules concerning the territory of the United
States was subject to restrictions of the Constitution protecting
property. In a word, Taney ruled that slaves were property,

not according to state law, but nationally. This was the kernel of the Taney decision, which burst like a bombshell on the nation on 6 March 1857.

'The most important decision ever made by the Supreme Court of the United States was pronounced yesterday,' said *The New York Times*. 'The supreme tribunal of the land decides that the Ordinance of 1787, as far as it prohibited slavery from the Northwest Territory, was unconstitutional; that the Missouri Compromise was unconstitutional; that Congress has no power to prohibit slavery from any portion of the federal territory, nor to authorize the inhabitants thereof to do so.'

Slavery had been given freedom of the public domain. Indeed, by inference, states themselves could no longer constitutionally exclude slavery. Since a man could safely take his slaves into states having anti-slavery legislation, it could be said there were no free states. Slaves were the same as any other kind of property, except that there were no laws requiring the return of strayed horses and cattle.

These extreme implications of the Dred Scott decision reflect the desperation of the times. Dred Scott sued too late, after emotion had taken its cancerous hold on reason — emotion of the kind that, injected into political issues, draws such hard and fast lines between good and evil as the Mason-Dixon Line.

Dred Scott was given his freedom immediately after the decision, but he could have won it had he sued earlier. Shortly after he first brought suit, the Wilmot proviso initiated the angry debates over slavery that became increasingly bitter at each renewal — over the Compromise of 1850, the Kansas-Nebraska Act in 1854, and, now, the constant struggle in Kansas Territory. By 1857, when the Supreme Court, seven to two, decided against Dred Scott and his race — and the basic American ideal of equal human right — slavery had become a political football, kept inflated by Northern self-righteousness and kept in play by the South's pigheaded championship of wrong.

The Taney decision was in keeping with the majority thinking of the day. The question with most everyone was not a question of whether or not Negroes were people. The question was Union.

It was a question of economics.

Northern politicians were forever intimating that slave labor costs nothing, and that its products competing with the products of free labor kept wages low. But actually slave labor had become so costly during the years the slave trade had been illegal that it was no longer profitable except for planters with great acreages of still-productive soil. That was a part of the South's desperation — worn-out soils and high-priced slaves. New soils that could support the expense of slaves bred in old areas were the South's great need. So the Dred Scott decision with its implied sanction of the expansion of slavery cheered the South. The Taney decision was bound to reopen the struggle for Kansas Territory, for it had given sanction to the proslave legislature's highjinks there.

The thing that had to be done then was to reverse the decision in the public mind. The powerful Northern press clamped down. For the first time editors who had prided themselves on their objectivity found themselves putting a foot in the same boat with Garrison, editor of *The Liberator* and high priest of disunion. They were to make Dred Scott a name never to be forgotten.

28

Four Governors Down and Two To Go

KANSAS TERRITORY would have done better if she had never had a governor, judging by the quiet that prevailed when she was governorless — between 10 March 1857, when Governor Geary slipped out of the Territory, and 27 May, when the new governor, Robert J. Walker, arrived at Leavenworth on the *New Lucy*.

There was not even an acting-governor on the grounds half that time, for Woodson had been given the better job of Receiver of the Delaware Lands. The new secretary of state, Frederick P. Stanton, did not arrive until mid-April and he was too cautious to plunge into territorial affairs. At least, he thought he was moving cautiously when he confined his activity to the apportioning of delegates to the constitutional convention which the Territorial Legislature had authorized.

Geary sent back a farewell message which did no credit to his deserved reputation as a to-the-point thinker on public affairs. He had suffered much, a collapse of purse as well as of ego, for he had defrayed a number of public expenses, including three months' pay to the two companies of militia that were kept mobilized.

He dwelt upon his unappreciated works and sacrifices in his farewell address and gave some valuable advice, though his only memorable words were a quotation from what Andrew Jackson had said at the time South Carolina threatened secession over the tariff: 'Mutual suspicions and reproaches may in time create mutual hostility, and artful and designing men will always be found who are ready to foment these fatal divisions. The world is full of such examples.'

Kansas Territory was long on 'artful and designing men.' They may have been busy that quiet spring of 1857 laying out Robert Walker's plat in their gubernatorial graveyard. Certainly popguns went off on both sides when Walker delivered his inaugural address.

'His lengthy address to the people, as usual with such documents, gave satisfaction to neither party,' free-soiler Charles Robinson commented. 'The free-state men were disgusted with his threats to enforce the territorial usurpation, and he gave too many promises of fairness to the "rebels" to suit the slave-state party.' And Robinson emphasized his own disapproval of Walker by repeating the gossip that the new governor's first act in Kansas Territory was to have '$250 worth of liquors distributed among the people in the streets of Leavenworth.'

South — a Richmond, Virginia, publication — denounced the new governor, saying that he had openly allied himself with the anti-slavery faction. 'No candid person can read his inaugural address and resist the conclusion that he goes out to Kansas with the deliberate design of wresting the Territory from the power of the South,' said *South*. 'It is idle to answer that his policy is opposed by the Black Republican party. The struggle between Walker and Robinson is not upon the issue of slavery or no slavery; it is competition for the glory of converting Kansas into a free State. The loss of Kansas would be a grievous calamity for the South; but to have it snatched from our grasp by the stealthy manipulation of a politician who affects a frank and honest purpose is an insult and wrong which we cannot bear with patience.'

The 'politician' Robert J. Walker was one of the most highly regarded men in the country. He was the son of a high federal judge and his wife was one of the Philadelphia Baches, a granddaughter of Benjamin Franklin. As a young lawyer, Walker made the first nomination of Andrew Jackson for the presidency. He was practicing in Mississippi when South Carolina sparked the nullification furore over the tariff. He took the stump against Calhoun's man Poindexter and won a seat in the Senate for himself. He took a leading part in the annexation of Texas and he was, according to *The New York Times*, 'the main instrument of making freedom of the northern portion of our newly acquired possession a condition of annexation.' Later, as Secretary of the Treasury under Polk, he initiated the 'revenue' tariff as distinguished from the protective tariff. Duties were cut more than half to the sound of cries of destruction from the Whigs. Senator Evans of Maine, party financial leader, went on record with a prediction that the next year's revenue would be less than $12 million, and Daniel Webster predicted it would be less than $14 million. Walker, the originator, predicted a jump to $30 million — and he hit it almost on the nose. The yield in 1847 was more than $29 million. And Walker was, according to *The Times*, 'the only financial minister whom the world has produced, who has advanced government stocks and maintained them above par during a foreign war and while it was borrowing money daily.'

This is the man who was welcomed to Kansas Territory with verbal brickbats. He spent most of his inaugural speech laying out a specific plan for so handling land grants that Kansas, when it became a state, might be free both of taxation and debt, but his listeners had ears only for what he had to say on the point of contest there, the slavery question.

He angered free-soilers by recognizing the Territorial Legislature as valid. 'If it is invalid, then we are without law and order in Kansas,' he said. 'All legal and judicial transactions are void, all titles are null, and anarchy reigns throughout our borders.' He would, he said, 'sustain the regular Legislature of the Territory in assembling its constitutional convention.'

He angered the proslavery boys by adding that he would protect all the people of the Territory 'in the exercise of their right of voting for or against that instrument.' Any constitution framed by the convention would be submitted to the people for their acceptance or rejection, he said.

He angered free-soilers by berating them for saying they would not vote for constitutional convention delegates because the election had been set by what they called the Bogus Legislature. 'The law has performed its entire and appropriate function when it extends to the people the right of suffrage,' Walker said. 'Those who abstain from the exercise of the right of suffrage authorize those who do vote to act for them. They are as much bound by the resulting legislation as if they had voted. Self-government depends on this principle.'

Walker annoyed proslavery men by raising the question of whether the climate of Kansas Territory was suited to slavery. And he turned right around and annoyed some free-soilers by saying that if 'slavery should not exist here, I trust it by no means follows that Kansas should become a state controlled by the treason and fanaticism of abolitionism.'

Robert Walker — described by Spring as 'an active, shrewd, tonguey, intellectual, withered little man' — was an able man, as had been, perhaps in this order: Geary, Shannon, Reeder. How long would he last?

II

ALL OVER THE country, people who could not read or write knew about Kansas. It was a word shouted in village churches and crackerbox sessions as well as in Congress and the press. It is testimony both to the deviousness and dexterity of local leaders on both sides that governing officers could continue to arrive in Kansas Territory only to find themselves completely in the dark about what was really going on.

Robert Walker probably expected proslave resistance to his determination on the question of referendum, but he must have been surprised at his hostile reception by free-soilers, to whom he promised elections free of fraud and a chance to accept or reject any constitution the proslave faction might frame.

Nobody but an insider could know what a bombshell Secretary of State Stanton had dropped into the free-soil camp just four days before Walker arrived in the Territory.

It was an innocent-looking bombshell — a simple announcement of the apportionment of delegates to the constitutional
convention. The explosive lay in the fact that Stanton had based
the apportionment on the deliberately defective census just
taken. Free-soilers had refused to register, expecting that federal territorial officials would not dare to call an election on the
basis of the scanty registration in free-soil communities. Stanton, new to the place, did dare to call an election on an apportionment that gave only twenty of the thirty-six organized
counties even a nominal representation. Nineteen counties south
of the Kaw, for example, were allotted only three delegates to
the thirteen delegates for the two proslavery counties of Leavenworth and Doniphan.

On 24 April, Stanton visited Lawrence and was entertained
at tea by Free State 'governor' Charles Robinson, who protested the census and the coming election.

'Bring me one man who has taken the proper steps to have
his name registered and been refused, and then see what becomes
of that officer,' Stanton said. 'The trouble is that you Free State
men are not willing to take any steps looking to the correction
of the evils you complain of.'

'Having determined to take no part in the election we
naturally are not solicitous about the purity of the voting lists,'
Robinson said, and added stuffily that businessmen had no time
to go hunting a census taker.

The election of 15 June, then, was a routine matter of de-
ciding which proslavery men would be delegates to the constitutional convention. Missourians stayed at home and only 2,200
proslavery residents bothered to vote. Alfred Johnson polled
only one vote but that elected him as one of the two delegates
from Franklin County. The convention itself was to be almost
as perfunctory, though it was to cause great reverberations.

III

THE FREE STATE LEGISLATURE met in Topeka on the ninth
of June but had to declare vacant the seats of thirteen absent

members to make a quorum. This fact was hidden from Governor Walker, who spent the four days this spurious legislature
was in session in Topeka, speaking publicly and privately and,
he thought, persuasively. He said that if their pretended legislature passed laws and tried to enforce them, there would be
trouble with the national government. And he again promised
that any constitution the Lecompton delegates wrote would
be submitted to a fair and full popular vote.

A big Free State party convention ran concurrently with
the legislative session. 'Walker with all his astuteness did not
wholly fathom the tremendous oratory,' wrote Leverett Spring.
'It was craftily handled so as to impress him with the conviction
that unless anti-slavery folk should receive fair treatment, revolutionary convulsions would certainly break out. The convention accomplished its purpose. Walker wrote his superiors in
Washington that had it not been for his intervention "the more
violent course would have prevailed, and the territory immediately involved in a general and sanguinary civil war." '

The old shell game was on again, with the new governor
as the gullible public.

IV

BOOMING LEAVENWORTH, where real-estate prices rose daily
and anyone could borrow gold without security or even a note,
elected its first Free State mayor, Henry J. Adams, late in June.
There was much armed bluster on both sides, but only one life
was lost. James Lyle, a young Georgian who was city recorder,
handed a proslave ballot to a German voter. The German tore it
to bits, saying, 'Do you suppose I'd vote that damned proslavery
ticket?' When proslavery bystanders set up a howl, free-soil
William Haller urged the German to stand his ground. Proslave
Lyle unsheathed his knife and turned to Haller; 'What is it to
you?' he demanded. Haller's answer was a quick plunge of his
knife into Lyle, deep enough to kill him.

In July, proslavery's Kansas National Democratic Party,
painfully so-named by a coalition of old-line Whigs and Demo-

crats, nominated candidates for the Territorial Legislature to be elected in October. And free-soilers began a series of bombastic meetings. They had sat out the constitutional convention election, but now they must decide whether or not to vote in the October election.

This was the year when, government surveys completed, pre-empted lands came up for final claiming and Indian trust lands came up for auction. In July, more than 2000 men gathered to bid on 100,000 acres put on the block at Osawkee in Jefferson County. Albert Richardson, who had just come to the Territory and was later to write a book, *Beyond the Mississippi*, was offered a $100 loan by a total stranger so he could get in on the grab. He took it. 'The constructive squatters respected each other's rights and protected their own,' he reported. 'The first man who ventured to bid against one of them was instantly shot down; so there was no further competition.' And he added, 'David's covetousness for the wife of Uriah was no stronger than the lust of the frontier Yankee for territory.'

In July, too, Governor Walker made his first call upon federal troops. One of his stipulations when he reluctantly took the governorship was that the famous Indian fighter, General William S. Harney, should be assigned to the Department of the West. President Buchanan had just written to the governor to say that General Harney had been selected to put down Mormon disturbances in Utah, but added, 'we must contrive to keep him with you, at least until you are out of the woods. Kansas is vastly more important at the present moment than Utah.' So Harney was at hand to take his dragoons to Lawrence where, Walker said, 'an act of rebellion' had been committed. Lawrence had refused to organize as a city under a charter granted by the Bogus Legislature and had set up an independent municipal government. 'Lawrence is the hotbed of all abolition movements in the Territory,' Walker wrote Secretary of State Cass. 'It is filled with a considerable number of mercenaries, who are paid by the Abolition Societies to perpetuate and diffuse agitation throughout Kansas, and prevent a peaceful settlement of this question.'

So 300 dragoons marched on Lawrence, but there was nothing for them to do when they got there. 'There was nobody to arrest, for no overt act had been committed, and there was nobody to fight, for nobody had taken up arms,' Richardson, who rushed down from the Osawkee sales, wrote.

And on the last day of the month, the Territory's first murder for money was committed. James Stephens was robbed and killed by John Quarles and W. M. Bays. 'Hitherto, every homicide in Kansas had resulted from the slavery issue,' wrote Richardson, who was in Leavenworth at the time. 'But here was a cold-blooded murder for money.' Neither Southerners nor Northerners liked that. Two thousand Leavenworth citizens met to mete out swift justice. Over the protests of proslave Justice Lecompte and free-soil Mayor Adams, the mob broke into jail, took out the murderers, and hanged them.

V

THE FREE STATE PARTY convened at Grasshopper Falls late in August to battle again the October election question. James Redpath, of the rabidly free-soil *St. Louis Democrat*, denounced participation as a 'backdown in principle.' But the convention ended by siding with Charles Robinson, who declared that 'men who are too conscientious and too honorable to change their tactics with a change of circumstance are too conscientious for politics.'

The Grasshopper Falls convention inexplicably authorized Jim Lane to put the party militia on a war footing and it passed a series of resolutions, two of which showed a profound distrust of Governor Walker. But free-soilers were soon to learn that Walker was a man who meant what he said. When the October elections rolled around, he stationed federal troops in the fourteen precincts where Missourians were most likely to vote. He was determined that these neighbors should keep their noses out of Kansas Territory's family affairs.

In stationing troops, he overlooked McGee County and the hamlet of Oxford in Johnson County, both pardonable oversights since McGee County in the southeast was Cherokee country with only a handful of white settlers and Oxford had, including stores and barns, only eleven buildings.

Then, the election returns came in. In McGee County, 1,226 votes blossomed in October where 14 votes had bloomed in June. And the hamlet of Oxford had a record turnout for any eleven-building town anytime, anywhere, with 1,628 votes cast.

Governor Walker, Southern Democrat, was faced with this crucial situation: If he let the McGee and Oxford returns stand, the Territorial Legislature would continue in proslave control; if he threw the returns out, territorial control would pass, for the first time, into free-soil hands.

Finally, Walker acted. He threw out the returns.

Proslavery men rushed to Lecompton to protest, spouted out their anger in fourteen furious resolutions. Justice Cato issued a mandamus ordering the governor to issue certificates of election to the unseated proslave candidates. Walker ignored the mandamus and one of the excluded candidates, ex-Sheriff Samuel Jones, strode into Secretary Stanton's office to demand that a certificate of his election be made out then and there. But the scholarly secretary was from Tennessee himself and not a man to be intimidated. He ordered Jones out of his office. Jones hesitated, hand on gun, then turned and left.

News of the affair spread quickly, and the next evening a company of free-soilers called on Secretary Stanton. They had come, they said, to take care of Jones. If it would be a convenience to have Jones out of the way and if Stanton and the governor would wink at the affair, they would be happy to hang the ex-sheriff that very night.

Stanton assured these obliging free-soilers that he was not the least afraid of Jones and, disappointed, they departed.

The whole affair enraged the small-statured but fiery governor. He armed himself with a small pepper-box pistol and said to Stanton, 'Come along and let's go see the Bengal tigers.'

They made a tour of the groggeries of Lecompton and in each and every one of them Walker demanded the attention of all present, then told his listeners exactly what he thought of them. If they had lost Kansas, it was through their own blundering excess of desire to possess her, he told them.

Walker had made a crucial decision, and he stood by it. The next Territorial Legislature would be comprised of nine free-soil councilmen to four proslave councilmen, and twenty-four free-soil representatives to fifteen proslave representatives.

The men of the South, in their ardor, had turned the tide against themselves.

VI

THE SOUTHERNERS still had a couple of cards up their sleeves. They had full control of the constitutional convention, soon to meet, and, by the Dred Scott decision, slavery had the freedom of this piece of public domain known as Kansas Territory. The Constitution of the United States, by this recent interpretation, upheld all acts of the Territorial Legislature to date regarding slave property. The only problem for the constitution framers, then, was how to perpetuate the status quo in such adroit phrases that anti-slavery voters would be trapped, should their constitution be referred to the people, as promised by the man who so recently had demonstrated his determination to keep his word.

This was the only concern of the Southerners. Once they got their constitution past the people of Kansas, they felt certain it would be passed by the still Democratic Congress and signed by the Democratic President, James Buchanan.

The Southerners had only this hope, but it held such promise that some free-soil men felt that the constitutional convention should not be allowed to meet. The leader of this faction, General James H. Lane, favored the wholesale slaughter of delegates, or so his enemies claimed, and their tale has been ignored by his Boswells rather than refuted.

The tale goes that Lane's slaughter plan was discovered by reporter Wattles of the New England Emigrant Aid Society's re-established *Herald of Freedom* and told to his editor, George Washington Brown. Brown says he grabbed his hat and rushed from one Lawrence store to another. Within an hour, some hundred substantial citizens had gathered in a vacant room over the Duncan brothers' store. Judge George W. Smith was made chairman and, on a motion by George Collamore, a committee headed by Columbus Hornsby was appointed to invite General Lane to attend the meeting.

Lane accepted the invitation with alacrity. He delighted in his talent for spellbinding and welcomed every opportunity to talk. But he was not invited to make a speech at this meeting. He was faced with a direct question on his plan to assassinate delegates to the Lecompton convention. At first he evaded the question, then admitted he did plan such an assassination.

A good many of Lane's boys had crowded into the assembly room, and at this point they cheered their hero so heartily that it was impossible for the meeting to go on. It was adjourned to meet that evening out of doors, in front of the Morrow House.

A large crowd gathered after supper.

Lane made his usual good case, for he was an orator who used every trick of the trade, even resorting to logic when necessary. When the opposition leaders spoke in a mild and conciliatory manner, he felt that he was gaining adherents to his plan, and he applauded louder than anybody when one of his lieutenants, Joel K. Goodwin, took the stand.

'Nothing but blood will restore tranquillity to Kansas,' Goodwin said. 'Nothing but blood will make Kansas a free state.' It was the Lane line and the cheers were hearty. 'I came here expressly to spill blood (cheers). It is not right that the whole country shall be convulsed, that disorder and violence shall be continued, that the perpetuity of the government shall be endangered by a revolution, when a little waste of worthless blood will restore order and tranquillity again (cheers on cheers). But I may differ with some of you as to the place to begin this bloodspilling business. No person has occasioned more strife, has been more fruitful cause of our disturbances than — James H. Lane!'

And Lane, stunned, listened as Goodwin went on. 'He demands blood. We all want it; but it is his blood that is demanded at this time; and if he presses on his assassination project, I propose that he shall be the first person to contribute.'

The general was so surprised and hurt by this reversal, suffered at the hands of a trusted lieutenant, that for once he had nothing to say. He just listened as the gathering reviewed the free-soil gains made in the recent election and decided to celebrate by holding a jubilation meeting in Lecompton on the day the proslave constitutional convention met.

General James H. Lane led this bloodless assault. 'There is nothing so difficult for a scoundrel to do as to meet the clear, honest gaze of the man he is trying to wrong,' wrote T. Dwight Thatcher in the 22 October issue of his *Lawrence Republican*. He pictured 'Sheriff Jones and his ilk' as 'gnashing their teeth in impotent rage as they listened to the burning words of the gallant Lane.'

But that was rhetoric. 'Jones and his ilk' spent the three days that the free-soilers were in Lecompton in convivial pre-convention planning. And when the free-soil orators were gone, the delegates met and set about to frame a constitution and a way to make free-soilers swallow the bitter pill.

VII

THE LECOMPTON CONSTITUTION closely resembled every other state constitution that has ever been framed. It even closely resembled the unsuccessful Topeka Constitution, except in its clauses concerning the Negro.

The free-soil instrument had barred people of Negro blood from ever living in Kansas. The proslave constitution not only would let Negroes live there but said, 'The right of a slave-holder to such a slave and its increase is the same as and as inviolable as the right of any property whatever.'

There had been a great influx of settlers that year, most of them from free-soil states. The delegates well knew that a constitution containing such a clause would stand no chance of acceptance by the people of Kansas Territory.

There was a long and bitter fight over whether or not to

send the Lecompton Constitution directly to Washington. Only the year before, Senator Seward of New York had insisted that the squatter sovereigns of K.T. should be allowed to make such a direct submission. But the constitution then in question was the Topeka Constitution, and its direct submission had been one of the factors in its failure. The real hurdle, however, was the local governor. Walker had promised the people that they would have a chance to vote on the Lecompton instrument, and he would see to it that they got that chance.

The convention finally found a tricky solution to its problem. It was a partial submission of its constitution to the voters. Citizens of the Territory of Kansas would be given a choice between two propositions: (1) constitution with slavery; (2) constitution without slavery.

If the first proposition should carry, then slavery would exist as legally in the new state of Kansas, when chartered by Congress, as it existed anywhere.

If the second proposition should carry, then slavery would 'no longer exist in the State of Kansas, except that the right of property in slaves now in this territory, shall in no manner be interfered with.' In other words, slaveholders living in the Territory when it became a state could be slaveholders as long as their slaves lived and produced their kind.

This alternative, free-soilers said, 'was like submitting to the ancient test of witchcraft, where if the accused, upon being thrown into deep water floated he was adjudged guilty, taken out and hanged; but if he sank and was drowned he was adjudged not guilty — the choice between them being immaterial.'

And several convention delegates were against this dodge. Judge Rush Elmore urged submitting the full constitution and letting the proslave cause stand or fall by that. And two of the delegates from Riley County were shocked by the fraud. 'I tell you this scheme of swindling submission will be the blackest in our history!' one of them cried. 'Those Black Republicans will get at the bottom of it so quick you'll never cease to hear from this dodge.' And the other said the compromise carried 'falsehood in letters of brass.' He assured the convention that he was a proslavery man and wanted to make Kansas a slave state, but that that would be impossible if they went through with this trick, which he was sure had been concocted by 'free-state Democrats.'

Opponents of the trick submission put up a stubborn fight, but they lost. Kansas voters were offered only these two propositions, and again free-soilers stayed away from the polls. The Lecompton Constitution 'with slavery' carried the Territory by an overwhelming majority and was submitted to Congress.

In the October election, in which free-soilers had participated, the Free State delegate to Congress was elected. N. J. Parrott defeated Epaphroditus Ransom, proslave ex-Governor of Michigan. So a free-soiler from Kansas Territory heard the President of the United States, in his message opening the Thirty-fifth Congress on 7 December 1857, endorse the proslave Lecompton Constitution. 'The Kansas-Nebraska Bill did not require the submission of any portion of the Constitution to an election, except that which relates to the domestic institution of slavery,' James Buchanan said, and he urged Congress to admit Kansas to the Union under the Lecompton instrument.

Another man who heard this message was Robert J. Walker, who had left Kansas Territory saying he would 'be absent on business for three or four weeks.' He never went back.

29

Voting Army Routed

ON THE DAY that President Buchanan endorsed the Lecompton Constitution, the new and free-soil Kansas Territorial Legislature met in special session.

The session had been called reluctantly by Secretary of State Stanton, acting-governor in Walker's absence. When free-soil leaders pressed for a session, he pointed out that the official terms of the elected Free State members had not yet begun. A special session, then, would mean a special session of the old pro-slavery Legislature. He was talked down on this point, and he called the new Legislature into session, but on the promise that it would act only in relation to constitutional convention election frauds and the full submission of the Lecompton Constitution to popular vote.

So, on 7 December 1857, free-soilers thronged Lecompton to cheer the Territorial Legislature which, Southerners said, 'had been dipped in the turbid waters of Black Republicanism' and, Northerners added, 'made clean.'

There was such a celebration that it took a day or two for a quorum of legislators to be rounded up. Then, the Lecompton Constitution was denounced and a date was set for a referendum on the full constitution. The day chosen was 4 January 1858, the date the proslave Lecompton convention had set for the election of state officers under its constitution.

This business disposed of, the Legislature should have

adjourned, as it had promised Stanton it would. But it took up another piece of business. Over Stanton's veto, it made the Free State Militia the official militia of the Territory and put James H. Lane in command, a position customarily reserved to the chief executive of a government.

Stanton had a feeling when he called the special session that he was proclaiming himself out of a job. And when the news of what had gone on reached Washington, he found that he had been right. He was removed from office on 16 December and General J. W. Denver, Commissioner of Indian Affairs, who happened to be visiting the numerous tribes in the Territory, was notified that he was to take over Stanton's duties.

And back in Washington, the President's endorsement of the Lecompton Constitution had sparked a debate that was again making congressional halls resound with the cry, 'Kansas, bleeding Kansas!'

II

JAMES DENVER WAS sworn in as Secretary of State, Kansas Territory, before Judge Cato on 21 December 1857. His first official act was to write Howell Cobb, Secretary of the Treasury, asking for $11,000 for legislative expenses. 'There is not a dollar on hand here,' he said.

While he was worrying about the finances of the Territory, free-soilers were debating about whether or not to vote in the election of state officers under the Lecompton Constitution. Charles Robinson again held that they should take part. They had followed his advice at Grasshopper Falls and gained control of the Territorial Legislature. Now, he argued, they should win the state offices under the Lecompton Constitution, in case Kansas was admitted under that instrument. But many of the free-soilers who met in Lawrence on the twenty-third of December to settle the question found the very thought of participating in an election set by the Bogus Legislature odious. They kept the argument going for two days — knowing perhaps what Jim Lane, who was not present, had up his sleeve.

The question of participation was about to come to a vote on Christmas Eve, when General E. B. Whitman dramatically entered the room. Panting, breathless, he raised his hand and cried, 'War has begun!' He had been twenty hours in the saddle, ridden a hundred miles with only one stop for food, he said. He had changed mounts four times to hasten the news that General Lane and 200 brave men stood embattled near Mound City. War, he said, had been made on peaceful citizens, who had implored Lane to take command.

'You stand here and talk about voting under the Lecompton Constitution, thinking thereby to defeat it, while your brethren in the southern part of the Territory are already in arms! The Lecompton Constitution!' he hissed. Then he raised his arm; 'Why, I would rather cut off this right arm than vote for any man under that constitution!'

A great shout went up and fiery Sam Wood stepped forward to call for volunteers to start for the battlefield at daybreak on Christmas morning.

When Charles Robinson suggested that the whole thing might be a ruse to influence the vote of the caucus, he was cried down. A vote was called for and it went as Jim Lane had wanted it to go — against participation.

But the conservatives, comprised largely of New England Emigrant Aid Society officials and partisans, did not take this defeat lying down. They repaired to the basement of the *Herald of Freedom* building and nominated a Free State ticket, headed by George W. Smith.

The day after Christmas, Jim Lane appeared in Lawrence, beaming. He had left his embattled troops where he found them — in his imagination — and had come back to gloat over the success of his ruse. His beam faded when he learned about the bolters. The fact that their ticket was being endorsed by all influential free-soil citizens, however, caused him to hop quickly on their bandwagon. Jim Lane was never a man to stick with a minority.

While these things were transpiring, the proslavery voting forces again prepared to enter the field.

On 4 January 1858, they attacked. They had enough striking power to come within a few votes of sweeping the election, but the Free State Party had the edge.

The Southerners lost the election. They also 'lost' the election returns, when news came that a congressional investigating committee was on its way to examine them.

The vital thing to the South was to get the Territory admitted under the Lecompton Constitution, and proof of ballot-box stuffing might be just the thing that would defeat that objective. When the Washington committee arrived and asked to see the returns, they could not be found. Their whereabouts was a mystery.

Surveyor General John Calhoun, as chairman of the Lecompton Constitutional Convention, was the man who would issue certificates of office should Kansas become a state under the constitution framed by that convention. He was, therefore, custodian of the election returns. But after four years of territorial life, he suddenly decided he had had enough of it. The Washington committee found that he had gone back to the States, leaving his chief clerk, General L. A. MacLean, in charge. MacLean told the congressmen that he had sent the election returns to Calhoun.

Sam Walker — now Brigadier General of the Territorial Militia, Sheriff of Douglas County, and Deputy U.S. Marshal — was told by William Brindle that the lost election returns were hidden in a woodpile near MacLean's office. And, in his capacity as sheriff, Walker armed himself with a search warrant and called upon MacLean.

MacLean was most co-operative. 'You are welcome to search, sir,' he said. 'I sent the returns to Calhoun. They are not here.'

'I think you are mistaken,' Sam Walker said. 'I know where they are.'

'Where?'

'Under the woodpile.'

'I forbid you to search!' cried MacLean, and he pulled out his pistol.

Walker told MacLean to put his gun away. Then, he calmly turned his back and walked to the woodpile where he easily found a candlebox and, in the candlebox, the lost election returns.

And that was the end of L. A. MacLean as a proslave force in Kansas Territory. He, too, went back to the States.

Many Southerners were getting disgusted with such monkeyshines. The ardent proslavery protagonist, Dr. John Stringfellow, put his *Squatter Sovereign* up for sale and went back to Missouri. He even wrote to the *Washington Union* protesting the admission of Kansas under the Lecompton Constitution. He said admission under this instrument would break down the Democratic Party in the North and seriously endanger the peace and interests of Missouri and Kansas, if not of the whole Union. The slavery question in Kansas had been 'settled against the South by immigration,' he said.

And in Congress, some of the most condemning voices raised against the Lecompton Constitution were Southern voices.

'I have grave misgivings whether the people of Kansas are of that character from which we may hope for enlightened self-government,' said Senator Biggs of North Carolina.

'The whole history of Kansas is a disgusting one from beginning to end,' said Senator Hammond of South Carolina.

'Why, sir!' cried Senator Iverson. 'If you could rake the infernal regions from the center to the circumference and from the surface to the bottom, you could not fish up such a mass of corruption as exists in some portions of Kansas!'

In the House, Southern settlers were reprimanded by Representative Atkins of Tennessee, but he also branded free-soil immigrants as 'struggling hordes of hired mercenaries carrying murder, rapine, and conflagration in their train.' And Representative Anderson of Missouri said he was certain 'no part of our Union has been settled by such an ungovernable, reckless people.'

Still, arguments in favor of admission were to fill more than 900 pages in the *Congressional Globe* and, after less than two months' debate, were to convince the Senate. There were thirty-three votes for admission to twenty-five against.

And this despite one of those strange-bedfellow shifts that are perhaps the strength of our democracy.

This one involved the great Democrat, originator of the Kansas-Nebraska Bill and inventor of popular sovereignty Stephen A. Douglas. Labeling the Lecompton business 'treachery and juggling,' the Little Giant set out to defend popular sovereignty against this assault from a new quarter, the South.

Representative James Hughes of Indiana, speaking at a Democratic meeting at Mozart Hall in New York on 2 March 1858, charged that Douglas had started this whole new agitation over Kansas because he was still disgruntled at not having been made the presidential candidate at Cincinnati.

'When the present session of Congress opened, with all this bright and glowing future before us — like a clap of thunder from the cloudless sky — from the Senate of the United States came the hoarse cry of discord,' Hughes orated. 'Kansas, bleeding Kansas — *terrima causa belli* — was rung out and borne on the breeze. Whose voice was it? Not that of the people of Kansas, not of abolitionists, not of Main Law fanatics, not of Republicans or freedom-shriekers — but the voice of Stephen A. Douglas, whilom the potent leader of democracy — our Joab — our mighty man of war!

'The nation was amazed. The Republican party, after the first transport of astonishment and delight, took formal possession of the fallen giant, notwithstanding the wry faces of some of their own leaders, who, like the Turk "will bear no brother near the throne," and now he who of late was their embodiment of evil "is become a god," and bestrides the great party of the North "like a huge Colossus." '

Once Mr. Hughes had cleared the oratory out of his system, he settled down to an able argument on the legality of the Lecompton Constitution, using the party line of tracing that instrument's history step by step.

Senator Polk of Missouri, in keynoting the pro-Lecompton stand, called that history 'A majestic spectacle of the people

marching in stately pace to the accomplishment of their purposes.'

The single tenable line of defense for the Lecompton Constitution was 'that it was the work of a legitimate convention
which observed all the indispensable formalities,' according to
historian Spring. 'The successive stages of its history were
elaborately rehearsed: The constitution dates back to the first
Territorial Legislature, which submitted to the people the question of calling a constitutional convention. Fifteen months afterward — a period ample for mature consideration — they re-
spond favorably at the polls. After a lapse of three months, the
question reaches the second legislatural session, which "bows to
the will of the people" and provides for an election of delegates.
Then between the legislative sanction and the election of delegates, four months intervene. Before the delegates meet and
enter upon their duties, a further delay of three months occurs.
They submit a single but vital article of the constitution to the
people for acceptance or rejection December 21st, and they
ratify it almost unanimously.'

The congressmen who used these arguments for the Lecompton Constitution of course never mentioned the reason for
'the stately pace.' No one called attention to the constant blood-
letting that kept the body politic of Kansas Territory too prostrate to move in anything but slow motion.

Congressmen opposing the Lecompton Constitution concentrated their attack on the fact that only a part of the constitution had been submitted to the people. But it was an argument
hard for them to make stick since they themselves had been
against any kind of referendum in 1856.

As Representative Hughes pointed out in his New York
speech, the men who in 1858 were insisting on full submission
of the Lecompton Constitution were the very men who had
fought from the first against letting Kansas settlers have
any say on the question of slavery. These men had fought the
passage of the Kansas-Nebraska Bill, maintaining that the
slavery question was one to be settled by congressional rather
than popular action. Now they were arguing for popular sover-

eignty in one breath, Hughes said, and declaring in the next that they would not vote to admit Kansas under the Lecompton Constitution 'if all the people desired it.'

The Senate finally voted to admit Kansas under the Lecompton Constitution, but the House turned the measure down and voted to refer this constitution back to the people. The Senate rejected the House measure and a committee of conference, comprised of members from both chambers, proposed a novel compromise bill called the English Bill.

An ordinance hooked onto the Lecompton Constitution asked for a much larger land grant than any state had ever received on admission, more than twenty-three million acres. The English Bill took a tip from this and hooked a land grant proposal to acceptance of the constitution. It offered the people of Kansas Territory much less land than they had asked for, not quite four million acres. If they accepted this reduced grant, they automatically accepted the Lecompton Constitution, and slavery. If they rejected it, they automatically agreed to wait until their Territory had a population of 94,000 before they proposed another constitution.

The only thing that could be said for the English Bill was that it gave people another crack at the odious, even to many Southerners, Lecompton Constitution. And the people turned down the constitution by a seven-to-one vote ratio.

30

New Roles for Old Rascals

ON 3 JUNE 1858, free-soil leader James H. Lane killed free-soil leader Gaius Jenkins over a claim dispute.

This incident symbolizes the change that was taking place in Kansas Territory. The struggle with proslave interests was not over, but as free-soilers gained the upper hand, free-soil feuds came into the open, often to be pursued with bold and ingenious trickery.

There were two sharply defined political factions on the free-soil side, the conservatives and the ultras, and these two groups were divided within themselves by the bitterest kind of personal enmities.

The conservatives, roughly, were comprised of the practical minded, the men who were as much concerned about the economic quarrel between North and South as about the inhumanity of human bondage. The feud within this faction was between the New England Aid Society brand, which seemed mainly concerned with personal gain but had a strong streak of righteous concern over the evil of slavery, and the Western-state brand, which was more honest, both in its unwillingness to compete with slave labor and its willingness to admit free-soil excesses. Charles Robinson epitomized the first group, Samuel Walker the second.

The antagonisms between these factions were there from the beginning. Lawrence was founded, as described earlier, on land swindled from its pre-emptors by the self-righteous, profit-minded agent of the New England Emigrant Aid Society, Dr. Charles Robinson. Free-soil men from the Western states also had come to take a stand against the extension of slavery and to find new opportunities for themselves, and they resented the monopolistic attitude of Easterners toward these impulses. Indeed the editors of the first two Lawrence papers, New England's *Herald of Freedom* and the West's *Kansas Free State*, spent more space on reviling each other than they spent on the common enemy, the South. Josiah Miller of the *Free State*, 22 October 1855, said of the *Herald's* editor, G. W. Brown: 'Mr. Elliott, our partner, on one occasion inquired of Mr. Brown what kind of morality he considered there was in publishing so many things about us that he knew to be false. Mr. Brown replied that he considered, in this difficulty between us, the end justified the means and that, therefore, he had a right to use those instruments that would most effectually accomplish the end desired, and consequently, was entitled to publish anything that would effectually injure us, no matter whether it be true or false.'

These were the conservatives.

When Josiah Miller's *Kansas Free State* folded, G. W. Brown put on his brass knuckles and went gunning for T. Dwight Thatcher, editor of Lawrence's new paper, the *Lawrence Republican.* Thatcher, who said of Brown, 'he stands the impersonation of a cringing sycophant, ready to kiss the foot that would tread upon his own and other people's necks,' was an ultra.

The ultras also differed greatly in their points of view but were at one in believing that slavery could be abolished only by what John Brown called 'remission of blood.' They ranged from such men as Brown and James Redpath, who hated slavery, to such men as Jim Lane and James Montgomery, who loved fighting.

Redpath admittedly came to Kansas to help create a military conflict between North and South, as did other Englishmen, including Richard Hinton, with whom he was to collaborate on a book about John Brown. Redpath said in his *Roving Editor*, 'I endeavored personally and by my pen to precipitate a revolution.' He joined Jim Lane's organization, the Danites, so-called because it resembled the Mormon disciplinary band.

Lane was thwarted in his plan to assassinate the delegates to the Lecompton convention, but that did not daunt him. He set to work on an even more magnificent plan. He and his Danites would wipe out all proslavery men still resident in the Territory. At a Danite meeting in Lawrence, early in 1858, Redpath listened with approbation while Lane named the generals who were to conduct the massacres at Atchison, Kickapoo, Leavenworth, and other proslave strongholds. But apparently Redpath was a man of words rather than of action. This professed revolutionist balked when Lane gave him the personal assignment of killing the ardently proslave junior editor of the *Squatter Sovereign*, Robert S. Kelley. Redpath was so shocked that he exposed Lane's mass murder plan. He denounced Lane and his plot in his own newspaper, the newly established, short-lived *Crusader of Freedom*. He wanted a revolution but was squeamish about its costs. He was and remained a John Brown idolater, but he refused to believe, against all evidence, that Old Brown was the Pottawatomie Creek butcher.

There were feuds between factions and feuds within factions. One of the most mercurial was that between the two high men of the New England Emigrant Aid Society, agent Charles Robinson and editor George Washington Brown. 'He would crawl on his belly to Jerusalem to save his miserable neck,' Robinson once said of Brown, and Brown said, in the Aid Society's *Herald of Freedom*, 23 May 1857, 'Circumstances have made Charles Robinson conspicuous in Kansas history and circumstances will confine him to oblivion.'

II

AFTER FREE-SOILERS WON the majority of seats in the Territorial Legislature and carried the election of state officers under the Lecompton Constitution, it was naturally expected that the

Free State Party would fold its rebel Topeka government, which had long been an embarrassment even to the most partisan Northern congressmen.

But there were those who, as Spring put it, 'still dreamed of some cross-cutting path into the Union.' Undaunted by the fact that the whole Topeka movement was considered rash and even treasonable by Washington, these partisans, in a joint meeting with the new Territorial Legislature, asked that body to vote itself out of existence and to transfer all its rights and prerogatives to the Topeka legislature. The Territorial Legislature, however purged in its membership, would always bear the onus of its origin, they said.

Members of that body were inclined to resent this charge. They rejected the Topeka proposal and, though they may have been motivated by an unwillingness to relinquish their own newly acquired power, the reason they gave for their refusal was wise beyond dispute. They said it would be political suicide for the free-soil cause if, having gained control of the only law-making assembly recognized by federal authorities, they threw it over in favor of what was considered a rebel assembly.

If the free-soil faction in control at the moment had listened to the free-soil faction that wanted to be in control, the delicate balance of the congressional scales, now weighing the Lecompton Constitution, might easily have been so weighted in that instrument's favor that Kansas would have been admitted as a slave state in 1858.

The Territorial Legislature's action, no matter what its motives, saved the day for the free-soil cause and, at the same time, dealt a death blow to the Topeka government. 'Governor' Robinson, in his message to the Topeka Legislature, which met 5 January 1858, urged that his government be kept. But the *Quindaro Chindowan* — a newspaper of a town Robinson had established just above Wyandotte to give free-soilers a Missouri River port — was the only newspaper to support his plea. The Topeka government reeled around for a while, then fell flat.

'The Territorial Legislature was now in undisputed control,' wrote Leverett Spring. 'Yet, though revolutionized in political composition, the quality of its political morality showed little betterment. The record it made was worse than indifferent.' Nine-tenths of its first session was taken up with minor bills incorporating cities and towns and private bills granting business charters. The few important bills it passed were, by territorial custom, vetoed by the governor and, by territorial custom, passed over the governor's veto.

First major act of the new legislature was a repeal of the first legislature's act to punish offenses against slave property. Denver, in his veto message, recognized the existing act as 'a very stringent one' but said he could not give his consent to the repeal of 'all laws on this subject, until there shall be some other enactment to take their place, so long as slavery is recognized and allowed to exist in this Territory.'

The next major move of the new legislature was to relocate the capital. It did not choose any established free-soil town but a place called Minneola, if 'an empty stretch of prairie grass, bugle brush, and weeds' can be called a place. Of course, it was busy becoming a place. The new capital's promoters — who comprised more than a two-thirds majority of the legislative body — had carpenters at work when they introduced the bill to make their own town capital of K.T. Yet flimsy as the specifications were, the building of the big balloon capitol had hardly begun when the acting-governor condemned Minneola with his veto, so quickly did he act against the bill creating her. And few more nails had been hammered when the legislator-promoters passed the creative act over his veto, so quickly did they act.

Denver was learning — as Reeder, Shannon, and Geary had learned before him — that a K.T. governor's veto was a sheer waste of ink. But this man had agreed to act as governor against his better judgment, and he kept putting off taking the oath as governor in order to force Washington to send another chief executive. He was in a good position to try to tame the lawless lawmakers. He refused to move his office to Minneola. He would not permit any public records to be moved there. And his stand was backed by U.S. Attorney General Jeremiah Black, who declared that the whole Minneola scheme was unconstitutional. Denver was backed, too, by the press. A large block of Minneola town stock had been set aside for local and Eastern journalists, but they were not going to buy. They decided, in a secret meeting at Lawrence, to assail the Minneola scheme with 'unsparing ridicule and execration.'

Sessions of the Territorial Legislature were limited by law to forty days. Toward the end of this session, this first legal free-soil body passed a bill calling for a constitutional convention. This was a surprise move and the strategy was to get the bill to Denver too late for him to act. But the new legislators were not well acquainted with the organic law. It permitted a pocket veto of any legislation that reached the chief executive within three days of the set adjournment date.

It happened that James Denver either thought that K.T. had had enough constitution-making for the moment or remembered that citizens had just agreed, by voting for the English Bill, to wait until the population grew before framing another constitution. Anyway, he gave the free-soil bill a pocket veto.

'But legislators who originated the enterprise of removing the capital to Minneola could not be thwarted by any such trifle as the pocketing of a bill,' Leverett Spring said. In the last hours of the session, James Denver received the convention bill endorsed as having been passed over his veto.

He sent for the presiding officers. The President of the Council, C. W. Babcock, the Speaker of the House, George Deitzler, and Chief Clerk C. F. Currier appeared, and the acting-governor held out the spurious document. 'Who is responsible for this?' he asked.

'Lane suggested it,' one of the men said.

'This is not the original bill,' Denver said. 'That is still in my hands, has never been out of them. This bill is a forgery. Now, I can make trouble for you, if I choose to do it. You have certified as to what is not true. The whole statement is false. But I have no wish to keep up the agitation. Two courses are open to you. Either you give me a paper setting forth the fact

that the original bill never was returned to the Legislature with
my objections and hence never was passed over my veto, or
destroy this counterfeit document here in my presence.'

'What shall we do with it?' asked Chief Clerk Currier.

'Destroy it,' said Speaker Deitzler.

The document was tossed into the executive stove.

But later that day, just before adjournment, this 'purged'
Legislature unanimously voted that the burned document had
been passed in due form. And, on 9 March 1856, delegates were
elected to a constitutional convention to be held two days later
at flimsy Minneola.

The first business taken up by the convention was the matter of immediate adjournment to warmer quarters. The debate
on this motion raged until five o'clock next morning; then the
Minneola shareholders, probably stiff with cold themselves, gave
in. The convention adjourned to meet again, after a good
night's sleep, at Melodeon Hall in Leavenworth.

Reconvened, delegates moved against both the 'free white
state' doctrine of the Topeka Constitution and the proslavery
bias of the Lecompton. An unqualified anti-slavery stand was
framed. It was, Spring said, 'an excellent constitution' doomed
'by the stigma of its origin.'

The voters of the Territory were as disgusted by 'the
Minneola swindle' as they had been by the 'Lecompton swindle.'
They rejected the Leavenworth Constitution by a 3 to 1 vote.
They gave, in effect, a vote of confidence to James Denver, who
had finally agreed to drop the 'acting' from his title and become
the fifth territorial governor. He was to serve as actual governor
for a shorter time than any of his predecessors, but he was destined to walk out of the Territory, not run.

III

ALL WAS PEACEFUL along the Kaw as the new legislature and
the new governor played the old territorial game of pass-veto-
pass. But that did not mean that Kansans were relinquishing
their role as 'an ungovernable, reckless people.' The center of

violence, tornado-like, had simply swept to another locale, to southeast Kansas Territory, where jayhawking had never taken a holiday.

George ('Murderer of Barber') Clarke was blamed by free-soilers for starting it all back in the fall of '56. He had made a raid then, had destroyed crops, stolen horses and cattle, and burned some free-soil cabins. 'Clarke's company,' said one of the victims, 'took everything they wanted, and I think they took things they did not want — to keep their hands in — had ribbons on their hats, side combs in their hair, and other things they did not need.'

After the Clarke raid, James Montgomery, a man of courage and craft, had gone to Missouri to get a list of the Missourians who had been in Clarke's party. He pretended to be a teacher looking for a job. He got a job and actually taught for two weeks. It took that long to get the information he wanted. When he had his list of ex-raiders, he closed the school and jumped into the role he was to play for years — that of retaliatory guerrilla chieftain. Twenty of Clarke's men were captured and stripped of all their removable property.

And the jayhawking spree was on.

Since the action of the comi-tragedy that played in Kansas Territory for seven long years now moved into the southeast theater, it might be well to go back even before Clarke's raid.

The southeast section, down around Fort Scott, was heavily proslave, but the men there missed out on all the thunderous doings in the valleys of the Missouri and the Kaw. When news reached them of John Brown's 'Dutch Henry business,' they were incensed but had no organization for retaliation. By the time news came that Missourians under John Reid were going to raid Brown's town, however, they could quickly muster a company. They did, and marched north to get in on the fight.

They were about three leagues distant from Osawatomie when nightfall came. They bivouacked and were about to eat their suppers when a party of some hundred settler-routing free-soilers descended upon them. They all quickly decamped, leaving their gear, including plates of food. They high-tailed it for home, arriving in Fort Scott toward midnight, their imaginations as lathered as were their horses' flanks.

Thinking their pursuers hard upon their heels, they aroused the town. The very sight of these heroes, with all the fears of pursuit upon them, threw the place in panic. As men, women, and children, hastily clad, fled their homes, rumor came that the expected slaughter and pillage had begun just north of town. And the townspeople, having no hills of consequence to flee to for refuge, gathered together and prayed. They were not attacked.

Initial blame for any situation involving more than one person is always difficult to establish. Opposite forces are somehow sparked into motion — and things happen.

Free-soiler James Montgomery believed, with John Brown, that the only way to beat the South was to force its settlers out of Kansas Territory. He had been intimidating proslave settlers on a small scale before the Clarke raid. After the raid he made a business of it. And since most proslave settlers in those parts had come to farm rather than to fight, Montgomery managed to drive out quite a number of them without much noise or bloodshed. Plundering and pointed words did the job. Montgomery, telling writer Albert Richardson about his home, called it a 'very good log house,' and added, 'A gentleman from Missouri built it, but soon after, he was unexpectedly compelled to leave the country and so I have taken possession until he returns' — a statement that seems to belie the free-soil view that Montgomery was compelled to organize a guerrilla band to protect himself and his neighbors.

Montgomery had things pretty much his own way in southeast K.T. He paid little attention to Lawrence as it symbolized free-soilism in Kansas Territory, and Lawrence paid little attention to him, until toward the end of 1857.

Then the Jayhawker captain began to meet with more resistance than he was accustomed to encounter. Maybe the Dred Scott decision was taking hold. Maybe it just happened. Anyway, Southerners he had run out started coming back to reclaim their claims. And they came back in such numbers that,

for the first time, Montgomery felt the need of assistance. He
sent a messenger to Jim Lane.

Lane ordinarily would have welcomed this invitation to
march, but Montgomery's request came at just the time he was
maneuvering to get himself made the governor's military superior. He could not leave Lecompton, but he did send help.
He sent Captain Abbott down to give 'all advisable aid.'

Southerners who came back to reclaim their lands were
claim-jumpers in Montgomery's eyes. He handled them as such,
setting up his own squatters' courts to give quick justice.

One of these claim-jumper disputes happened to come to a
crisis just as Abbott arrived, and he was made judge of Montgomery's impromptu court at his camp on the Little Osage.

News of this unconventional court came to the ears of
United States Marshal Blake Little in Fort Scott, and he quickly
deputized a small posse and rode north.

The court, when informed of Little's approach, abandoned
its judicial role and prepared to fight. But the marshal simply
asked Montgomery for an explanation.

The slight guerrilla chieftain had a low, musical voice and
was a persuasive talker. And he could rely on the fact that news
not only traveled slowly in Kansas Territory but was never to
be trusted, compounded as it was of fact and fancy. He told
Marshal Little that the legislature then in session had repealed
the entire code established by the previous legislature. He convinced the marshal that there were no laws for him to enforce,
so Little rode back to Fort Scott. He told the story there and
learned that he had been duped. He then deputized a posse of
forty men and returned to the woodland court of the man who
pictured himself as the Robin Hood of the southeast.

The bench was a split log against the side of a log cabin.
The court, on this mild December day, sat on tree stumps and
leaned and lounged against trees.

Marshal Little posted his posse in the wood; then he strode
up to the bench and turned to face the self-constituted court.
'Gentlemen, you will understand that you are dealing with the
United States and not with border ruffians,' he said. 'You will

learn that there is a difference between them. I order you to surrender and prepare to accompany me to Fort Scott.'

The court expressed itself as unwilling to submit to arrest.

'I will give you half an hour, gentlemen,' said the marshal. 'You will agree to come with me, then, or I'll blow you all to hell.' And he walked off to join his posse.

The court recessed. Some of its members retired into the cabin and others stationed themselves behind trees.

The half-hour passed. There was no word from the court and the marshal ordered his posse to charge.

Most of his possemen were town loafers who had ridden out for a lark. They charged the cabin happily enough, but they did not like it when a dozen or so Sharp's rifles barked out. Most of the men wheeled their horses, kicked them in the flanks, and headed for home. Some stayed to return the volley, but they lit out, too, when the answering round came.

The alleged claim-jumper was convicted and encouraged to leave the Territory for a healthier climate.

These were the preliminaries to the next big bloody act about to take place in Bourbon County.

31

Bi-annual May Massacre

IN THE SOUTHEASTERN COUNTIES of the Territory the stage was set in that spring of 1858 for the bi-annual May massacre.

James Montgomery had done a good job of clearing that section of Southerners who had come to the Territory with the simple idea of making a home. But the Southerners who had come to make Kansas a slave state were less easily scared. George Clarke had become a resident of Fort Scott and, though he had become inoperative as an offensive force, he gave counsel to the proslavery circle that held forth in the barroom of the McKay Hotel. And up in Linn County, the proslave confab center was the big log house of Captain Charles A. Hamilton, wellborn and wealthy Georgian. This restless and adventurous young man had arrived in Kansas Territory too late for the bloody doings of '56 and had never been able to organize a force large enough to put a scare into Montgomery's Jayhawkers, much less combat them. When the proslavery cause took such a definite decline early in 1858, he became desperate. He compiled a list of obnoxious free-soil men in his neighborhood and laid a plan for capturing them and executing them.

This death list in some way got into the hands of Montgomery, who made a swift plan to strike before Hamilton did. And his plan would have succeeded had it not been for earlier events.

Late in March, two free-soilers named Denton and Hedrick

were killed down near Fort Scott. Free-soil gangs moved to hunt
out the killers, destroying as they went, and Governor Denver
sent federal troops down to restore order. The dragoons, under
Captain Weaver, attempted to arrest some free-soil guerrillas
they met up with in the streets of Fort Scott. This move had
been anticipated. The dragoons were fired upon from concealed
positions and had to take cover.

At least that is the story as it was edited for Eastern consumption. The admirers of James Montgomery — William
Tomlison, his biographer, and James Redpath — make this
'first time in American history that Federal troops were resisted by citizens' sound much worse.

Montgomery, Tomlison said, 'saw the necessity of striking
a blow that would destroy the charm of the invincibility which
was supposed to reside in gilt buttons with an eagle stamped on
them; and accordingly used to his utmost endeavor to come in
collision with the dragoons.' But the federals were wary, they
'cared not to come in conflict with an enemy of whose prowess
they had heard so much.' Then in April, accident gave Montgomery 'the opportunity he had so long desired.'

He was looking for some stolen horses 'under the very guns
of the Fort' when proslave scouts told the dragoons of his whereabouts. Captain Anderson and some thirty men set out after
Montgomery.

The guerrillas were headed for a timber belt on a tributary
of the Marmaton and as they neared it, the chieftain 'held saddle
council with his little band of followers.' In the ravine, they
quickly dismounted and formed a line, a line of eight.

'On thundered the dragoons, their sabres drawn,' wrote
Tomlison. Montgomery yelled an order to halt. The dragoons
came riding on. 'Halt!' cried Montgomery. The dragoons were
close now and one of Montgomery's men, 'a brave but somewhat
profane young man, in the excitement of the moment, exclaimed,
"Halt! G** d*** you, Halt!"'

As the dragoons bore down, 'the little handful of heroes
passed a volley of balls from their Sharp's rifles into the ad-
vancing troops,' then opened fire with their revolvers.

'The gallant dragoons wheeled and fled,' leaving their dead and wounded. 'Anderson lay under his horse, which had fallen upon him and was apparently lifeless. The blood oozed from the wounded men lying in all positions, upon the velvety sward. The rifles, revolvers, etc., looked very tempting to some of the boys and they begged permission to step out and pick them up, but their leader would not allow it. It was Uncle Sam's property, he said, and they were Uncle Sam's boys themselves, and it was not right to steal from the old gentleman, but when the old gentleman got so out of place as he did that afternoon, it was perfectly right to *learn* him his place.'

Friends of Montgomery deemed 'it policy to ignore his connection with the skirmish of Yellow Paint,' Tomlison reported, commenting, however, that it did free-soilers a world of good to have it 'satisfactorily demonstrated that a Sharp's rifle ball, carefully directed, would have the same effect upon a dragoon as on a common man.'

When the two dead and four wounded federal soldiers were brought to Fort Scott, Captain Weaver set out to patrol the countryside, looking for Montgomery. He found him on the first of May, just as he was laying siege to the log house of Charles Hamilton. When the dragoons rode up, the siege ended abruptly and Montgomery, skilled in evasion, made off.

He rode off to further depredations during that merry month of May. He plundered the store of James Wells at Willow Springs, stole a horse from a Mr. McKinney, and set fire to his house. 'The policy seems to be to rob, pillage, and drive out every proslavery man in Kansas, and Montgomery and his banditti are the instrumentalities employed for that purpose,' commented the New England Emigrant Aid Society's *Herald of Freedom* on 22 May 1858.

New intelligences had been sent to Denver, and he deputized Samuel Walker as a U.S. Marshal and sent him down to arrest Montgomery and his gang.

Meanwhile, Hamilton seemed to have given up his deadly scheme. Montgomery's attack on the Southerner's stout house had apparently had a chastening effect. Hamilton's conduct became so mild and reassuring that precautions were relaxed.

He did have a slight brush with blacksmith Eli Snyder, however. Hamilton was riding to Chouteau's Trading Post one day, and he met Snyder walking along the road with a shotgun under his arm.

'Where are you going?' Hamilton asked. 'You are going to Trading Post.'

'If you know better than I do,' said Snyder, 'why do you ask?'

'If you don't look out,' said the Georgian, 'I'll blow you through.'

Snyder hoisted his shotgun to his shoulder. 'If you don't leave, I'll tumble you from your horse,' he said.

Hamilton left, but he came back. About a week later, he appeared at Snyder's smithy. He sent in one of his well-armed companions to bring Snyder out.

'A man wants to see you,' the henchman told the smith.

Snyder was pounding out a horseshoe and he gave another blow, then tongs in hand, followed the henchman out-of-doors. 'Good morning, Mr. Hamilton,' he said.

'I've got you,' Hamilton said.

'Yes? What do you want?' asked Snyder. And as Hamilton and his men drew their pistols, Snyder struck the nearest horse such a resounding whack on the rump that all the horses shied and threw the pistols out of aim. The shots went wild.

Snyder dashed into his smithy to get his shotgun.

Hamilton and his men were ready for him when he came out. Their pistols cracked and his shot went wild. As the wounded smith made a dash for his cabin, his young son leveled a double-barreled shotgun from the window. 'Burn the devils,' cried his father, as the first barrel spat buckshot. 'Cut away at them with the other barrel!' And the peppering shot did the trick. Hamilton and his men rode off.

But getting Snyder was not the only thing planned for that nineteenth day of the mad month of May. Other roundup parties were at work and they showed up at an appointed meeting place with a good number of men, from whom Hamilton selected nine.

The nine chosen to serve as an example for the rest were taken to a gulch on the Marais des Cygnes, as the upper Osage had been named by the French because it was a breeding ground for swans.

The free-soilers were lined up against the dirt embankment.

A firing squad fell into line.

'Gentlemen,' said one of the free-soilers, 'if you are going to shoot, take good aim.'

'Ready,' said Hamilton.

One of his men wheeled his horse.

'Brockett, goddamn you, wheel into line!' cried Hamilton.

'I'll be damned if I'll have anything to do with any such goddamned piece of business as this,' said Ruffian Brockett.

Hamilton shrugged, pulled out his own revolver, took aim and fired. A volley of shots followed and all of the lined-up men fell to the ground. William Stillwell, Patrick Ross, William Colpetzer, Michael Robinson, and John F. Campbell were dead. The Hairgrove brothers, William and Asa, Charles Reed, and Asa Hall were only wounded but they pretended to be dead when their assailants gave their pockets a hasty frisking, before riding off.

This cold-blooded slaughter, which took place nearly two years to the day after Old Brown's bloody trek down the Pottawatomie, became known as the Marais des Cygnes massacre. John Greenleaf Whittier memorialized it as that in the September issue of the *Atlantic Monthly*, in a nine-stanza poem that began, 'A blush as of roses, where roses never grew! Great drops on the bunch grass, but not of the dew!'

Established citizens, on both sides of the border, looked upon the massacre as an uncivilized and frightful outrage. And James Montgomery took advantage of this anger. He knew that Sam Walker was in those parts with orders to arrest him, so he quickly became a leader of the outraged people, attending as many squatter protest meetings as he could.

It was at such a meeting at Raysville, some dozen miles north of Fort Scott, that Deputy Marshal Walker caught up with his man. But this is what happened:

Walker saw the gathering at the edge of town and naturally looked into it. He and his small posse dismounted, tied their horses to a hitching rail, and joined the crowd.

An acquaintance of Walker's spotted him immediately and came over. 'What are you after?' he whispered.

'I've come to take Montgomery,' Walker said.

'You can't do that! That thing's out of the question.'

Marshal Walker said nothing. He listened to the speaker on the stump call for the extinction of Fort Scott, 'infamous nest of border ruffianism.' And after a while Walker turned to his acquaintance, 'I don't know Montgomery and I don't wish to have him pointed out,' he said. 'If he is, I shall have to make an effort to take him.' The man gave Walker a relieved grin and they both sat down.

Sam Walker heard himself taken over the coals, by inference if not by name. There was considerable talk about the Lecompton government and how it sent down officers to arrest free-state men, yet ignored the sink of iniquity that was Fort Scott. There, even now, hid some of the men who had been in Hamilton's firing squad on the Marais des Cygnes, but did any officer of the law dare go in and arrest them?

Sam Walker got to his feet. 'I'm an officer of the law,' he said. 'Provide me with the proper warrants for the arrest of these men and I will serve them.'

Word spread that this was the famed Sam Walker himself, and a cheer went up. The outraged people had an officer of the law on its side at last. Warrants now became the only problem. When nobody with the authority to issue the proper warrants could be found, Sam Walker said, 'Give me a common justice's writ and I'll go, even though as a federal officer I have no business to serve it.'

Next day, Sam Walker rode into Fort Scott. He divided his men and had them surround the home of proslavery Sheriff

Hill, the McKay Hotel, and the home of General George Clarke, veteran troublemaker.

Everywhere, proslave residents and visitors, forewarned by scouts, were very much in evidence. The streets swarmed with armed men and most of them followed Sam Walker to the home of Clarke. There were more of them than there were of Walker's men when that brave fellow went up to knock on Clarke's door.

There was no answer.

The marshal took out his pistol and knocked with its butt.

There was no answer.

The marshal was about to knock again, and harder, when Clarke stuck his head out of an upstairs window. 'I promise to surrender,' he said. A moment later he came out onto his piazza, with his wife on one arm and a daughter on the other. He demanded to see the marshal's papers.

Walker had no intention of showing them, for, as Spring put it, they were 'of no more account than a handful of pages plucked from the life of Jack the Giant Killer.' Sam Walker drew his pistol. 'I'll give you two minutes to surrender!' he thundered.

There was a deadly silence. It was so quiet that you could hear the clicks as proslave thumbs pulled back gun hammers.

'I saw nothing except the ruffian before me,' Walker said. 'I was told that proslave rifles were pointed at me while my escort aimed at Clarke. It was a mighty solemn state of affairs. Two minutes, I think, must have almost expired when Clarke, white as a sheet, handed over his carbine.'

Clarke was one of several prisoners rounded up and when they got out of town, Walker also arrested Montgomery, who was a member of his own posse.

All of these men managed to escape, however — just how was never made public. But Sam Walker had not had time to get back to Lecompton when Montgomery swooped down upon Fort Scott in the dead of the night, secured the sentinels, and set fire to the town. As the townspeople came out of their houses, they were greeted by a fusillade of shots from a near-by ravine. The citizens quickly sought cover and returned fire. There was a spattering answer, which the Fort Scotters returned, and then the free-soilers rode off.

But by the middle of June things were calm enough for Governor Denver to make a peace tour of the southeast. He told settlers that both sides were deserving of censure, so both would be treated without regard to former differences. In the interest of future peace, he proposed the election of new county officers in those parts, the patrolling of the border by federal troops, a delay in the execution of old writs until they were re-examined by a competent tribunal, and the dispersion of all guerrilla bands.

It was a popular speech. Delegates from Kansas Territory crossed the border to meet at West Point with some 200 men of Missouri. Both gave pledge in writing against invasion of either side by the other and the Missourians promised to help bring Captain Hamilton and his mates in massacre to justice.

That might have been the end of the struggle if John Brown had not received a setback in the East. His first plot against Harpers Ferry was revealed by an unfaithful lieutenant and, to throw off suspicion, he paid another visit to Kansas Territory. He arrived about a month after Governor Denver's peace tour. Before he left, he cut his mark again.

32

Five Governors Down and One To Go

THE LASSO OF CIVILIZATION was being whirled with an eye toward Kansas Territory, but she was to do a lot of snorting both
before it caught her, and afterward.

Men were at work stringing telegraph wires to Leavenworth from Lexington, Missouri. Lieutenant Colonel J. E.
Johnston, of the First Cavalry, reported to Secretary of Interior Floyd that southern Kansas seemed to offer a practicable
route for construction of a railroad to the Rio Grande. There
was a lot of railroad talk in the air. It was to be some time before
the first rails were laid on Kansas soil, but the idea of taming
this wild cayuse with steel bands was getting into full swing.

The biggest towns in the Territory were incorporating
into cities — not only the familiar places but the less spectacular
Geary, Elwood, Olathe, White Cloud. There were 175 corporate
town companies in the Territory, and twenty newspapers.

You could hardly say that any place with the stretch of
Kansas Territory, spreading 700 miles from east to west and
200 miles from north to south, was getting filled up, but it was
getting used to the sight and smell of man. In fact, the root of
all evil had just been discovered on the western rim and a few
men began to move west in the summer of 1858.

A decade before, Cherokee Indians, far from home, had
picked up quartz studded with gold on the banks of the Cache-
le-Poudre, a western tributary of the South Platte. The word

got back to their relatives in Georgia, but it was not until early in 1858 that Russell Green and a party of gold-seekers reached the Rockies. They found a little gold on Cherry Creek. But that summer a Delaware Indian, Fall Leaf, appeared in Lawrence, K.T., with some scale gold which he said he had found while hunting on the headwaters of the Arkansas.

Gold had been discovered in west Kansas Territory!

The news hit the headlines and, uncharacteristically, exerted a peaceful influence. Two days after the Marais des Cygnes massacre, which earlier would have brought free-soilers out in an avenging body, a party of twenty men left Lawrence for 'the gold region in the vicinity of the Rocky Mountains in Kansas.'

The drift westward had begun. And one of Governor Denver's last official acts was to authorize the organization of Arapahoe County, K.T. The county covered the Pike's Peak region and though more than 300 miles of treeless, white-manless plains lay between it and the nearest organized county to the east, it had a much larger population than that county in no time at all.

Civilization had Kansas Territory flanked and was about to move in on her. It would find Kansas Territory a lot of horse for one civilization to handle.

II

'A HOUSE DIVIDED against itself cannot stand,' lawyer Abraham Lincoln of Springfield quoted to a convention of Illinois Republicans in his hometown on 17 June 1858. The American government could 'not permanently endure half slave and half free,' he said. 'We are now far into the fifth year since a policy was inaugurated with the avowed object and confident promise of putting an end to slavery agitation. Under the operation of that policy, that agitation not only has not ceased, but has constantly augmented.'

He was speaking of Kansas Territory, about a month after the Marais des Cygnes massacre and just at the time that John

Brown was making his way down from the abolitionist port of
debarkation, Tabor, Iowa, to pay his last and only historically
important visit to these parts.

Old Brown had a plan now for freeing the black man. It
was to free, by violence, enough slaves that they themselves
could fight to free the others. And to give them a place of refuge,
he planned to set up a republic in Canada. He had the place
picked and the officials chosen. And he was building an army
when his drillmaster, Hugh Forbes, turned traitor. Forbes told
a senator about Brown's plan.

Old Brown, faced with the accusation, denied it. He said
he was simply organizing a company of settlers to take to Kansas. And since a return to Kansas Territory was forced upon
him, he made it fit into his major plan. He needed not only to
throw off suspicion but to test his plan. Kansas Territory was
the place for that, but he would have to move carefully.

He played the part of the patriarch. He called upon the
Free State leaders with whom he had always been at odds. 'You
have succeeded in what you undertook,' he told Charles Robinson. 'You aimed to make Kansas a free state and your plans were
skillfully laid for that purpose. But I had another object in
view. I meant to strike a blow at slavery. Nothing but war can
extinguish slavery and the sooner war is inaugurated, the better.' He talked as if his part were done, gave no hint of his plans.
Privately he dubbed Robinson 'a weather-cock character, a perfect old woman.'

He played the part of the father, working in the fields with
his sons. He gave them the family news. It happened to be good,
for Old Brown, practiced at raising money for arms, had given
a thought to his family. 'For a thousand dollars cash, I am
offered an improved piece of land which might enable my family,
consisting of my wife and five minor children (the youngest not
yet three years old) to procure a subsistence should I never return to them; my wife being a good economist and a good old-
fashioned business woman,' Brown wrote Amos Lawrence of
Boston, and he added this hooker: 'She has gone through the
past winter in an open cold house, unfinished outside and not

plastered.' He got the thousand dollars and Mrs. Brown and the children now lived in a warm house at Mount Elba, New York.

John Brown was in the Territory but behaving himself. Kagi, Secretary of War of his Canadian Republic, Richard Realf, private crusader of Lady Byron and John Brown's Secretary of State, and some of his other men were with him. They worked on their plan and their military training, but they did no jayhawking.

Montgomery, whom Old Brown called 'the only soldier I have met among prominent Kansas men,' was behaving, too. Governor Denver could write Secretary of War Cass in September, 1858, to commend Captain Weaver on the fine job he and his border patrol were doing in maintaining peace in southern K.T.

September saw the exodus of the last of the ardent pro-slavery leaders. The doughty ex-sheriff, Sam Jones, was appointed Collector of the District of Paso del Norte and left for Texas that month. Raider-general George Clarke was made a purser in the Navy, work he certainly could not pursue in K.T., and the once hated Colonel Henry Titus left for Sonora. Any trouble to be made would have to be made by free-soilers.

Denver sent his resignation to the President on 10 October 1858, but said he would stay on the job until his successor arrived. And a few weeks later he notified Washington that he intended to release Captain Weaver's company from border patrol on 6 November. No orders were received to the contrary and the dragoons returned to Fort Leavenworth.

It just happened that right after the federal patrol was withdrawn, James Montgomery was notified that he had been indicted for destroying a ballot box at Mound City back in January. His reaction to the news was to go on a jayhawking spree.

Weary of it all, Denver left the Territory in the hands of Secretary of State Hugh B. Walsh, who immediately wrote to Washington. 'The notorious James Montgomery, encouraged by the support of the leading Republican press in the territory, has recommenced his system of marauding and plundering in the county of Linn,' he said.

House after house was robbed and, finally, proslavery men retaliated. When Poyner and Lemon came to Fort Scott to report that they had been robbed, a party of horsemen set out. The free-soiler they wanted to get was Benjamin Rice, who had been indicted for the murder of a Southerner named Travis, by a free-soil jury, but had never been jailed. They found Rice, but these southeastern Southerners never had the old border zip. They did not string up Rice — they just jailed him in Fort Scott.

The old patriarch, John Brown, was itching to get back into action. When he heard that Montgomery planned to ride into Fort Scott to rescue Rice, he hastened down to see that the thing was done right. Montgomery let him go along, but on the understanding that he was to stay in the background. 'There wouldn't have been one stone left on another if I had let him have command,' Montgomery said. And it was quite a gentle raid. The murderer Rice was rescued from jail with virtually no resistance. Only J. H. Little was rash enough to fire upon the raiders. His shot was returned, right through the heart, and, as a further punishment, his store was plundered of some $7000 worth of goods.

This taste of blood made Old Brown eager to get on with his work.

Three days after Samuel Medary arrived in Lecompton to take up his duties as the sixth territorial governor, Old Brown gave him the violent welcome traditional to K.T. It was two days before Christmas — the season of peace on earth and toward all men good will — when John Brown marched his men down the Little Osage into Missouri. At the border he divided his company into two squads that they might move quickly down both banks of the stream, taking and destroying as they went. They came back with eleven slaves belonging to three families and all other removable property, from horses to clothing, of those families and a dozen more.

This was a slave-stealing rehearsal, not a murder march. It brought sudden death to only one man, David Cruise, 'a plain and unoffending farmer,' according to free-soiler George Crawford of Fort Scott, who went to John Brown after his raid to protest it.

'We're settlers and you're not,' Crawford told Brown. 'You can strike a blow and leave. The retaliatory blow will fall on us.'

John Brown was very much hurt by this reproach, but even more by a similar reproach from his close friend, Augustus Wattles. 'It's no pleasure to me, an old man, to be living in the saddle, away from home and family, exposing my life,' he said. 'If free-state men feel they no longer need me, I will be glad to go.'

So Old Brown went. He went as far as Sugar Creek, to the north of Fort Scott and about twelve miles from the border. There he set up camp. He sent out word that he would resist any officers sent to take him, and put his men to work building fortifications — to keep the law out and his frightened captives in.

33

The Time Is at Hand

NEW YEAR'S DAY 1859, a Thursday, was publication day for the *Herald of Freedom*, and it again gave free-soilers of southeast K.T. a verbal thrashing.

It quoted a Mound City resident who said, 'Little did I think in '56 that professedly Free State men would be guilty of the same crimes for which we denounced the proslavery men of that year' and a Moneka clergyman who declared it 'a strange sight to see peace men, those who in the States were members of peace societies, laboring to inaugurate civil war, with the expressed object of working a revolution throughout the nation, ultimating in the dissolution of the Union.'

John Brown never had belonged to a peace society. His God was a wrathful God who would accept no token of faith that had not been dipped in blood. The preacher must have meant that one-time preacher, James Montgomery. He had belonged to peace societies. And he was willing to have peace now — on his own terms. He answered a plea from Governor Medary with an offer to suspend his depredations if the governor would promise, 'in black and white,' that no Montgomery man would be arrested for any past action and that the proslavery men they had driven out of the Territory would be kept out.

Medary gave this message to the Legislature when it convened early in the new year. It quickly passed an amnesty bill forgiving past offenses. But no legislature could guarantee that proslavery men who had been driven out of Kansas would stay out, so Montgomery had to continue to discourage Southern immigration. He did it by making forays into Missouri.

And Captain Eli Snyder, the brave smith of Trading Post, attacked a cabin used as Ruffian headquarters in Missouri. The Missourians returned fire and refused to surrender, so the cabin was fired and four men perished in its flames.

Governor Stewart of Missouri sent appeals to Governor Medary and to the President of the United States. And an aroused Missouri Legislature framed an act to raise a militia in her southwestern counties to disperse the outlaws from southeast K.T. The committee to which the bill was referred, however, came out with a singularly dispassionate report against it. 'A militia formed of the kindred and neighbors of the murdered and robbed would be hard to restrain from acts of summary punishment, should any of these desperadoes fall into its hands,' the committee held. 'And it would likewise be difficult to teach such troops the line of our jurisdiction, and in the excitement of inflicting a merited punishment on some offender, it would be hard for them to comprehend the deplorable evils of an armed invasion of a sister territory by the militia of a State.'

Governor Medary tried to act with a matching justness. He, too, telegraphed the President. He reported Kansas at fault in the border troubles and said he had asked the commandants of both Leavenworth and Riley to send military assistance. And he appealed to the Territorial Legislature to take action against Montgomery and Brown. 'Good citizens who formerly sustained these men,' he said, 'beg to have something done to stop "Jayhawking," as they term it, or, they say, their counties will be depopulated.'

But K.T.'s Legislature was busy playing politics. The feuds within feuds made dealing out patronage a ticklish matter, with no assurance that things would turn out as intended. Take the office of state printer, for example. Two-thirds of the legislators appointed T. Dwight Thatcher of the *Lawrence Republican* to that job, but he never got a lick at the gravy. By organic law, the secretary of state controlled printing and he authorized

Joel Goodwin to place jobs. Goodwin gave them all to the 'State Printer's' arch rival, G. W. Brown of the *Herald of Freedom*.

The solons were busy, too, passing divorce laws. They passed so many making divorce and remarriage easy that 'one wag in the House,' Legislator Albert Richardson reported, 'introduced a bill declaring marriage abolished in Kansas and free love established in its place.'

The Legislature finally did take time to vote to sustain Governor Medary in 'any legal measures to restore peace.' But it offered no help. The governor was strictly on his own in matters concerning war and peace.

And the governor thought, for one whole day, that he could handle the situation. He counted on federal aid. One January day, Washington authorized him 'to offer a reward of $250 each for the apprehension of Capts. Montgomery and Brown.' But the very next day Medary learned that Washington had ordered federal dragoons, so recently re-assigned to border patrol, back to Fort Leavenworth.

Montgomery celebrated this removal with such a jayhawking spree that more than a hundred Fort Scott residents signed a petition asking the governor to establish martial law. The Missouri Legislature had dropped its fight-back bill, but it now offered $3000 for the arrest of John Brown.

The sizableness of the sum may have been the thing that made Old Brown prepare to leave the Territory. The inaction imposed by being on the defensive may have made him restless. Or he may have planned all along to stay in Kansas Territory only until about the end of January. He had demonstrated that he could capture slaves in order to set them free, and he may have felt ready to get on with his major work.

Whatever the cause of Brown's sudden departure from his stronghold on Sugar Creek, it caught Governor Medary by surprise. He sent word to Colonel Edwin Sumner, again commandant at Leavenworth, that Brown was in Calhoun County on his way to Nebraska and asked him to furnish the bearer, Marshal P. T. Colby, with enough military force 'to secure' the captain.

Sumner assigned troops and the chase began. The Brown party, which included the eleven slaves, came close to being overtaken at Holton, K.T., but Old Brown, who knew the country well, took advantage of the deep-creased face of the land and outrode his pursuers. He won what came to be called 'The Battle of the Spurs,' and from Nebraska on it was easy going. He conducted the underground to Canada himself and the whole operation, from the taking of the slaves to setting them free, was so much in pattern with his dream that his plan for sparking a revolt among all slaves took new impetus. His attempt to set up a freeing center at Harpers Ferry was to come that fall.

Meanwhile, back in Kansas, things happened just as George Crawford of Fort Scott had told John Brown they would. Free-soil residents were held accountable for visitor Brown's excesses, and George Crawford was one of the men who paid.

A party of proslavery men — led by Brockett, the Ruffian who had refused to fire at Captain Hamilton's shooting party on the Marais des Cygnes — called upon Crawford in his Fort Scott store. They told him to leave town.

Crawford had a good business, and he was reluctant to give it up. He told them that he had not approved of John Brown's tactics and had said so to his face. 'Should I have to pay for his mistakes, gentlemen?' Crawford asked.

'You're a free-state man, aren't you?'

Crawford nodded.

'Well,' said Brockett, 'when a snake bites me, I don't go looking for that particular snake; I kill the first snake I come to.'

Mr. Crawford left town.

By and large, though, Kansas Territory's proslave settlers were in a poor position for retaliation; they were so outnumbered. When the Legislature granted amnesty to Montgomery and his men, it, in effect, licensed him to meet his own second demand, of keeping proslave settlers out of the Territory. The amnesty act had no tense. Future political offenses were apparently forgiven along with past ones. Montgomery and his lieutenant, Charles Jennison, were free to continue to harass proslavery settlers, new and old.

The Southerners, now, had no leaders. The strategists had given up the hope of making Kansas a slave state. They were centering their strategy on Washington. The Dred Scott decision had given slavery freedom of the public domain, so the thing to do was to keep Kansas in the public domain, keep it from becoming a state.

In Kansas Territory, the now free-soil Legislature, just before adjournment on 11 February 1859, passed an act abolishing slavery. Governor Medary gave it the traditional pocket veto, since it was not within this body's power to abolish slavery. But the solons also venerated tradition. They ignored the governor's veto and celebrated by tossing the slavery enactments of the Bogus Legislature into a midnight bonfire.

Since the Taney decision, even free Negroes had not been safe in Kansas Territory. One of the acts of the Legislature was to vote $1000 to defend Dr. John Doy and his son Charles, who had been captured while driving thirteen free Negroes to safety in Iowa.

An attempt had been made to take two freedmen, Claude Fisher and William Riley, to Missouri to be sold back into slavery. That had frightened other free Negroes in the vicinity of Lawrence, so the Doys had offered to drive them to safety. The free papers the Negroes carried meant nothing to the Ruffians who challenged the party. The Negroes and the Doys were taken across the Missouri to Weston and put behind bars in the Platte County jail.

The K.T. Legislature authorized Governor Medary to appoint counsel for the defense of Doctor Doy. And the counsel appointed was the man who in five years of generally malignant territorial history had been the man most maligned — ex-Governor Wilson Shannon, who had recently returned to hang up his shingle in Lawrence.

There were new cries of federal partiality to the proslave cause when Governor Medary's choice of counsel was announced. Wilson Shannon had been called 'the sodden tool of the slave power' by such commentators as Mrs. Charles Robinson and reporter William Phillips. Of the recorders of the day, only George Brewerton had seen Wilson Shannon as a man sincerely concerned with finding a middle ground on which the opposing extremes might come to a peaceable agreement. The Doy trial, on 4 March 1859, two months after the arrest, was a test of this Wilson Shannon.

The case was tried in St. Joseph, Missouri, before a court of Southerners. The charge, of course, was Negro stealing. 'If we allow our negroes to be stolen with impunity,' said Prosecuting Attorney Colonel John Doniphan, 'our fair-skinned daughters will be reduced to performing the contemptible drudgery in the kitchen.' It was a powerful argument, but Wilson Shannon was able to break it down enough to hang the jury.

John Doy went free, though in keeping with the spirit of the time and place, not for long. Two months after the charge of Negro stealing had been dropped, he was re-arrested and, this time, convicted. He was sentenced to five years, but, also in keeping with the spirit of the time and place, he was rescued from jail and sent by underground to Iowa.

II

By MIDSUMMER, 1859, things were very quiet in Kansas Territory. James Montgomery had things arranged pretty much to his liking. He could conduct his operations against proslavery men with so little opposition that it was generally said that the struggle for Kansas was over.

When John Brown burst into national prominence that fall with his abortive attempt to free the slaves at Harpers Ferry, people were to say that peace had come to Kansas because John Brown had left there. This was not true. He had played no more real part in Kansas history with his Pottawatomie Creek slashings than Captain Hamilton had with his Marais des Cygnes mowdown. Among the men of violence, Captain Montgomery was the man who year after year kept proslavery votes to a minimum, and he was to continue his good work long after John Brown's body began to molder in its grave. As late as the fall of 1860, his man Jennison saw fit to kill off three proslavery men who still stubbornly stayed in the Territory — Jim Moulton and well-to-do Samuel Scott, for reasons unrecorded, and Russell Hind, who at least was given squatter trial before he was hung. Montgomery explained this hanging to District Judge Hanway. 'Russ Hinds, hung on the 12th day of November, 1860, for man stealing,' he wrote. 'He was a drunken border ruffian, worth a great deal to hang but good for nothing else. He had caught a fugitive slave, and carried him back to Missouri for sake of a reward. He was condemned by a jury of twelve men, the law being found in the 16th verse of Exodus xxi (And he that stealeth a man, and selleth him, or if he be found in his hand, he shall surely be put to death).'

It was open season on man, then, a year after John Brown's death, just as it had been and was to be all through the territorial period of Kansas. In fact, private killings were not to become outlawed there until the wholesale slaughter of war was in order — Carl Horne, sentenced to hang in Leavenworth on 7 December 1861, was the first Kansan to be legally punished for murder.

John Brown played virtually no part in Kansas history, but no one can deny that he cut quite a figure on the larger stage of American history. There have been a number of planned martyrdoms throughout recorded time, but certainly none more carefully worked out or more effectively executed than John Brown's.

So much has been written about him from hindsight, that it is difficult to realize he was not a national figure before or after the Pottawatomie Creek massacre. He was not well known when he returned to Kansas Territory in 1858. The first time his name gained any degree of prominence was when he made his raid into Missouri to capture slaves in order to free them.

That raid put the name of John Brown on the marquee, ready for lights. When Old Brown took leave of his friend

Wattles, he said he was going to leave Kansas, probably never to return. 'I consider it my duty to draw the scene of the excitement to some other part of the country,' he said.

God's Handyman, long convinced that he had been chosen to free the slave, felt that the time was at hand. The spotlight was on him and all he needed now, to achieve martyrdom, was death, under the right circumstances. He may have bungled the Harpers Ferry raid more than he had intended. It would not bear study — from the nonsense of selecting the best-treated slaves thereabouts to arm for freedom through the helter-skelter killings to the delaying action he had to play to get captured.

Overpowering the watchman at the Harpers Ferry arsenal was simple, but the way the slaves of George Washington's great-grandnephew, armed with pikes to help fight for freedom, hovered around their master for protection must have been disappointing. Shooting into the dark at every human sound — what did John Brown think when he learned that his first fatality was a free Negro, Sheppard Heyward, baggagemaster who had gone out to look for bridge-watchman Pat Higgins when he heard the shot that creased Pat's skull. Sheppard Heyward, who took a long time to die, was a freeman so respected as a townsman that the mayor, Fontaine Beckham, lost his own life because he went to look for this Negro. Did John Brown mourn these, or his own freedman raider, Dangerfield Newby, or the townsman Boerley, or the faithful Kagi, or Dauphin and William Thompson, Leeman, Taylor, or Washington's Negro Jim, all killed — or even his own sons, Watson and Oliver, both mortally wounded?

If he did, he did not show it, then or ever.

There were three avenues left open for escape, even after the Virginia militia got itself organized. The old raider, John Brown, knew them all and probably could have escaped without any avenue. He did not want to escape. That was plain from the way he ignored the repeated warnings of the devoted Kagi. The time for martyrdom was at hand. And everything worked out as if he had engineered it. He was captured and jailed, tried, convicted, and sentenced to hang by the neck until dead — and

at just the right tempo, fast enough to keep public interest
mounting, yet slow enough to give him time to say those noble
things expected of martyrs.

It was his role and he stuck to it. When a whisper came of
a plan to rescue him from his captors, he publicly asked that any
and all such plans be abandoned. 'I am worth now infinitely more
to die than to live,' he said. The pin-prick bravado of Harpers
Ferry was beginning to fester just as he had planned. Southern
Senators shouted his name so that it echoed throughout the land
and brought countless Northern minds to his defense. The very
incomprehensibility of the Harpers Ferry episode had caught
the public fancy. The John Brown legend was building, even
before he died.

It had a couple of close squeaks at the time. Some enter-
prising journalist had looked at the long-ignored minority report of the Committee to Investigate Kansas Territorial Affairs
and learned of John Brown's guilt in the Pottawatomie Creek
massacre. The item was given little space but it came to the
attention of Judge Russell of Boston, who was so upset by it that
he traveled to Charleston to get the old man's denial. He got it.
John Brown denied his guilt. 'But,' he said, 'I think here in jail
as I believed in Kansas, that the act was just and necessary.'

Old Brown had said to blacksmith Eli Snyder at Trading
Post that 'the Dutch Henry business was at the right time.' He
often referred to the massacre with approbation, but he knew
better than to admit responsibility for it. One wonders why he
did not destroy one of the last letters he received before he swung.
Perhaps it was a final impudence, an expression of the contempt
for man that people steeped in causes so often have. Perhaps he
knew even then that the legend of John Brown had grown beyond the fact of John Brown, so that people might read the letter from Mahala Doyle, when published, without having it make
the slightest impression on the armor of their opinion.

John Brown wrote his own epitaph. This was Mahala
Doyle's:

'Sir: Although vengeance is not mine, I confess that I do
feel gratified that you were stopped in your fiendish career at

Harpers Ferry, with the loss of your two sons. You can now appreciate my distress in Kansas when you then and there entered my house at midnight and arrested my husband and two boys and took them out into the yard and in cold blood shot them dead in my hearing. You can't say you did it to free our slaves; we had none and never expected to own one . . .'

III

THE YEAR 1859 brought the first train to the western border of the United States, on rails newly laid across northern Missouri, from Hannibal to St. Joseph. And the Pacific coast was brought closer in time by the initiation of the Pony Express from St. Joe to San Francisco that April.

Railroad talk in Kansas Territory grew louder. The Legislature granted a charter to the Atchison and Pike's Peak Railroad Company. But all travel was to continue to be by stage and occasional steamboat for some years to come.

Most recorders of day-by-day living had folded their diaries and gone back east by this time. The weather was no longer a matter of record, but squatters must have had a wet spring that year. Four steamboats got as far up the Kaw, in dry years dammed by sandbars, as Lawrence in May, and one, the *Gus Linn*, actually paddled nearly 150 miles farther inland, past dying Lecompton and growing Topeka, past old St. Mary's Mission and the settlements of Wamego, St. Georges, Manhattan, Ogden, past Fort Riley to Junction City and up the Smoky branch for thirty miles. It must have been a wet spring.

There were telegraph wires right in Kansas Territory. They followed the Missouri from Wyandotte to Leavenworth and would carry a message to Washington in less time than it took to ride into town. With this innovation, the *Leavenworth Herald* went daily.

All these things were a source of wonder and pride to the men and women who by now were considered old-timers. But the same month that saw four steamboats unload at Lawrence, brought a famous visitor to the Territory who seemed to find the going rough. Horace Greeley had extolled the promise of Kansas for five solid years. Now he paid his first visit to it. He liked 'natural Kansas' much better than he had expected, he wrote. The timber was 'more generally diffused' than he had expected. 'The country is more rolling than I had supposed. I consider Kansas well watered — no prairie State better. Springs, streams, creeks, rivers are quite universal.' But he could not say much for domesticated Kansas. He was amazed at the rapid drop-off in civilization as he moved westward. 'Room bells and baths made their last appearance at Leavenworth,' he said. Barbers disappeared at Topeka, and bootblacks at Junction City. One gathers that the great 'Go West, Young Man' editor was glad to get back East.

The country, however, was full of young men used to shaving themselves and going without shoeshines, and the Territory kept growing. It had grown to such an extent by 1859 that a whole mess of new treaties had to be made with the Indians. The Great White Father was busy that summer signing scraps of paper. The Swan Creek and Black River bands of Chippewas agreed to share their thirteen sections of land in Franklin County with Munsee, or Christian, Indians. And the Sacs, Foxes, and Kanzas all agreed to fancy language that added up to less land.

The Territory, despite Greeley's dim view of it, was, in squatter eyes, shaping into something that looked like a potential state. The Territorial Legislature, in its midwinter session, had, in keeping with territorial tradition, set up a series of elections to arrange for a constitutional convention and the day after the Fourth of July delegates convened in Wyandotte. By the end of the month the Wyandotte Constitution was framed, after heated debates which threw out proposals to exclude free Negroes from the State of Kansas, to give women the right of suffrage, and to prohibit the sale of intoxicating beverages.

The instrument was adopted by the voters of Kansas Territory in October 1859.

Then 'Hon. Abe Lincoln,' as the *Leavenworth Times* called him, arrived in St. Joseph, Missouri, on December first and was met by his kinsman, Mark W. Delahay of Leavenworth, and D.

W. Wilder. That night at Elwood, K.T., he gave, according to
Wilder, a speech 'substantially the same as he made soon afterward at the Cooper Institute, New York, and one of the ablest
and clearest ever delivered by an American statesman.' The
next day, the day John Brown was executed, Lincoln spoke at
Troy, Doniphan, and Atchison. And December third he spoke
at Stockton's in Leavenworth.

On 14 February 1860, Kansas Territory's Wyandotte
Constitution was introduced in the Senate of the United States.
It was reported out of the Committee on Territories, on 29 March
1860, with a recommendation for admission of Kansas into the
Union.

The South was still stubborn. It had given up making a
slave state of Kansas Territory. Its tactic, then, was to keep
Kansas a territory for as long as possible — forever, if it could
be done. Green of Missouri, leader of the opposition to admission, did not attack the Wyandotte Constitution. He raised the
question of whether or not Kansas Territory was physically fit
to become a state, because she had so little arable land.

Washington Irving was quoted. A quarter of a century
before, Irving had predicted that most of the country now disputed would, by its nature, 'form a lawless interval between the
abodes of civilized man.' Here, he said, 'may spring up new and
mongrel races, the amalgamations of the debris and abrasions
of former races civilized and savage — the descendants of wan-
dering hunters and trappers; of fugitives from the Spanish and
American frontiers; of adventurers and desperadoes of every
class and country, yearly ejected from the bosom of society into
the wilderness.'

Could Americans doom their kith and kin to such a land?
Green raised the question and hammered at it. He insisted that
if Kansas were to be admitted, she must be given 30,000 square
miles from the southeastern portion of Nebraska Territory.
'Without this addition, Kansas must be weak, puerile, sickly, in
debt, and at no time capable of maintaining herself,' he said.

Nature did her best to sustain Green's argument. A great

drought descended on Kansas Territory in 1860. Month after month for more than a year no rain fell. Local sprinkles did no more than torture the thirsty earth. Parched, it cracked open to expose all planted seed to shriveling heat. There was an exodus back East and those who stayed sent appeals for food. The New York Legislature alone appropriated $50,000, and altogether nearly ten million pounds of seed, food, and clothing were sent. 'Kansas will never become free or slave state until all the rest of the world is overpopulated!' cried one of the defeated. 'Nobody who has the strength to walk, or money to pay for conveyance, will stay there long.'

Ammunition for Senator Green. Doubt that Kansas was physically worthy of sisterhood in the great family of states was added to long-held doubts about the moral fitness of her citizens. Many Northern congressmen hesitated to vote for her admission, and Southern congressmen were determined that she should not become a state. 'I will not consent that Texas shall associate with such a State as this would be,' said Lone-Star Senator Wigfall. 'The inhabitants are outlaws and land pirates. The good men were abandoned by the government and driven out. Ruffianism is all that is left, and are we to associate with it?'

Kansas was the general subject for pity or contempt, as the drouth held into the winter of 1860.

The people who stayed in Kansas Territory liked neither the pity nor the contempt. The first railroad iron had been laid on Kansas soil at Elwood early in the dry year of 1860 and its completion to Wathena, four miles away, was a cause of celebration. And crops in good years could not be beat. When Medary resigned as governor on 10 January 1861, Acting-Governor George M. Beebe, in taking the reins, exhorted Kansas Territory to thumb her nose at everyone and become an independent nation.

'If God in his wrath shall tolerate the worst portent of this tempest now so fiercely raging,' he said, 'Kansas ought and I trust will, declining identification with either branch of a contending family, tending to each alike the olive offering of goodneighborship, establish, under a constitution of her own creation, a Government to be separate and independent among nations.'

But Acting-Governor Beebe was not only too wordy, he was too late. The gestation period of a giant is seven years and it had been seven years on 4 December 1860 since the idea of Kansas was conceived.

34

The Giant Is Twins

A PRINCIPLE had been defeated in Kansas Territory. It was the principle upon which the South had based all its hopes of expansion, the principle of squatter sovereignty or self-determination by new states of whether they were to be slave or free.

When the North took over in Kansas Territory in 1858, all Southern hopes of maintaining a balance of power were dashed. The South made no objection that year to the admission of Minnesota as a free state or to the admission of Oregon in 1859. Yet the dawning of the fateful year of 1861 found Kansas still a territory. Why?

The South was at the North's mercy in Congress, and was to forever be. The North had the votes to resolve all North-South issues, yet with slavery the great issue to be decided, the North, with her usual crass righteousness, put a high-tariff plank in Abraham Lincoln's platform. 'This is a contest involving protection and the rights of labor,' said governor-candidate Austin of Pennsylvania, campaigning for Lincoln and himself. 'If you desire to become vast and great, protect the manufacturers of Pennsylvania. All hail Liberty! All hail Freedom! Freedom to the white man!'

Freedom to the white man! That was the attitude throughout much of the North and the South knew it. There was little real concern over the plight of the Negro or of any exploited class, black, red, or white. Yet the North persisted in its holier-than-thou attitude. Its powerful press and pulpit, through seven long years in Kansas Territory, had blazoned Southern excesses and suppressed news of Northern excesses. The North had made Kansas an emotional word, a portentous symbol.

No one can deny that the institution of slavery was an insult to human dignity, a blot on democracy. Southerners knew it as well as Northerners, as their bluster at the outset of the Kansas territorial period well shows — people always yell louder when they appear or feel to be in the wrong than when they appear or feel to be in the right.

Southerners knew in their hearts that slavery was an indefensible institution. They felt in the wrong. Yet they knew, too, that there was as much wrong on the other side. They were being called un-American brutes by men whose ancestors had sold into slavery the descendants of Chief Massasoit, great friend of the Pilgrims, by men whose ancestors had kept slaves as long as they were profitable, by men living on fortunes built by the slave trade, by men whose ports were still outfitting slave runners, by men interested only in subjugating the South financially, by men who for seven long years had tailored news to suit their purposes.

Families well grounded in self-respect can work out their problems peaceably. But all members of this family had degraded themselves either by defending wrong or by feigning right. They had lost their self-respect in Kansas Territory and they hated it, as the scene of their degradation. They feared to birth Kansas as a state because they knew, by then, that she would bring with her a monster twin, a hate-nurtured giant named Civil War.

The Southern states looked upon Abraham Lincoln as midwife-elect to these monster births. South Carolina, Alabama, Florida, and Mississippi protested by withdrawing their legislators from Washington.

The North had a clear legislative advantage, but it was with reluctance that she admitted bitterly contested Kansas Territory to statehood on 29 January 1861. Then, in a frantic attempt at reconciliation, this Northern Congress sent to out-

going President Buchanan the proposed Thirteenth Amendment to the Constitution referred to at the beginning of this
book, the amendment clearly designed to establish slavery in
the United States forever. Ohio ratified this amendment less that
two weeks after it was passed and Lincoln's home state, Illinois,
was to join border Maryland in ratifying it nearly a year after
Kansas' lusty, hideous twin, Civil War, had been born.

Three kith-kill-kin years were to pass before the Thirteenth Amendment as it stands today was passed — the amendment that abolished human slavery from the bounds of our
Union — and they were to tear wide open the unhealed wounds
of 'Bleeding Kansas.'

II

THE USUAL GANG of the not-too-sanctimonious were gathered
in Room 7 of the Eldridge House, favorite carousal place in
strait-laced Lawrence, K.T. It was the evening of 29 January
1861, and about nine o'clock, Daniel Anthony came striding in.
He stamped the snow from his boots and called for attention.
'Gentlemen,' he said. 'The President of the United States today
signed the bill admitting Kansas to the Union.' And he held up
a copy of the *Leavenworth Conservative*, which screamed,
'Extra! Kansas Admitted!'

Men ran into the streets to shout the news. Townspeople
already in bed, got up, dressed, lighted all their lamps and
candles, and joined the gathering throng in the streets. 'Old
Sacramento,' the cannon that had served as threat, booty, and
peace barter in the recent territorial days was loaded and fired.
And when the blustering cold forced a retreat indoors, men and
women went from house to house celebrating.

'Toasts were drunk, songs were sung, speeches were made,'
Judge Simpson was to recall. 'And — well, the truth is, that my
recollection is not good after midnight. You must recollect that
the main question was admission, not prohibition.'

Kansas was a state — an infant giant, though smaller than
expected. She had gained no land from Nebraska Territory and

she had lost much land to the public domain. She had lost her most populous county, Pike's Peak (or Arapahoe), with 34,000 people or more than there were in her three leading eastern counties, Leavenworth, Douglas, and Doniphan. She had lost the Rockies and 22,000 square miles of plains. But Kansans were glad enough to give up the gold mines to be rid of some of that arid stretch of buffalo sod, broken only by sage and soapweed, known as the Great American Desert. They saw no future in this land and gave no thanks to Texas for the nearly 8000 square miles of it that she had ceded from her old Republic to square off K.T.'s southwest corner.

Kansas, however whittled down, was still a giant in size and potential productivity. Conceived in cold calculation, born in a rending hatred, she was to be baptized in blood. It was not a christening. It was a deep-river baptism.

III

The Civil War was fought, and won, in the East by accepted rules, by chessboard maneuvers to gain position through surprise flank movements and well-planned and well-executed frontal attacks, and to hold position through fortification, troop placement, and anticipation of enemy moves.

Many men from Kansas went off to be chessmen in these important plays, far more per capita than from any other Northern state. Every quota sent by the Union Kansas met doubly, for the new state was peopled by men who had come there to fight against slavery.

Many Kansans were assigned to formal fighting, but others were incorporated under local commands and fought the war out in the same roles, now legalized, that they had played in the curtain-raiser. Men who had been raiders were now authorized to wear the uniform of the Union Army. Many of them did not bother, any more than did their brothers across the border bother to don the gray of their Confederacy. Frontier dress lent itself well to guerrilla tactics.

There were formal moves and battles west of the Mississippi

— Wilson's Creek, Fayetteville, Big Blue and Little Blue, Cabin Creek to name a few. Halleck and Hunter commanded the Union forces and Price, Cabell, Marmaduke, and McIntosh were among the Confederate generals. There was some standard warfare, but most Civil War engagements west of the Mississippi were fought along guerrilla lines. It was the kind of warfare in which the civilian population suffered more than the military, and for the most part it is remembered in national annals by the name it made the most notorious — Quantrill.

A study could be made of this man and his madness, and it might turn out to be a simple study of retaliation. There is considerable evidence to support the contention that this bushwhacker's fiendish sack of Lawrence in 1863 added up to no more brutality than had been imposed on Missouri and Arkansas civilians by Jim Lane's unauthorized brigade and by that flying squadron known as the Kansas Redlegs, a brutal band that flaunted its identity by wearing red morocco leggings.

Kansas — so given to elections that one squatter predicted native Kansans would be born equipped with ballot boxes — had set its state government in motion immediately upon its admission in 1861. Dr. Charles Robinson, once jailed as usurper to the office of Governor of Kansas Territory, was inaugurated as Governor of the State of Kansas ten days after she was admitted and the Kansas Legislature, quickly called into session, confirmed Samuel Pomeroy and James H. Lane as United States senators.

Jim Lane tossed off his cowhide vest, donned his black broadcloth, and was soon operating on a large scale in Washington. He turned soldier again when Lincoln was inaugurated and threats were made against the new President's life. The soldiers bivouacked in the East Room of the White House were Kansans under Lane's command. And when war came, Lane camped on Lincoln's doorstep until he got himself made a brigadier general — then he went out to operate on his own.

He sold Abe Lincoln a grandiose scheme for an expedition into the southwest. Or thought he did. The Union commanders west of the Mississippi were never informed of Lane's claimed status and therefore resented what they called his 'jayhawking' of a general's rank. They spiked his expedition, so he set out on his own campaign into neighboring Southern communities.

He plundered on a grand scale. Butler, Parkville, and Osceola were, as Lane put it, 'cleaned out.' Even his chaplain was caught up in the spirit of thievery, according to Leverett Spring, and plundered Confederate altars for his unfinished church back home.

Jennison's Redlegs were operating at the same time. No estimate was made of the total number of citizens killed, but community after community reported losses by the score. And throughout Missouri and northern Arkansas, chimneys marking the sites of destroyed homes were called 'Jennison Monuments.'

Generals Hunter and Halleck wrote numerous protests to General McClellan about the activities of these 'Kansas jayhawkers and robbers' but got no answers. General Hunter finally declared Kansas under martial law because the activities of Lane and Jennison were 'seriously compromising the Union cause in border Missouri.' Governor Robinson took a hand. He appointed Frederick Stanton to Lane's neglected Senate seat. That sent 'The Grim Chieftain' scurrying back to Washington, but Jennison's Redlegs kept up their operations and, when Robinson's term as governor was up, Lane came back.

And the name of Quantrill came to be heard in the land. His lightning raids into Kansas began to be felt — little raids that were to fade into nothingness in the flaring light of his major opus.

As a single incident in the whole bloody history of Kansas and the whole bloody course of the Civil War, none exceeds the second sack of Lawrence for unvarnished terror and brutality.

At sunrise on 21 August 1863, Quantrill and his band of nearly 200 horsemen topped the rise a mile to the east of the sleeping town. A halt was called as some men rebelled against their leader's plan. He bullied them into line. They rode on. They were half a mile from the village, when Quantrill yelled.

'Charge!' And the bushwhackers spurred their horses and swooped down into town, shooting as they went.

Quantrill made headquarters at the Whitney House and sent criers out to announce that they had come after Redlegs and sent patrols out to seek and kill the wanted men. The destruction that followed gives credence to the charge that the guerrilla chieftan's order was 'to kill every man and burn every house.'

Slated victims — including Jim Lane, Number One on their list — lit out for the ravines, and many of the men who perhaps deserved to die escaped. Some of them were saved by the quick-wittedness of their women.

One man, whose name was obscured in the first telling and therefore lost, escaped because his wife was quick to notice a love of flowers in the leader of the detail assigned to kill her husband. She saw a flower in the squad leader's hat and came out into her yard, which was ablaze with late August bloom. 'Good morning,' she said. 'You've come to see my flowers.'

It was a surprise counterattack. The guerrilla halted to look about, with apparent enjoyment.

'What do you think of them?' she asked.

'They're fine, ma'm,' he said. 'They are too damned pretty to be burned.' And he turned to his men. 'I'll shoot the man who touches them. March on!'

This was the only happy moment in that ugly morning of panic, flight, and courageous resistance, of bluff and defeat, of senseless death — all to the sound of clattering hooves, crackling flames, of screams and groans.

One hundred and eighty-three men and boys met sudden death that morning.

The streets were full of distraught wives and mothers, women whose men lay dead, whose homes were burning, when Quantrill, having lunched, appeared on the Whitney House piazza. He looked at the burning town, the weeping women, then went down to mount his horse.

He swung into the saddle. His men mounted their horses. Their work was done. They were ready to go.

Quantrill wheeled his horse and swept off his hat. 'Ladies,' he said, with a bow, 'I now bid you good morning. I hope when we meet again, it will be under more favorable circumstances.'

Some said Jim Lane assembled a fighting crew and rode after Quantrill but was never able to overtake him. Other men claimed that Lane and the Redlegs started after Quantrill when he was safely out of reach and that they entered Missouri and slew every man that they came to, without inquiring into his politics.

IV

KANSAS WAS four years old when the Civil War came to an end. And in that brief time she had suffered not only four more years of blood and thunder but also a bond-issue scandal and an impeachment trial.

Horace Greeley had in a way predicted it all on his visit in 1859. 'The twin curses of Kansas, now that Border Ruffians have stopped ravaging her,' he said, 'are Land Speculators and One Horse Politicians.'

These were her twin curses from the beginning. They remained her twin curses throughout the war, and afterward.

No other state had been moved to try to impeach her first governor. Charles Robinson underwent that ordeal and, in the light of full evidence, he was guilty of speculating with state funds if his auditor and secretary of state were guilty. They were impeached. He was acquitted. But he must have been guilty in the eyes of the voters, for they never again elected him to any important office, though he kept trying. The number of legislators who voted for his acquittal and were immediately given some kind of political or military office may have made the voters suspicious. Or perhaps too many of them wondered how he acquired 2160 acres of the richest bottomland in Kansas. He should have explained to those envious men that the farm was not his. It belonged to his wife. The Kansas Pacific Railroad had sold it to her, title clear, for the sum of one dollar.

Corruption charges in connection with Indian contracts

were never proved against Senator James Lane. But three months after the charges were made in the Senate of the United States, he was dead — by his own hand.

Land Speculators and One Horse Politicians. Blood and thunder, drouth and exploitation. Certainly no new state ever chose a more fitting motto than did young Kansas. *Ad Astra per Aspera.* It had been and would always be 'To the stars by hard ways.'

A Footnote Bibliography

TEXTBOOK KANSAS HISTORY has a complete Northern bias. A middle-of-the-road suspicion that the Southerners could not have been as black as they have been painted, or the Northerners as white, sent me digging into the literature of territorial days, first for my own instruction, then to write this book.

References, blow by blow:

PROLOGUE

ABORTIVE THIRTEENTH AMENDMENT, 1950 *World Almanac,* 102.

– 1 –

FAMILY TREE

History of the United States (1874), Samuel Eliot.
Rise of the New West (*American Nation,* XIV, 1906), Frederick J. Turner.
Slavery and Abolition (*American Nation,* XVI, 1907), Albert B. Hart.
America's Tragedy (1934), James Truslow Adams.
True History of the Civil War (1903), Guy Carleton Lee.
History of Kansas (1868), John Halloway.
The Kansas Crusade (1889), Eli Thayer.
Growth of the American Republic (1950), Morison and Commager.
Ordeal of the Union, I and II (1947), Allan Nevins.
A Basic History of the United States (1944), Charles and Mary Beard.
Bulwark of the American Republic (1937), Burton J. Hendrick.
Leavenworth Herald file, Library of Congress.
'The Railroad Background of the Kansas-Nebraska Act' (*Mississippi Valley Rev.,* June 1925), F. H. Hodder.

SLAVERY A MUTUAL PROBLEM — *Eliot,* 369, says that from early colonial days 'anti-slavery meant opposition to an evil from which all parts of the country were suffering and to the relief of which all must contribute. Slavery was to be removed gradually and with compensation to the owners of slaves emancipated . . . All this changes in the second period, from 1831 on.' Also, *Turner,* 151–2; *Hart,* chap. IV; *Adams,* 69.

DUKE OF YORK'S ROYAL AFRICAN COMPANY — *Halloway,* 39, says Queen Anne wrote the Governor of New Jersey in 1702 to give 'due encouragement to the slave merchants and in particular to the Royal African Company.' And *Lee,* 34–5, says, 'No clause in the Treaty of Utrecht was more jealously guarded than that which gave her [England] the exclusive right of selling Africans in the Spanish West Indies and on the coast of America.' In 1775, the Earl of Dartmouth said, 'We cannot allow the colonies to check or discourage in any manner a traffic so beneficial to the nation.'

SOUTHERN MOVES AGAINST SLAVERY — *Lee,* 39–43; *Adams,* 69.

THE TARIFF, COTTON GIN, AND SHIFTS IN SENTIMENT — *Lee* discusses all the factors involved in the growing schism between North and South, but says, 19, 'Public opinion in the north, however, where domestic servitude was not profitable, grew more and more opposed to the institution, especially after the discovery that slavery and the tariff were irreconcilable.' Tariff legislation, 108–11. Effects of the cotton gin, *Turner,* 45–6, includes export figures from Pitkin's *Statistical Rev.* (1835), 518. The tariff and nullification, chap. XIX, *Turner.* Also *Eliot,* 362–8; *Hendrick,* 218–22; *The Beards,* 252–4; *Morison-Commager,* 475–85, 638–9. *Nevins,* I, ignores the tariff; II, 269, gives it only brief mention as a factor.

ABOLITION MOVEMENT — *Eliot,* 370–71, gives anti-slavery society figures, tells of the meeting of Lundy and Garrison and its eventual effect on Southern sentiment. *Eli Thayer,* wrote his book to prove that Eli Thayer had more to do with setting the slaves free than any other one man, including Abraham Lincoln. 'It is supreme folly to attribute the secession to the election of Mr. Lincoln,' he says, 242: 'had the South won Kansas she never would have attempted secession.' The burden of proof is on Mr. Thayer and his copious quotes from the press of a century ago make his book a valuable source. Also see *Lee,* 64–5. *Morison-Commager,* 548, minimize the effect of abolitionist screams on Southern nerves, as does *Nevins,* I, 144–9, who maintains that debate over the admission of Missouri had caused Southerners to 'develop and clarify their arguments and that the theory of slavery as a positive good was fully formulated before Garrison started *The Liberator.*'

SLAVERY IN THE NORTH — *Lee*, 24–53, quotes Lalor's *Cyclopedia of Political Science, article Slavery* on slavers outfitted in Port of New York.

GRADUAL EMANCIPATION AND ITS PROBLEMS — *Eliot*, 369; for full discussion see *Nevins*, I, 500–535.

MISSOURI COMPROMISE AND COMPROMISE OF 1850 — All histories. *Lee*, 93–5, quotes both Whig and Democratic platforms of 1852, says the compromise measures (1850) were 'accepted by both parties as oil allaying troubled waters.'

KANSAS-NEBRASKA BILL — *Morison-Commager*, I, 620, attribute Douglas' puzzling act in reviving the slavery issue to his interest in a transcontinental railroad that would take a northern or central route. They see it as a bid for Southern support in opening new territories. *Hodder*, 1–22, reviews Douglas' early interest in a transcontinental road and his special interest in having Chicago as the great terminal. He sees the introduction of the Kansas-Nebraska issue as a quick counter-move against Secretary Jefferson Davis, who was pushing for a southern railroad to California. *Nevins*, II, 82–7, 104, finds the railroad question only a minor clue to Douglas' action; fully discussed, 88–121. Many historians see Douglas' championship of the squatter-sovereign principle simply as a backfiring bid for Southern support to attain his consuming passion, the presidency of the United States.

– 2 –

THE PARENT STOCK

Kansas, the Prelude to War for the Union (1885), Leverett W. Spring.
Three Years on the Western Border (1856), John McNamara.
Wars on the Western Border (1859), George Douglas Brewerton.
The Truth at Last. History Corrected. Reminiscences of Old Brown (1880), G. W. Brown.
False Claims Truthfully Corrected (1902), G. W. Brown.
Reminiscences of Gov. R. J. Walker (1902), G. W. Brown.
The Kansas Crusade (1889), Eli Thayer.
The Kansas Conflict (1889), Charles Robinson.
'The Rise and Fall of the Kansas Aid Movement' (*American Hist. Rev.*, IV, 1935), Ralph Volney Harlow.
An Appeal to the Record (1903), William Esley Connelley.
The Narrative of John Doy of Lawrence, Kansas (1860), John Doy.

NEWS THAT KANSAS IS OPENED REACHES MISSOURI — *Spring, 24–8.*
Spring is the only impartial historian of this period. He was still close
to the subject and to Dr. Charles Robinson, who was influential in the
management of both Kansas University, where Spring taught, and the
Kansas Historical Society. *McNamara,* 22–4. This Episcopal clergyman was a colorful, only mildly editorializing reporter, and it is a
shame he stayed less than a year after the Territory opened. *Brewerton*
is a rich source of border flavor.

II

WEBSTER, SEWARD, AND WADE QUOTES — *Spring, 5; Thayer, 12–*
13.

NEW ENGLAND EMIGRANT AID SOCIETY — *Thayer,* 23–30, gives
its organization and plan. His book was one of a raft of I-Done-Its by
members of the Society. His special hate was William Lloyd Garrison,
while the local boys hated John Brown. The *G. W. Brown* volumes are
all apoplectic. *Robinson's* is poorly written but a valuable source, since
it is largely comprised of letters, speeches, and territorial press quotes.
Critical of the Aid Society: The *Harlow* article. *Connelley,* 109–30 —
in fact the whole book — is vituperative but valuable because his material is largely comprised of clips from the territorial press. *Doy,* 19–
21, tells how he and his free-soil neighbors were cheated out of the
site of Lawrence by the Robinson party. The Aid Society's proprietary
attitude toward the land and timber claims of other free-soil squatters
aroused the ire of the *Kansas Free State.* The 30 July 1885 issue gives
an especially detailed account. *Spring,* 29–36, is impartial in his ap-
praisal.

– 3 –
SEEDBED

Notes of a Military Reconnaisance (1848), Lt. Col. W. H. Emory.
Kansas and Nebraska (1854), Edward Everett Hale.
The Kansas-Nebraska Handbook (1857), Nathan Parker.
Kanzas Region (1856), Max Greene.
Kansas: Its Interior and Exterior Life (1856), Sara L. Robinson.
Six Months in Kansas (1856), Hannah Anderson Ropes.
The Annals of Kansas (1875), Daniel W. Wilder.
History of the State of Kansas (1883), A. T. Andreas.

Kansas the Prelude to War for the Union (1885), Leverett Spring.
Wars on the Western Border (1859), George Douglas Brewerton.
Life Beyond the Mississippi (1867), Albert D. Richardson.
History of Kansas, Information Regarding Routes, Laws (1854), New
   York Kansas League, George Walter.
Howard Report (*Report* 200, 34th Congress, 1st Session).

TOPOGRAPHY AND AGRICULTURAL PROSPECTS — *Emory*, 10–15;
Hale, 83–128; *Parker*, 12–23. Greene gives the most thorough first-hand
description.

BEAUTY — *Greene* and many others, notably *Mrs. Robinson* and
Mrs. Ropes.

EARLIER HISTORY — *Hale*, 9–16; *Spring*, 17–22; *Wilder*, 5–31;
Andreas, 44–57. *Greene's* Santa Fe Trail information, 73–85, is especially interesting. *Brewerton*, also author of *A Ride With Kit Carson*
(1848), tells the Little Aubrey story in his *Wars on the Western Border*, 123–4.

INDIAN TREATIES — *Wilder*, 32–6, gives dates. *Greene*, 25–35, talks
about tribes; 37–8, Indian lands; and 99–102, briefs terms of 1854
treaties. *Andreas*, 58–74. *Hale*, 17–60, quotes many authorities on the
various tribes, puts the land ceded by the emigrant tribes (eastern
tribes earlier removed to Kansas) at more than 13,000,000 acres.

SQUATTING — *Parker*, 30–35, gives steps for pre-empting public
lands. Also *Richardson*, 137–41; *Doy*, 11–12. *Greene*, 38–9, puts the
Indian-Squatter problem in a nutshell: 'The entire extinction of the
Indian "tribe system" of land title, by the close of 1856, may be counted
on with as much certainty as anything in the future can be. But the
pioneer who would make sure of his preemption, must obtain copies of
the treaties when they are consummated if he would "squat" intelli-
gently. These considerations are not, however, of any real importance,
and need not deter a person from settling where he may prefer; as a
small fee, of ten dollars or so, will propitiate the owning tribe.' *Greene*
appends, 174–85, the organic law of the territory, the national Home-
stead Law, and the local squatter laws.

ROUTES AND FARES — *Parker*, 24–6; *Walter* pamphlet.

FIRST CENSUS AND ELECTION — *Spring*, 40–43, *Wilder*, 41, gives
votes by districts and number of resident votes. Nevins, *Ordeal of the
Nation*, II, 313, must have got this November, 1854, election confused
with the later elections. There were visiting voters, but the free-soil-

biased *Howard Report* says, 'Of the legal votes cast, General Whitfield received a majority.'

– 4 –

THE MIGHTY SEED

Annals of Kansas, D. W. Wilder.
A Journey Through Kansas (1854), Rev. Charles Boynton and T. B. Mason.
Three Years on the Western Border, John McNamara.
Conquest of Kansas (1856), William Phillips.
Kansas, Leverett W. Spring.
Reports of the Special Committee on the Troubles in Kansas Territory (*Report* 200, 34th Congress, 1st Session) referred to as *Full Report* 200.
Howard Report (*Majority Report* 200, 34th Congress, 1st Session).
Senate Report 34 (34th Congress, 1st Session), referred to as *Report* 34.
Kansas Conflict (1889), Charles Robinson.
Kansas, or, Squatter Life and Border Warfare in the Far West (1858), Thomas H. Gladstone.
An Appeal to the Record, William E. Connelley.

THE CAPITAL, LEAVENWORTH — *Wilder,* 38. Also *McNamara,* who was in and out of the place all the time as a missionary to K.T. And *Boynton and Mason,* who came representing the Kansas League of Cincinnati.

SECRET SOUTHERN ORGANIZATION — *McNamara* tells many 'sound on the goose' anecdotes and gives more first-hand information on the Blue Lodge than does any other source. *Spring,* 41.

SECRET NORTHERN ORGANIZATION — Most chroniclers of the day were writing to arouse the North to send more support in men and arms. They soft-pedalled the Kansas Regulators or Kansas Legion. *Phillips,* 148, acknowledges the organization's existence but says only the rougher element belonged. The *Howard Report* ignored the testimony of Andrew J. Francis, who said that the free-soil leaders, Robinson, Reeder, and Lane were present when he was initiated. But the testimony is given in *Full Report* 200, 910–21. And *Report* 34, 27–30, quotes at length a pamphlet containing the constitution adopted by the Legion on 4 April

1855. This document was taken from George F. Warren who attempted to 'conceal and destroy same by thrusting it in his mouth.' The historical impression has been that free-soilers did not form a military organization until long after the voting invasion of March, 1855, indeed not until the threat on Lawrence the next winter. The first encampment of the Kansas Legion, however, was held 8 February 1855. Robinson, *Kansas Conflict,* does not mention the Legion.

II

EARLY TERRITORIAL NEWSPAPERS — *Wilder,* 43–4; *Brewerton,* 390–92.

FIRST GENERAL ELECTION — *Spring,* 43–51. *McNamara,* who watched the voting army depart, 142–7. *Gladstone,* 241–2, gives a colorful eyewitness account by Rev. Frederick Starr. A good part of the 1206-page *Full Report* 200 is devoted to eyewitness testimony. *Phillips,* 91–7, gives the version of the story Tom Thorpe told. Thorpe's published testimony, *Full Report* 200, 1134, is in the spirit but colorless.

III

NEW ELECTIONS — *Spring,* 52, says new elections were held in eight districts. *Full Report* 200 says six.

ILLEGAL FREE-SOIL VOTERS — The *Kansas Free State* was attacked by the *Herald of Freedom* for telling about the illegal Northern voters. The *Free State,* 7 April 1885, retorted that the *Herald's* editor had said to a pre-election convention, 'Be of good cheer, for 300 Eastern emigrants are on their way and will be on hand for election day.' See *Connelley,* 88–9.

– 5 –

ONE GOVERNOR DOWN AND FIVE TO GO

Kansas, Leverett W. Spring.
Ordeal of the Nation, II, Allan Nevins.
Three Years on the Western Border, John McNamara.
Leavenworth Herald file, Library of Congress.
Kansas: Its Interior and Exterior Life, Sara L. Robinson.
Six Months in Kansas, Hannah Anderson Ropes.
Annals of Kansas, Daniel W. Wilder.

Life of Gen. Jas. H. Lane, Liberator of Kansas (1897), John Speer.
Wars on the Western Border, George Douglas Brewerton.
Kansas Conflict, Charles Robinson.
The Gun and the Gospel (1899), Rev. H. D. Fisher.
Kansas Territorial Governors (1902), William E. Connelley.
Kansas Historical Collections, XII, referred to as *KHC,* XII.
Senate Report 34 (34th Congress, 1st Session)

REEDER'S TRIP EAST — *Spring,* 52; *Nevins,* 386–7.

LEAVENWORTH — *McNamara,* 56–7, gives the background on the McCrea-Clark killing, says that Clark, angered by McCrea's free-soil talk at a squatter's meeting, moved toward him 'with club upraised' and that McCrea shot in self-defense. Dragoons from Fort Leavenworth rescued the killer from a lynch-minded mob. The news notes on Leavenworth's growth are from the *Leavenworth Herald.*

LAWRENCE — At this point, *Sara L. Robinson,* wife of Charles, enters the scene as an eyewitness diarist and free-soil propagandist. She describes Lawrence as she first saw it, 35ff. Another record-keeping resident was *Mrs. Ropes,* who tells the story about the couple who woke up to find a rattlesnake in bed. Their name was Chubb.

FREE STATE POW-WOW — *Wilder,* 51; *Speer,* 34–7.

REEDER'S TOWN — James Christian, proslave member of the Bogus Legislature but a much respected citizen of Lawrence often quoted by Charles Robinson, described Pawnee and the session there to *Brewerton,* 283–91. *Nevins,* 387, is wrong when he says, 'A good stone assembly hall, with ample accommodations for board and lodging was available.' The assembly hall did not get a real roof or window pane until it was sixty or seventy years old and was preserved as a landmark.

CONWAY — *Robinson's* version, 152–3, of the Conway defiance is used. Free-soilers made such point of the interference of prominent Missourians in territorial affairs that Robinson's praise, 417, of the part Kersey Coates of Missouri played in free-soil affairs is interesting.

REEDER REMOVAL — *Wilder,* 51–5; *Spring,* 56. *Connelley,* 28–30, admires Reeder but says his course at Pawnee 'is incapable of explanation or justification.' Also *Fisher. Nevins,* 389, digests the correspondence between Reeder, Indian Commissioner G. W. Manypenny, and Indian agent George Clarke printed in the *National Intelligencer,* 21 June 1855. But there must have been more to it than there revealed. Major Montgomery was tried and court-martialed for his part in the deal, *KHC,* XII, 333–6. Also see *Senate Report* 34, 18.

– 6 –
FALSE VIRTUE

Life and Letters of John Brown (1885), F. B. Sanborn.
Kansas: Its Interior and Exterior Life, Sara L. Robinson.
Kansas Conflict, Charles Robinson.
Annals of Kansas, Daniel W. Wilder.
Went to Kansas (1862), Miriam Davis Colt.
Kansas, Leverett Spring.

FREE STATE MILITARY ORGANIZATION — See *Secret Northern Organization,* this bibliography, chapter 4. To refute *Sanborn's* statement that his hero, John Brown, had taken arms to his sons in Kansas before Sharp's rifles got there, *Robinson,* 120–27, publishes Amos Lawrence's correspondence dated early in the summer of 1855. There was an order for 'one hundred Sharp's rifles packed in casks, like hardware' and a letter from E. D. Ladd telling of the arrival 'on the *Emma Harmon* of five boxes of books, which on being opened proved to be instead of *books,* one hundred Sharp's rifles, capable of discharging 1000 shots a minute.'

TERRITORIAL LEGISLATURE — *Wilder,* 52–3, names all members, their professions, ages. The 'Act to punish offences against slave property' is given in full, 57–8. *Spring,* 53–8.

AGUE AND DEATH — Newly broken lands produce a miasma which was a pioneer bugbear. *Greene,* 18, predicted there would be ague when Kansas Territory's lands were broken but 'no danger of shaking to pieces.' Some did shake to pieces. One was the husband of *Mrs. Colt,* who wrote of frontier hardships.

– 7 –
'A BLOODY ISSUE!'

Kansas (1885), Leverett W. Spring.
Conquest of Kansas (1856), William Phillips.
Annals of Kansas (1875), Daniel W. Wilder.
Life of Gen. Jas. H. Lane (1897), John Speer.
Life Beyond the Mississippi (1867), Albert D. Richardson.
The Gun and the Gospel, Rev. H. D. Fisher.

SHANNON WELCOME — *Spring,* 82–3.

PARDEE BUTLER — Classic story with all free-soil chroniclers. *Phillips,* 145–8, gives fullest account.

II

BIG SPRINGS CONVENTION — *Wilder,* 60–61, full resolutions. *Phillips,* 120–24, reports meeting; picture of Lane, 139–40. John Speer, editor of the *Kansas Tribune,* which he was to move from Lawrence to Topeka in October, was also present. His report, *Lane,* 45–7. See *Spring,* 63–8. For a word picture of Lane see *Richardson,* 44–6. Speer calls Lane 'one of the most abstemious men I ever saw,' but another admirer, *Reverend Fisher,* speaks of his 'censurable mirthfulness' in the company of politicians. And that is James H. Lane, politician, in a nutshell.

LANE'S BLACK LAW — *Kansas Free State,* 24 September 1855, carried a letter from Charles Stearn, the one dissenter to Lane's Black Law. 'All sterling anti-slavery men, here and elsewhere, cannot keep from spitting on it,' he said, 'and all pro-slavery people must, in their hearts, perfectly despise the base sychophants who originated and adopted it.'

– 8 –
THE SPARK AND THE TINDER

Conquest of Kansas, William Phillips.
Kansas, Leverett W. Spring.
Annals of Kansas, Daniel W. Wilder.
Kansas Conflict, Charles Robinson.
Appeal to Reason, William E. Connelley.
Rascals in Democracy (1942), William Clugston.
Life Beyond the Mississippi, Albert D. Richardson.
Kansas: Its Interior and Exterior Life, Sara L. Robinson.
Kansas Territorial Newspapers, Library of Congress file.
True History of the Kansas Wars (1856), O. N. Merrill.
Wars on the Western Border, George Douglas Brewerton.
Reports of the Special Committee on the Troubles in Kansas Territory (1856), referred to as *Full Report* 200.
Herald of Freedom file, Library of Congress.

(*Note on Sharp(e)'s Rifles:* Without exception, the writers of that day
spelled Sharp's with an 'e.' But Bannerman's, famous firearms store in
New York, while acknowledging this spelling, lists them as Sharp's
rifles. That is the spelling on the guns.)

LAUGHLIN-COLLINS KILLING — *Phillips,* 141–4, devotes considerable space to this killing, without proving anything. Both were members of the Kansas Legion but Collins hated Laughlin because he told
proslavery men about this secret organization. They quarrelled —both
were armed, both shot, and Collins was the one who got killed.

THE TOPEKA CONVENTION — *Phillips,* 127–40, covered it well; the
good anecdotes are his. Other accredited reporters present were James
Redpath, *Missouri Democrat* (free-soil) and John Speer's brother Joseph of the *Chicago Tribune. Spring,* 69–72. *Wilder,* 74–88, gives the
full text of the Topeka Constitution.

FREE-SOIL AND SEX — *Robinson,* 175–80, includes the story about
Jim Lane and Mrs. Lindsay. Jim Lane was not the only free-soiler
involved in scandals with women. A diligent researcher could do a book
on the subject. *Connelley,* 17, calls the circumstances of Robinson's
relations to women 'unfit for publication' and adds, 'The case of a lady
now supposed to be living in Cambridge, is perhaps the most notorious.'
On page 78, he tells how Mrs. G. W. Brown came home from a trip east
to raise money to re-establish her husband's destroyed *Herald of Freedom* plant to find her husband involved with one of his clerks, who became Mrs. G. W. Brown the second. Samuel Pomeroy's interest in the
fairer sex became a matter of public record, according to *Clugston,* 60.
Richardson, 148, reports the interest of free-soil solons in an easy
divorce and, 143, tells a juicy tale about how the wife of one free-soil
politician tried to run away with another prominent free-soil leader.
Unfortunately, he mentions no names.

LAW AND ORDER PARTY — *Wilder,* 70; *Phillips,* 148–50; *Sara Robinson,* 115–17; *Spring,* 84; *Leavenworth Herald.*

II

COLEMAN-DOW KILLING AND BRANSON RESCUE — *Phillips,* 152–
61; *Sara Robinson,* 104, 111. Textbook Kansas history has relied on
these propaganda sources. Both of these writers gloss over the claim
dispute, picture Dow as a quiet, peaceable fellow. Neither of them tells
of the visit the free-soil intimidators made to Hargis and Buckley. Of

the score of books that came out of this period, only one was written by a Southern settler, and he was neither an 'ultra,' as extremists of both sides were called, nor, unfortunately, an able writer. *Merrill*, 1–16, tells the story in a plodding, sincere way. It is the same as that told to *Brewerton*, 150, by Governor Shannon. Brewerton was the only real newsman to visit Kansas Territory. He interviewed tirelessly on both sides, made no editorial comment. *Redpath* called him proslave but the free-soil partisan, *Wilder*, 94, reviewing his book in 1875, said, 'He was not a partisan, and his book is valuable now because he wrote down the Northern and Southern version in the very words of the leading actors.' *Brewerton's* interview with Coleman, 223–31, gives an interesting insight into squatter law in operation and is important because this killing was crucial in territorial and national history. It was screamed as a wanton, unmotivated murder in the Eastern press, and the events that ensued were used by the Free State leaders as the reason for their formation of a military organization. Coleman, by the way, told substantially the same story some months later to the Congressional Investigation Committee, *Full Report* 200, 1052–6. The majority report did not mention his version.

BURNING OF PROSLAVE HOMES — *Herald of Freedom*, 29 November 1855, surmised that proslave men set the fires. *Phillips*, 186, says, 'There's little doubt that Southerners set the fires.' Mrs. Robinson ignored the burnings. Free-soil Vigilante Bercaw told *Brewerton*, 280–82, about the first attempt to fire Coleman's home and certainly does not question but what the same men set the three fires that night. Sam Wood tells the same story in a letter about the Branson rescue written to A. Wattles in 1857 and printed years later by *Robinson*, 184–6. *Spring*, 86, simply says, 'A proposition to fire their deserted cabins was discussed and rejected, though the adverse decision did not keep them from being burned that night.'

III

SHERIFF JONES SUMMONS A POSSE — *Phillips*, 162–3; *Spring*, 90–91, *Brewerton*, 167, tells the story about the old fellow with the flintlock and, 159–67, gives his interview with Shannon on events leading up to the actual march on Lawrence.

– 9 –

'THE WAKARUSA WAR'

Wars on the Western Border, George Douglas Brewerton.
Life of Gen. Jas. H. Lane, John Speer.
Conquest of Kansas, William Phillips.
True History of the Kansas Wars, O. N. Merrill.
Kansas: Its Interior and Exterior Life, Sara L. Robinson.
Kansas Conflict, Charles Robinson.
Reports of the Special Committee on the Troubles in Kansas Territory
  (1856), referred to as *Full Report* 200.
Roving Editor, or, Talks with Slaves in Southern States (1858), James
  Redpath.
The Public Life of Captain John Brown (1860), James Redpath.

I AND II

SHANNON'S STORY OF 'THE WAR' — *Brewerton,* 167–90, includes correspondence.

ROBINSON'S STORY OF 'THE WAR' — *Brewerton,* 293–8.

As REPORTED AND REMEMBERED — *Phillips,* 163–202; *Speer,* 51–62. John Speer was the free-soil patrolman who got his horse shot from under him. *Merrill,* 22–30; *Mrs. Robinson,* 112–40; *Robinson,* 191–201. Testimony of numerous witnesses on both sides on the whole affair, from the murder of Dow to the murder of Barber, *Full Report* 200, 1040–1128.

III

THE YANKEE LADIES' AID — *Brewerton,* 270–75, tells the story with all the Pickwickian flavor that was the style among journalists of that day.

IV

YANKEE DOODLE — Again *Brewerton's* version, 203–10.

THOMAS BARBER — That the death of one man is more important to a cause than the death of dozens was never better illustrated. Incalculable capital was made out of the virtually accidental killing of Thomas Barber. George Clarke was forever afterward to be referred to as Murderer-of-Barber Clarke. *Mrs. Robinson,* 144–6, makes it a cold-blooded murder, indeed, as does *Phillips,* 211–15, though he does quote the proslavery story, which was substantially the same as the versions told

Brewerton, 319–22, by the dead man's brother, and 326–7, by Thomas Pierson, both of whom were with him at the time he was shot. *Brewerton* called upon the widow and his report, 228–31, is touching. Barber was given a martyr's funeral, reported at tearful length by Mrs. Robinson and Mrs. Ropes. Also see *Full Report* 200, 1121–5.

PROSLAVE LEADERS MEET — Senator Barber of South Carolina gave Atchison's position in a congressional speech on 5 March 1856. *Spring* mentions it, 11; *Phillips,* 237.

JOHN BROWN'S FIRST APPEARANCE — Englishman James Redpath went to St. Louis to get a job as Kansas correspondent for the strongly free-soil *St. Louis Democrat* so that he might, as he says in his *Roving Editor,* 300, endeavor 'personally and by my pen, to precipitate a revolution.' He idolized John Brown, though their paths seldom crossed. He gives the fullest account of Old Brown's first public appearance in K.T. — *Capt. John Brown,* 86–92. When a New York publisher asked Redpath to do a life of John Brown as a Republican campaign document, he declined. 'I would not help light cigars from the fire above the altar,' he said. He finally wrote the book because he found a publisher who shared his high devotion to his hero.

– 10 –

EXPLODING PEACE PIPE

Conquest of Kansas, William Phillips.
Wars on the Western Border, George Brewerton.
Life of Gen. Jas. H. Lane, John Speer.
Kansas: Its Interior and Exterior Life, Sara L. Robinson.
Kansas Conflict, Charles Robinson.
The Public Life of Captain John Brown, James Redpath.
Kansas, Leverett W. Spring.
Kansas Territorial Newspapers, Library of Congress file.

NEGOTIATIONS AND THE PEACE TREATY — *Phillips,* 218–23; *Brewerton,* 191–4; *Speer,* 62–4; *Mrs. Robinson,* 146–9; *Robinson,* 201–6.

FREE-SOIL AND PROSLAVE REACTION — *Phillips,* 222–7; *Redpath,* 88; *Spring,* 98–101. Robinson gives the full text of the peace treaty, but time apparently obliterated the objections made by his free-soil compatriots. He does not mention them.

THE WEATHER — *Phillips,* 226. And Shannon told *Brewerton,* 196, that it seemed 'as if the very elements' fought for him.

II

PROSLAVE CASUALTIES — *Mrs. Robinson,* 150; *Phillips,* 232.

PRISONERS OF WAR — *Mrs. Robinson,* 152–3, 156; *Phillips,* 229–30; *Brewerton,* 387–9. *Brewerton,* 78–83, tells of meeting the released Pomeroy, 'burly and dark complexioned,' as Pomeroy was on his interrupted way East and Brewerton was on his way to Kansas Territory.

FREE-SOIL CELEBRATIONS AND THE GOVERNOR'S SUDDEN DEPARTURE — Gleeful capital was made of Governor Shannon's authorization of the Free State militia. *Phillips,* 227, makes no mention of the circumstances under which the trick document was obtained, says, 'In consideration of the troubled state of the territory, the governor commissioned,' and so on. *Robinson,* 206, says, 'While being entertained by the citizens of both sexes, an alarm was raised . . .' *Speer,* 64–5, says Lane got Shannon drunk ('while he pretended to drink') and obtained the prized authorization, adding, 'It was not ten minutes after Lane got this order, till he was in the streets in great glee, exclaiming, "We are now United States dragoons." ' *Mrs. Robinson,* 153–6, includes party preparations. She credits her husband with getting the order. Governor Shannon told just how the order was obtained in a written statement to *Brewerton,* 196–200. 'It did not for a moment occur to me that this pretended attack upon the town was but a device to obtain a paper from me that might be used in my prejudice,' he said. Next morning, 'upon the most diligent inquiry, I could not learn that any force whatever made its appearance before Lawrence.' Mrs. Robinson is sarcastic about the governor's being called away before the big party. The *Herald of Freedom,* 13 December 1855, was slyly jubilant, said of Governor Shannon, 'He came, learned the facts, and, like an honorable man, has done what he could to retrace his steps.'

– 11 –

BLOODY NEW YEAR

Annals of Kansas, Daniel W. Wilder.
Conquest of Kansas, William Phillips.
Life of Gen. Jas. H. Lane, John Speer.
Wars on the Western Border, George Brewerton.
Kansas, Leverett W. Spring.

WEATHER — Everybody, especially *Mrs. Robinson,* who gives a day-by-day report. Buffalo item, *Brewerton,* 215. *Spring,* 102–4.

ELECTIONS AND MURDER OF REESE BROWN — *Phillips,* 234–46. His account is used, though he calls the murdered man E. P. Brown. His name was Reese P. Brown, according to *Speer, Wilder, Spring,* and the *Kansas Historical Society. Speer,* 72–3, was on patrol with Brown during the 'war.'

WEEKLY MAIL — *Wilder,* 88.

— 12 —

HATREDS HOTBEDDED

'Rise and Fall of the Kansas Aid Movement' (*American Hist. Rev.,* IV, 1935), Ralph Volney Harlow.
Kansas: Its Interior and Exterior Life, Sara L. Robinson.
Conquest of Kansas, William Phillips.
The Buford Expedition to Kansas (*Alabama Hist. Soc.,* 1900), Walter Fleming.
Kansas, Leverett W. Spring.
True History of the Civil War, Guy Carleton Lee.
Ordeal of the Nation, II, Allan Nevins.
Wars on the Western Border, George Brewerton.
Went to Kansas, Miriam Davis Colt.

GERRIT SMITH QUOTE — *Harlow.*

ATCHISON QUOTE — *Mrs. Robinson,* 179–80.

WAS THE PRESS OF THE *Territorial Register* DESTROYED? — Everyone, except Phillips, says that the print shop of Leavenworth's *Territorial Register,* run by Lincoln's kinsman, Mark W. Delahay, was destroyed that winter. *Phillips,* the most prejudiced writer of them all, had enough of the real reporter in him that facts observed were inclined to anchor his imagination. He happened to be in Leavenworth at the time. He tells of the talk about dumping the press, 237, but says, 'Delahay's office was not mobbed,' and he tells what saved it.

BUFFORD EXPEDITION — *Fleming* also tells about the Rush Elmores and their slaves and the question Judge Elmore raised about the economic feasibility of slavery in Kansas.

FREE-SOIL MOVES — *Spring,* 104–5, 164–7; also *Harlow.*

BEECHER BIBLES — *Spring*, 165; *Lee*, 114–15; *Nevins*, 431.

PRESIDENTIAL PROCLAMATION — Many sources. *Brewerton*, 370–71, gives the proclamation in full.

OTHER NORTHERN SETTLEMENT COMPANIES — *Harlow* tells of the various settlement companies. *Miriam Davis Colt* records the disappointments of the Vegetarian colonists.

LECOMPTON, THE NEW CAPITAL — *Brewerton*, 135, describes Lecompton in its building stage. It was mostly comprised of a general store which 'seemed to contain a little of everything, but more particularly cheese and corn whiskey.'

TOWNS IN 1855 — *Mrs. Robinson*, 188–9, 210–15. *Brewerton* describes all the towns he visited and the territorial newspapers, *Library of Congress* newspaper files, report local progress.

– 13 –

HOW TERRITORIES BECAME STATES

Crime Against Kansas (1856), Charles Sumner.
Senate Report 34 (34th Congress, 1st Session).
Cong. Globe, 34th Cong., 1st Session, Appen. 544.
Kansas Conflict, Charles Robinson.
Annals of Kansas, Daniel W. Wilder.
Ordeal of the Nation, II, Allan Nevins.
Memorial of the Senators and Representatives and the Constitution of the State of Kansas; also the Majority and Minority Reports of the Committee on Territories (1856).
Life of Gen. Jas. H. Lane, John Speer.
The Senate Bill for Admission of Kansas as a State, Democratic campaign bulletin, 1856.

TECHNIQUES OF ADMISSION — Thoroughly discussed in the long congressional debate over Kansas Territory's prayer for admission under the Topeka Constitution. *Sumner* rehashed the admission of Michigan. The answers made by Senators Cass and Stewart, *Cong. Globe*, clearly state the statehood technique. *Report* 34, 34–5, goes into detail on the admission of a number of states.

THE PRESIDENT'S MESSAGE — Full text, *Robinson*, 225–6. *Wilder*, 90; *Nevins*, 417–24. The Committee on Territories to which the message was referred made *Senate Report* 34, at the Senate's request.

PRESENTATION OF THE TOPEKA CONSTITUTION AND THE DEBATE —
In the Memorial, 41, Mr. Grow says 'The population of Kansas, from
the most reliable sources of information, is nearly or quite equal to
the present fractional ratio for a member of Congress.' Mr. Zollicoffer,
minority, 51–2, says, 'The population in October last was 25,000, or less
than one-third the number (93,420 inhabitants) requisite to entitle
Kansas to a representative in Congress, and he gives a table showing
that the 18 states previously admitted had populations well above the
ratio of representation when admitted. *Speer* passes over Lane's ex-
periences in presenting the Topeka Constitution in Washington. *Spring,*
74–8, tells about it. *Robinson,* 228, disposes of the whole business in
two paragraphs. The Democratic campaign bulletin is largely devoted,
9–30, to sections of the debate on the bill. The modern historian who
has treated this most fully is *Nevins,* 424–8.

– 14 –

HARROWING TIME

Kansas: Its Interior and Exterior Life, Sara L. Robinson.
Kansas, Leverett W. Spring.
Life of Gen. Jas. H. Lane, John Speer.
True History of the Kansas Wars, O. N. Merrill.
'Letter from Col. Axala Hoole, 1856,' *Kansas Quarterly,* February 1934.
Life Beyond the Mississippi, Albert D. Richardson.
Conquest of Kansas, William Phillips.
Kansas Historical Collections, IV, referred to as *KHC,* IV.

SHARP'S RIFLES — *Mrs. Robinson,* 191; *Spring,* 166.
CONGRESSIONAL INVESTIGATION COMMITTEE: It interviewed 323
witnesses. Historians calling Report 200 the *Howard Report* refer to the
majority report as mentioned under Chapter IV. The reference used in
this book, *Full Report* 200, includes the majority and minority reports
and the sworn testimony of the witnesses.
ATTEMPTS TO ARREST SAM WOOD AND SAM TAPPAN — *Speer,* 76–8,
gives a participant account of these events. *Merrill,* 35–8, was there,
too, and his account is substantially the same as Speer's, except that
being a Kentuckian he quotes the free-soilers as using some pretty
rough language. Since free-soil literature quotes all Northerners in
gentlemanly tones and makes ruffians of the Southerners, it is interesting

that another proslave fragment would lead the reader to believe that
the Yankees may have done some cussing. *Colonel Axala Hoole,* writing
to his mother from Lecompton, K.T., on 3 April 1856, commented that
all the men in Lawrence were profane. He also said he had seen catfish
weighing as much as a hundred pounds caught in the Kaw, but that
does not brand him as an exaggerator. *Richardson,* 115–16, tells of a
catfish that got stranded on a sandbar on the far side of the river from
Lecompton. It was found to weigh 117 pounds. That Governor Shannon accepted Sheriff Jones's story of being set upon by an armed band
is shown in his letter to Secretary of State Marcy, 27 April 1856, *KHC,*
IV, 405–13.

JONES'S RETURN WITH THE DRAGOONS AND THE ATTEMPT TO ASSAS-
SINATE HIM — Lt. James McIntosh of the dragoons immediately reported on the search and the shooting of Jones to Governor Shannon in
a dispatch dated 30 April 1856, *KHC,* IV, 418–19. *Speer,* 79–80, tells
of the posse's fruitless hunts, does not mention the shooting of Jones.
Phillips, 254–7, gives a full account and says the shot was fired by a
rash free-soil boy. *Mrs. Robinson,* 199–208, took heartily to the view
that the shot was fired by a proslavery man. She even tells how a couple
of strangers stopped at a home near Lawrence and asked whether
Jones was in town. The answer was in the affirmative. 'The taller man
then said, "I am a pro-slavery man, but Jones will never leave town
alive." ' *Spring,* 109–11, tells of free-soiler Filer's confession twenty-
five years later.

II

GRAND JURY SESSION — *Spring,* 111–12, 118; *Phillips,* 267–70;
Mrs. Robinson, 218–19; *Merrill,* 39–40.

REVEREND PARDEE BUTLER, CHAPTER II — *Phillips,* 259–62,
quotes Butler directly.

FREE STATE LEADERS HEAD EASTWARD — *Spring,* 112–16; *Phillips,* 270–76. *Mrs. Robinson,* 219–20, tells of her husband's arrest but
does not mention being with him and being allowed to go East. Perhaps
she feared that her diary, scheduled for publication that fall, would
lose its on-location authority, though of necessity at this point, she
drops the day-by-day form with its comments on daily living. She
takes the diary form up again when she returns some weeks later. Her
husband's telling the story of his arrest, 238, says, 'As Mrs. Robinson
was not regarded as a fugitive from justice, she was permitted to go on.'

DONELSON'S PROCLAMATION — All sources give this. The only thing they disagree on is his name. The wide use of Phillips as the chief source on this period is reflected in the use of his notion of the marshal's name and his calling R. P. Brown 'E. P. Brown.' He always called the marshal J. B. Donaldson (as do Mrs. Robinson, Spring, and today's historian, Allan Nevins). That was the territorial auditor's name. Wilder made it Donalson, but in official documents it is always, or almost always, I. B. Donelson. His first name was Israel. All name spelling in those days seems to have been done by ear.

– 15 –

FIRST SACK OF LAWRENCE

Conquest of Kansas, William Phillips.
Kansas Conflict, Charles Robinson.
Kansas: Its Interior and Exterior Life, Sara L. Robinson.
Kansas, Leverett W. Spring.
History of the South, Rhodes.
'David R. Atchison' (*Missouri Hist. Rev.,* 1930), Theodore Atchison.
Appeal to the Record, William E. Connelley.
Kansas Historical Collections, iv, referred to as *KHC,* iv.
Life of Gen. Jas. H. Lane, John Speer.

THE POSSE — The *Lecompton Union* (proslave), 21 May 1856 gave a full account of the march on Lawrence, said the posse was 'eight hundred strong, cavalry, infantry, and six-pound cannon.' Also see *Phillips,* 304–9.

THE ATTACK — Letter from Lawrence Committee on Safety to the marshal, 22 May, 1856, included in *Robinson's* account, 251–6. Shannon's letter to Franklin Pierce with appended communiques, 31 May 1856, *KHC,* iv, 414–20. *Mrs. Robinson,* 240–48, apparently got her fill-in from *Phillips,* 288–304, from the way she spells the marshal's name and because she uses Phillips' imaginary Atchison quote. But she adds some of her own embroidery. She says the Ruffians fired point blank at a group of women but missed aim. Both 'facts' are uncharacteristic of the Missourians. Atchison's actual efforts to quell the mob: *Spring,* 120–28. The *Squatter Sovereign,* 24 June 1856, says Atchison 'exhorted the men above everything to remember that they were marching to enforce, not to violate, the laws.' Apparently, Atchison never was as ruffianish as the Eastern press pictured him. *Rhodes,* 62, quotes him as saying, at the time of the passage of the Kansas-Nebraska Bill, 'We must meet them peaceably at the ballot-box and out-vote them. If we cannot do this, it is an omen that the institution of slavery must fall in this and other states, but it would fall after much strife, civil war, and bloodshed.' A descendant, *Theodore Atchison,* says Atchison was President of the United States for a day because inaugural day fell on Sunday in 1849 and President Taylor could not be inaugurated until Monday. Vice-President William R. King had died and Atchison as President of the Senate was, at that time, next in line. He was often called vice-president by the chroniclers of the time.

FREE STATE HOTEL — The Grand Jury's charge that the Free State Hotel was built as a fortress was passed over with scorn by the free-soil propagandists. *Speer,* 22–23, prints this note, written 21 October 1894, by Ben Johnson who erected the hotel: 'Friend Speer: I received a line from you asking about the walls of the Free-State Hotel. The building was fifty by eighty feet, four stories high. The basement walls were two feet thick; first story twenty inches; the balance eighteen inches thick. The parapet walls in front above the roof were two feet, running bevel all around the building, making the sides and rear from two to six feet high, with portholes six feet apart, sixteen inches large on the inside, and four inches on the outside, mortared over to prevent observation from the without side. Shape of opening: (diagram).'

ROBINSON DAMAGE CLAIMS — *Connelley,* 23–6, goes thoroughly into Robinson's claims for damages. Robinson was finally awarded $23,953.

– 16 –
BIT PLAYER, JOHN BROWN

The Public Life of Captain John Brown, James Redpath.
Kansas, Leverett W. Spring.
History of the State of Kansas, A. T. Andreas.
Conquest of Kansas, William Phillips.
With John Brown in Kansas (1910), Luke Parsons.
Howard Report and Full Report 200 (34th Congress, 1st Session).
John Brown and the Legend of '56 (1942), James C. Malin.
Appeal to the Record, William E. Connelley.
John Brown (1900), William E. Connelley.
Kansas Conflict, Charles Robinson.
The New York Times, May–June 1856, New York Public Library.

Kansas: Its Interior and Exterior Life (1856 and *Enlarged Edition,*
   1899), Sara L. Robinson.
John Brown and His Men (1899), Richard Hinton.
John Brown, Liberator of Kansas and Martyr of Virginia (1910), F. B.
   Sanborn.
John Brown (1950), Oswald Garrison Villard.

OLD BROWN'S CONTEMPT FOR THE FREE STATE PARTY — *Redpath,*
88; *Spring,* 148.

FREE-SOIL GUERRILLA ACTIVITIES — *Redpath,* 98–9, says John
Brown, Jr., heard that Lawrence was threatened and marched with more
than sixty men to defend the town. When he learned that the safety
committee intended to offer no resistance, he headed back toward Osawatomie, 'but ere he reached it and disbanded, his father, with a company of seven men, left his camp and began in right earnest the war of
liberty.' This supports considerable other evidence that free-soilers
were on the offensive before the sack of Lawrence, though this event is
generally cited as the thing that set fire to John Brown and other free-
soil guerrillas. *Andreas,* 895, tells how proslave Reverend Martin White
was shot at and run out of the Territory a month before the sack of
Lawrence. *Phillips,* 313–16, tells several gay guerrilla stories, including
the one about the three Southerners killed from ambush. See also affida-
vits of five proslave victims of free-soil raids, *Full Report* 200, 1199–
1205.

POTTAWATOMIE CREEK MASSACRE — *Luke Parsons,* 11–13, was
one of the men who helped Old Brown sharpen his broadswords and
saw him set out on his murder march. Townsley, who was sent along as
guide to the butcher party, made a full confession, 6 December 1879,
at Lane, Kansas; briefed by *Spring,* 144, and quoted verbatim at some
length by *Robinson,* 265–7. *Spring,* 137–52, writing in 1885, says 'It
was a misfortune that Howard and Sherman, Republican members of
the Congressional Committee, should have declined to explore this
ghastly affair.' Mordecai Oliver did explore it and briefed the testimony of the survivors in his minority report. Their full testimony was
appended to *Full Report* 200, 1193–9, printed in 1856. But though the
Howard Report was widely used, in evidence against the South,
no one has used the minority report with any real desire to get
at the truth. As late as 1942, *Malin,* 757, disposed of the minority report in a paragraph mentioning that there was such a report.
He either never read it or failed to see how the stories told by the

survivors paralleled the Townsley confession. But then *Malin,* 386–7, gives little weight to that confession. If he had paid more attention to Townsley's emphasis on Brown's insistence that Townsley stay with the party because he was needed to point out proslave homes, Malin could have avoided the painful research for his Chapter xxxi. There he tries to establish the fact that the murders ('not unique in brutality,' to *Malin,* 753) might, by a stretch of coincidence, have been committed over claim disputes. Yet only one of the survivors could name the grizzled leader. James Harris did recognize old man Brown and his son, Owen Brown. Harris must have told James Glasswell, the stranger who was spared, because Glasswell told James Christian of Lawrence a few days after the massacre that John Brown had led the murder band. *Connelley (John Brown),* 185–251, makes no excuses. He sees John Brown's action as a master stroke that set men free of the 'bogus laws.' And he has only contempt for the men who, later, jealous of Brown's fame, pretended shock at his deed. He points out in his *Appeal,* 11, that it was known the next day that John Brown was the perpetrator of the deed. To see how the massacre was handled by the New York papers, comb through the May–June, 1856, files at the New York Public Library. Be sure to use a fine-toothed comb, or you won't find a mention.

NEIGHBORS OF THE MURDERED MEET — *Phillips* sits this one out; *Spring,* 147–8; *Andreas,* 132.

JOHN BROWN HATERS — The *Herald of Freedom,* 7 February 1857, months after the massacre, called John Brown 'noble-minded and generous.' The editor who wrote these words spent his last days writing diatribes against this man (see Chapter II, bibliography). He said he did not know at the time that Old Brown was connected with the murders, but G. W., as has been mentioned, was a famous liar. *Luke Parsons* says that Robinson defended the act in those days, said it was justifiable. 'It was generally approved by the Free State party,' Parsons said, still feeling in 1910 that 'those deaths saved a lot of lives.' But *Robinson,* 265–301, writing in 1889, gave an impressive body of evidence to show that the Pottawatomie Creek massacre changed proslave bluster to violence in Kansas Territory. The most interesting shift was that made by *Mrs. Robinson.* The *Enlarged Edition* of her book has a 32-page appendix of evidence against John Brown, as a man and as a force in Kansas political history. One quote is from a letter in the *North American Review,* 1883. 'I knew the old scoundrel long before the war, long before Kansas was known,' wrote N. Eggleston, of Solon,

Ohio. 'He tried to blow up his mother-in-law with powder, he was guilty of every meanness. He involved his father at one time in ruin . . . His swindling operation in Franklin, Portage County, O., would make another chapter. The last time I saw him was at Brockaway's Hotel in Cleveland, where he had a large number of Missouri horses selling. Brockaway told me they were stolen and I heard the question put to Brown and he didn't deny it. If New England can't find better material to make heroes of than John Brown, she had better go without them.'

JOHN BROWN IDOLATERS AND APOLOGISTS — *Redpath,* 119, devotes few words to the massacre, says Old Brown was twenty-five miles away at the time. *Redpath,* 374, again denies John Brown's connection with the affair. *Hinton,* 60–92, devotes all those pages not to the massacre but to an attempt to justify it. He thinks of everything, even threatened violations of free-soil women by the Pottawatomie Creek farmers. *F. B. Sanborn,* 247–82, begins his chapter thus: 'John Brown will mean little to those who do not believe God governs the world . . .' If your stomach can take it, read through to the next page and you will see, 'Such a deed must not be judged by every day rules of conduct . . .' This researcher stopped there. Still, in 1943, *Villard,* 148–88, with all the facts before him, could say, 'Without clear appreciation of what happened on the 24th and 25th of May, 1856, a true understanding of Brown the man cannot be reached. The actual details have been veiled for more than half a century in a mystery which the confession of one of the party only partially dispelled.' His bibliographical reference on 'one of the party' is page 1206 of *Full Report* 200. In my book, printed by the same Washington printer, Cornelius Wendell, page 1206 is the last page and contains only one paragraph, which attests the signature of Thomas J. Goforth by John R. Swearingen, Clerk.

– 17 –

BATTLE OF BLACK JACK

Conquest of Kansas, William Phillips.
The Public Life of Captain John Brown, James Redpath.
Kansas, Leverett W. Spring.
Kansas Historical Collections, IV, referred to as *KHC,* IV.
Kansas Historical Collections, XII, referred to as *KHC,* XII.
The Truth at Last, G. W. Brown.

THE HUNT AND THE BATTLE — *Phillips*, 331–42; *Redpath*, 120–35; *Spring*, 152–8.

JOHN BROWN'S INSANITY — *G. W. Brown* virtually devotes his book to the subject. Also see Eli Moore letter, *KHC*, XII, 338–46.

RELEASE OF PATE BY COLONEL SUMNER — *Redpath*, 137–40; *Spring*, 158–62; *KHC*, IV, 439–41.

– 18 –
AT HOME AND ABROAD

Kansas, or Squatter Life and Border Warfare in the Far West, Thomas H. Gladstone.
Kansas: Its Interior and Exterior Life, Sara L. Robinson.
The Border Ruffian Code in Kansas, Republican campaign document, 1856.

PRISONER ROBINSON IN LEAVENWORTH — *Gladstone*, 50–58.

PRISON LIFE — *Sara Robinson,* back home again, 272, 296–7, 300–306.

II

BACK IN THE STATES — The platforms of the three main parties and the acceptance speeches of their candidates are to be found, strangely enough, in a pamphlet entitled, *The Border Ruffian Code in Kansas*. Since this pamphlet carries an advertisement headed 'Republican Documents Now Ready' and signed 'Greeley & McElrath, Tribune Office, New York,' it is an easy guess that the pamphlet was a Republican campaign pamphlet.

– 19 –
HEAT LIGHTNING

Kansas, Leverett W. Spring.
Conquest of Kansas, William Phillips.
Spencer Kellogg Brown, His Life in Kansas and Death as a Spy (1903), G. G. Smith.
Kansas: Its Interior and Exterior Life, Sara L. Robinson.
Annals of Kansas, Daniel W. Wilder.
Kansas Historical Collections, IV, referred to as *KHC*, IV.

TISCHMAKER DEATH — *Spring,* 180, tells how free-soilers crept into Franklin 'with the stealth of Indians,' but 'the brisk rifle practice in the darkness, accomplished nothing beyond the killing of one of the defenders and wounding of others.' Tischmaker was the name of the man who was killed. It was come upon by accident and is recorded here because dead Southerners so seldom seemed to have had names. Full account of this first attack on Franklin, *Phillips,* 243–9.

MAJOR HOYT KILLED — Much was made of the shooting from ambush of Major Hoyt. No mention was made of the fact that Hoyt was once caught smuggling Sharp's rifles and released. *Smith* tells this episode in passing, 53–7.

SAM WALKER AND TITUS — *Phillips,* 320–22; *Spring,* 182–5.

DISPERSION OF THE TOPEKA LEGISLATURE — Military correspondence, including Jefferson Davis' disapproval of Sumner's using U.S. troops, *KHC, IV,* 446–52. *Phillips,* 392–406; *Mrs. Robinson,* 310–15; *Spring,* 129–36.

ARMY APPROPRIATION BILL — *Wilder* entries, 103–4. There were evidences of worry about the appropriation in many of the intra-military communiques that summer, *KHC, IV,* 474–5. On the day the bill was held up, Senator Douglas reported a bill authorizing the people of Kansas Territory to form a constitution as a ticket for admission into the Union. It immediately passed the Senate but was killed by the House. The House countered with a substitute bill reorganizing the Territory. It was killed by the Senate.

– 20 –

TWO GOVERNORS DOWN AND FOUR TO GO

Kansas, Leverett W. Spring.
'Rise and Fall of the Kansas Aid Movement' (*American Hist. Rev.,* IV, 1935), Ralph Volney Harlow.
Annals of Kansas, D. W. Wilder.
The Public Life of Captain John Brown, James Redpath.
Life of Gen. Jas. H. Lane, John Speer.
Kansas Conflict, Charles Robinson.
Kansas: Its Interior and Exterior Life, Sara L. Robinson.
Kansas Historical Collections, IV, referred to as *KHC, IV.*
Dictionary of American Biography, Shannon, Wilson.

SLAVES IN KANSAS TERRITORY — *DeBow's Review*, August 1856.

KANSAS RELIEF — *Harlow; Spring*, 163; *Wilder*, 102.

LANE'S ARMY — *KHC*, IV, 471–4; *Spring*, 169; *Redpath*, 145; *Speer*, 111–13; *Robinson*, 298–313; *Platte County Argus Extra*, 18 August 1856.

ATTACKS ON FORT FRANKLIN AND FORT WASHINGTON — *Speer*, 114–15; *Spring*, 181–2.

FALL OF FORT TITUS AND 'PEACE,' — *Robinson*, 311–13, prints letter written in 1884 by a participant, James Blood. *Spring*, 182–6; *Mrs. Robinson*, 325–7.

GOVERNOR SHANNON RESIGNS — *Spring*, 187, quotes Shannon on the governorship of K.T. *Wilder*, 21 August 1856 entry, says Shannon is notified of his removal. Spring simply says he resigned. Shannon's resignation letter dated 18 August (*KHC*, IV, 403) says he has heard unofficially that he has been removed. The *Dictionary of American Biography* says he forwarded his letter of resignation 18 August 1856, and three days later received notice of his removal. The Shannon letter to General Smith is given in full, *KHC*, IV, 461–2.

FREE-SOIL PILLAGE OF TECUMSEH — Military dispatch, *KHC*, IV, 489; also *Spring*, 178.

FUGIT SCALPS AN ABOLITIONIST — *Wilder*, 105, dates the event, 19 August 1856. Fugit was arrested later in Missouri, according to the *St. Louis Democrat*, 27 May 1857. The murdered man was a newcomer by the name of Hopps, Hoppe, or Hops, depending on which writer you read. *Mrs. Robinson*, 328, calls the Ruffian Fugert.

– 21 –

'REIGN OF TERROR'

Geary in Kansas (1857), John H. Gihon, M.D.

Kansas, or Squatter Life in the Far West, Thomas H. Gladstone.

Kansas Historical Collections, IV, referred to as *KHC*, IV.

The Public Life of Captain John Brown, James Redpath.

Kansas, Leverett W. Spring.

Spencer Kellogg Brown, G. G. Smith.

Life of Gen. Jas. H. Lane, John Speer.

Kansas Conflict, Charles Robinson.

Annals of Kansas, D. W. Wilder.

MISSOURI'S CHOICE FOR GOVERNOR — A new on-the-scene recorder is about to appear and, luckily, for William Phillips' *Conquest of Kansas* has gone to press and Mrs. Robinson is writing her last chapters. *John H. Gihon, M.D.*, private secretary of Governor Geary, 128–31, says the proslavery party wanted Calhoun as governor. He quotes at length a letter published, he does not say where, over the name of Atchison and other Missouri leaders, which protests the appointment of Geary, a man 'ignorant of our condition, a stranger to our people.'

WOODSON AND HIS PROCLAMATION — *Gladstone*, 12, was impressed by the 'tall, somewhat handsome' Woodson, said he 'did not join in all particulars the extreme party.' Free-soil residents felt otherwise. His proclamation against them was widely published. Full text, *KHC*, IV, 470–71.

MARCH ON OSAWATOMIE — *Redpath*, 146–51; *Spring*, 190–91; *Smith*, 67–81. There is an interesting account in the diary of Spencer Brown, O. C. Brown's fifteen-year-old son who was made captive by the proslave forces. Since his father was with Lane's army and his mother had gone back East, he lived for some time 'in captivity' with a doctor's family in Missouri, fell in love with the doctor's daughter.

WOODSON AND COLONEL COOKE — *Spring*, 192. Cooke's action commended, *KHC*, IV, 481–3; complete military correspondence on the period, *ibid.*, 471–88.

LANE'S MARCH ON LECOMPTON — *Speer*, 115–22, gives the fullest account. Another member of Lane's Army, O. C. Brown, wrote about the march to his wife; see *Smith*, 98–101. James Blood's letter, *Robinson*, 308–13. Military correspondence, above. Also *Spring*, 192–4.

JEFFERSON DAVIS COMMUNIQUE — *Wilder*, 105; full text, *KHC*, IV, 426.

WOODSON REPLY TO LAWRENCE — *Spring*, 192.

ORIGIN OF THE JAYHAWKER NICKNAME — *Spring*, 240.

II

GOVERNOR GEARY'S TRIP TO K.T. — *Gihon*, 103–21.

MAJOR HACKETT AND CAPTAIN SACKET — Captain Sacket's dispatches, *KHC*, IV, 489, 495. Probably Gihon's 'Major Hackett.' It is interesting to note that Gihon in his background material, 12–103, gives the goriest free-soil versions. In events observed first-hand he becomes noticeably more two-sided.

– 22 –

HARVEST TIME

Geary in Kansas, John H. Gihon.
Kansas, Leverett W. Spring.
Kansas Historical Collections, IV, referred to as *KHC*, IV.
The Public Life of Captain John Brown, James Redpath.
Life of Gen. Jas. H. Lane, John Speer.
Kansas Conflict, Charles Robinson.
John Brown, F. B. Sanborn.
NOTE: The complete executive minutes of the Geary Administration are to be found in *KHC*, IV, 520–742.

LECOMPTON — *Gihon*, 122.

GOVERNOR'S FIRST OFFICIAL MOVES — *Gihon*, 123–34; *Spring*, 197–8.

FIRST EXCITEMENT AT LAWRENCE — *Gihon*, 134–40, includes Geary's appeals to Colonel Cooke. The colonel's report to Fort Leavenworth describes the condition of Lawrence, *KHC*, IV, 497–8.

HARVEY'S ATTACK ON HARDTEVILLE — Geary's dispatch to Secretary of State Marcy, *Gihon*, 155. *Redpath*, 159–60. *Speer*, 123–4, says five proslave men were killed, but military reports, *KHC*, IV, 502–4, 510–11, say one.

WOODSON'S POSSE AT LAWRENCE — *Gihon*, 148–57, most colorful account, includes Shannon's report to State Department. Military reports, *KHC*, IV, 498–501. *Redpath*, 158–70, credits John Brown with saving Lawrence. *Sanborn* uses Redpath version. *Robinson*, in refutation, 324–8, reprints letter by Joseph Cracklin, captain of the Lawrence Stubbs, published in the *Lawrence Tribune* in 1881. *Spring*, 198–201, says Old Brown was there but that he did not do much but give shooting advice. *Spring*, 208, tells the good story of what Sam Walker, a man among pharisees, said to Geary and what Geary said to him.

– 23 –

GEARY TRIES TO GOVERN

The Public Life of Captain John Brown, James Redpath.
Geary in Kansas, John H. Gihon.
Kansas, Leverett W. Spring.
Annals of Kansas, D. W. Wilder.

Kansas Historical Collections, IV, referred to as *KHC*, IV.
The Hyatt Manuscripts of the Kansas Historical Society, 1875.

JOHN BROWN BEFORE THE MASSACHUSETTS LEGISLATURE — *Redpath*, 176–84, full text. Also *Wilder*, 115–17.

GEARY ATTEMPTS TO REFORM THE JUDICIARY — *Gihon*, 113–14, 157–66; *Spring*, 202–3.

THE MURDER OF BUFFUM AS A CASE IN POINT — *Gihon*, 166–81.

ARMY REFUSES FURTHER CARE TO PRISONERS — Colonel Cooke and General Smith agree that the Army's custody of Harvey's men 'embarrasses the troops and diminishes their efficiency,' *KHC*, IV, 501, 538.

CRIMINAL CONVICTIONS MAY 1854 to OCTOBER 1856 — *Spring*, 203; also *KHC*, IV, 605.

II

'PEACEABLE IMMIGRANTS' — *Gihon*, 187–91; *Spring*, 170–72; military reports, *KHC*, IV, 512–17, 609–12, particularly, 516. *Redpath*, 171–2, quickly passes over the immigrant party he led. 'It was intended to stop and disarm my train, but a few forced marches defeated that design. It was known that another large train was coming in after me; this train several companies of cavalry and artillery marched northward to arrest,' he says, then adds that 'as soon as the military supplies had been stored,' he left Topeka.

FREE-SOIL RAID OF U.S. ARSENAL — *Spring*, 172; also the *Hyatt Manuscripts*. These accounts were written by a number of Northern settlers for the Englishman, Thaddeus Hyatt, who had been sent by the National Kansas Committee in 1856 to investigate things.

CAPITAL GROGGERIES — *Gihon*, 194.

III

THE GOVERNOR'S TOUR — *Gihon*, 195–204.
BACK TO BUSINESS — *Gihon*, 204–5.

– 24 –

THE NATIONAL ELECTION

Kansas, Leverett W. Spring.
The Border Ruffian Code in Kansas, Republican campaign pamphlet, 1856.

The Issue Fairly Presented. The Senate Bill for the Admission of Kansas as a State. Democracy, Law, Order and the Will of the Whole People Against Black Republicanism, Usurpation, Revolution, Anarchy and the Meager Minority, Democratic campaign pamphlet, 1856.

Kansas Conflict, Charles Robinson.

True History of the Civil War, Guy Carleton Lee.

Growth of the American Republic, i, Morison-Commager.

Ordeal of the Nation, ii, Allan Nevins.

THE 'TEMPORARY LUSTRATION OF NATIONAL POLITICS' — *Spring,* 209. Two pieces of campaign literature at hand bear Spring out. The titles have a diatribish sound, but the arguments inside are made by a passionless presentation of evidence. The Republican campaign pamphlet contained not only, as mentioned in the bibliography for chapter XVII, the platforms of the parties and the acceptance speeches, but also the territorial slave code and a dissection of the Toombs Bill by W. Y. Roberts, Free State pretender to the lieutenant-governorship of Kansas. The Democratic pamphlet is a carefully documented review of the Kansas admission question, introduced thus: 'We shall not undertake to determine why the God of nature made the African inferior to the white man; or why He permitted England to fasten the institution of slavery upon the colonies against their repeated and earnest remonstrances. Nor can we tell what Heaven in its wisdom may intend to work out in the relations of master and slave, as they now exist in several of the United States. This, however, we do know and will add, that when these States, as independent parties, agreed to come under a common Constitution and into a common Union — it was on terms of perfect equality, for the mutual and equal benefit of all, and that African slavery was one of the recognized subjects of that compact.' *Robinson,* 339 says that Geary was sent to K.T. to 'quiet disturbances that the election of Buchanan might be secured.'

NATIONAL BACKGROUND — *Lee, True History,* 123-6; *Morison-Commager,* 624-5; *Nevins,* 495-514.

– 25 –
OUT LIKE A LAMB

Geary in Kansas, John W. Gihon.
Kansas Historical Collections, IV, referred to as *KHC,* IV.
The Kansas Region, Max Greene.
Three Years on the Western Border, John McNamara.
Annals of Kansas, D. W. Wilder.
Kansas, Leverett W. Spring.
Kansas Conflict, Charles Robinson.

GEARY POINTS WITH PRIDE — Reports to Washington, *Gihon,* 209–14.

PETITION OF SQUATTERS ON INDIAN LANDS — *KHC,* IV, 641–2, 655, 700.

INDIAN TRUST LANDS — *Greene,* 102.

ILLEGAL SETTLING AT LEAVENWORTH — Fullest discussion, *Mc-Namara,* 63–75.

PUBLIC LAND SALES AT LEAVENWORTH — *Wilder,* 117; *Gihon,* 210–12; *KHC,* IV, 638, 657–9, 661.

A ROBINSON PLOT WITH GEARY? — *Spring,* 204, accepted the Robinson story, evidently told to him personally, for the account in *Robinson,* 340, differs only in detail. Nothing in the wealth of material on the Geary administration substantiates the tale.

FREE STATE LEGISLATURE LACKS A QUORUM — *Spring,* 204–5; *Gihon,* 214–16; Geary's report to Secretary March, *KHC,* IV, 688–9. The legislature did organize on the second day; some men were arrested by Sheriff Jones but were immediately released by Judge Cato on $500 bail.

LAW AND ORDER BRIBE — *Gihon,* 357.

II

THE TERRITORIAL LEGISLATURE SETS ITS TONE — *Gihon,* 218–20.

– 26 –
THREE GOVERNORS DOWN AND THREE TO GO

Geary in Kansas, John W. Gihon.
Kansas Historical Collections, IV, referred to as *KHC,* IV.
Kansas, Leverett W. Spring.

LECOMPTON AND THE SOLONS — *Gihon,* 220–27.

SHERRARD — *Gihon,* 227–44; also *KHC,* IV, 708–10.

CENSUS BILL — *Gihon,* 260–70; full text veto message, *KHC,* IV, 717–21.

GEARY WRITES AMOS LAWRENCE — *Spring,* 207.

ELMORE-KAGI FRAY — *Gihon,* 271; *KHC,* IV, 704.

PETITION OF THE PRISONERS AT TECUMSEH — *Gihon,* 271. There are a number of communications about the treatment of prisoners in the executive minutes, *KHC,* IV. In one, Geary refuses to give Sheriff Jones permission to use balls and chains.

GEARY RESIGNS — *Gihon,* 391, gives Geary's resignation letter. To keep it secret, Gihon mailed it just before the mails closed. 'The post-master's son and L. A. MacLean, the latter being always in the office at the opening and closing of the mails, were the only persons present. Yet in the morning, the subject of the governor's letter to Washington was the subject of universal conversation throughout the town,' Gihon said.

GEARY SAYS GOOD-BY TO SAM WALKER — Gihon skips this; *Spring,* 208, tells it.

– 27 –
THE DRED SCOTT DECISION

'A Legal View of the Case of Dred Scott as Decided by the Supreme Court,' *The Law Reporter, June 1857.*

Some Phases of the Dred Scott Case (*Mississippi Valley Hist. Review,* XIV, *No.* 1), F. H. Hodder.

Emergence of Lincoln (1950), Allan Nevins, 84–7, 90–118.

True History of the Civil War, Guy Carleton Lee, 126–8.

Growth of the American Republic, Morison-Commager, 625–6, 629, 636.

New York Newspapers, March 1857, New York Public Library files.

– 28 –
FOUR GOVERNORS DOWN

Geary in Kansas, John W. Gihon.

Kansas Historical Collections, IV, referred to as *KHC,* IV.

Emergence of Lincoln, I, Allan Nevins.

Kansas Conflict, Charles Robinson.

Kansas, Leverett W. Spring.
Annals of Kansas, D. W. Wilder.
Life Beyond the Mississippi, Albert D. Richardson.
Life of Gen. Jas. H. Lane, John Speer.
History of the State of Kansas, A. T. Andreas.
Reminiscences of Gov. Walker, G. W. Brown.

GEARY'S FAREWELL — *Gihon,* 308–27; also *KHC,* IV, 738–42.
WALKER'S INAUGURAL — *Gihon,* 328–48, full text.
REACTION TO WALKER — *Gihon,* 303–8; *Robinson,* 351; *Nevins,* 144–7, 155.

II

THE CENSUS AND ELECTION — *Chicago Tribune* account, reported by Horace White, of the tea party at Robinson's, reprinted by *Robinson,* 345–50. *Spring,* 215–16. See Nevins, *Lincoln,* I, 148–9. Names of delegates and votes each received, *Wilder,* 127–8.

III

FREE STATE LEGISLATURE 'MEETS' — *Wilder,* 126. *Spring,* 214–15; Speer, 135. *Richardson* now comes to Kansas Territory. He was at Topeka 9 June 1857 and described the Free State leaders, 43–9.

IV

HEADLINE NEWS: LEAVENWORTH ELECTS A FREE STATE MAYOR — *Gihon,* 299–301; *Richardson,* who was there, 64–6.
THE NATIONAL DEMOCRATIC PARTY OF KANSAS — An historic convention was held by the Law and Order party at Lecompton early in 1857; reported by *Gihon,* 253–8. There was great astonishment when Dr. John Stringfellow, an old-line Whig, as were the majority of those present, proposed that they call themselves National Democrats. 'Democratic' was a bitter pill for many of them to swallow, but it seemed to best encompass their proslave stand.
OSAWAKEE LAND SALES — *Speer,* 136–7; *Richardson,* 70–71.
GENERAL HARNEY AND THE LAWRENCE REBELLION — Assignment of Harney, *Wilder,* 128, and *Nevins,* 144. *Richardson,* who left the land sales to defend Lawrence against General Harney, 74–6.

V

GRASSHOPPER FALLS CONVENTION — *Richardson*, 83–6; *Speer*, 136; *Wilder*, 133; *Andreas*, 126; *Robinson*, 357–9.

WALKER THROWS OUT ELECTION RETURNS — *Spring*, 218; *Wilder*, 151–2.

VI

DID JIM LANE PROPOSE TO SLAUGHTER DELEGATES TO LECOMPTON? — *G. W. Brown*, 104–15; Joel Goodwin letter, *Robinson*, 373–4. Lane's Boswell, *Speer*, 137–9, does not mention the slaughter idea. He simply reports that between five and six hundred free-soilers, led by Lane, went to Lecompton despite 'almost impassable roads, from the recent rains and mud.' Editor Thatcher's comment on Lane's speech adds weight to Speer's view, since Thatcher bore no love for Lane.

VII

LECOMPTON CONVENTION — *Spring*, 220–24; *Nevins*, 229–34. See *Wilder*, 134–48, for full text of the Lecompton Constitution.

GOVERNOR WALKER GOES EAST — *Wilder*, 152; *Spring*, 226. *Richardson*, 76, says, 'Governor Walker kept this pledge and Buchanan remorselessly removed him.'

BUCHANAN'S ENDORSEMENT OF LECOMPTON — 'Seldom in the history of the nation has a President made so disastrous a blunder,' says *Nevins*, 239. And it was recognized as such, at the time, by all but Buchanan himself and perhaps the Southern Cabinet members who influenced him. It lost Stephen A. Douglas to Southern democracy or, as *Richardson*, 87, put it, 'began that rupture in the democratic party which resulted in the election of Abraham Lincoln and the southern rebellion; and thus the Lecompton convention has a national and historic interest.' Also *Spring*, 230–32.

NOTE: For the national reaction to the Walker administration, see *Nevins*, 148–75, 234–9.

– 29 –

VOTING ARMY ROUTED

Life of Gen. Jas. H. Lane, John Speer.
Kansas Conflict, Charles Robinson.
Emergence of Lincoln, I, Allan Nevins.
Annals of Kansas, D. W. Wilder.

Life Beyond the Mississippi, Albert D. Richardson.
Reminiscences of Gov. R. J. Walker, G. W. Brown.
Speech of Hon. James Hughes (1858), a pamphlet.
Kansas, Leverett W. Spring.

SPECIAL SESSION OF THE TERRITORIAL LEGISLATURE — *Speer*, 142–6, and most importantly, 163–74, because he gives the battle between Governor Denver and Lane over Lane's unauthorized activities as militia major-general. *Robinson*, 374–5, 377–8; *Spring*, 226–7; *Nevins*, 266–7.

II

THE NEW GOVERNOR AND TERRITORIAL FINANCES — *Wilder*, 155.

TO VOTE OR NOT TO VOTE — *Speer* passes over the contention that Lane tried to stampede the pre-Christmas meeting of the Free State party into not voting to elect officers under the Lecompton Constitution. *Richardson*, not present, gives a meager account, 101–2. *Spring*, 228, simply says that a meeting was held. The unreliable *G. W. Brown*, 136–43, is relied on, for *Robinson*, 375–7, adds his own note on Lane's beaming return to town and reprints G. W.'s version.

ELECTION OF 4 JANUARY 1858, AND THE LOST RETURNS — *Richardson*, 99–104, apparently is *Spring's* source, 229–30.

THE LECOMPTON STORM — John Stringfellow admits defeat, *Wilder*, 16. *Spring*, 231–6. For a full account, see *Nevins*, 239–301. The Hughes speech is quoted at length because it gives the arguments of those who favored admitting K.T. under the Lecompton Constitution. He discusses, 10–11, the Douglas enabling act of 1856 and quotes Seward's amendment to permit a direct submission from any constitutional convention to Congress.

ENGLISH BILL — Full text, *Wilder*, 165–7; *Spring*, 235–6; *Nevins*, 297–301.

– 30 –

NEW ROLES FOR OLD RASCALS

Life of Gen. Jas. H. Lane, John Speer.
Kansas Conflict, Charles Robinson.
Life Beyond the Mississippi, Albert Richardson.
Reminiscences of Gov. R. J. Walker, G. W. Brown.
The Truth at Last, G. W. Brown.
False Claims Truthfully Corrected, G. W. Brown.

The American Ten Years War (1906), Denton J. Snider.
Annals of Kansas, D. W. Wilder.
Kansas, Leverett W. Spring.
Public Life of Captain John Brown, James Redpath.
History of the State of Kansas, A. T. Andreas.
Appeal to the Record, William E. Connelley.

LANE-JENKINS KILLING — *Speer* devotes 35 pages, 187–218, 337–9, to explanations and testimony to prove that the claim was Lane's and that he killed in self-defense. *Robinson,* 421–4, seeks to prove that Lane was entirely in the wrong. *Richardson,* 113–14, though no admirer of Lane's, except as an orator, said, he 'did exactly what two out of three frontier settlers would have done under the circumstances.' This was not the free-soil attitude toward the Coleman-Dow killing.

FREE-SOIL FACTIONS — *Robinson,* though writing to discredit Lane and John Brown, took a few side swipes at such talking and writing abolitionists as Martin Conway, T. Dwight Thatcher, William Phillips, and James Redpath. All of G. W. Brown's books had the same purpose. It was in his *Reminiscences of Governor Walker* that he publicly joined hands with his hated colleague, Charles Robinson. 'Without Charles Robinson's hearty cooperation from that time forth, I heartily believe Kansas would be a slave state today,' he said. T. Dwight Thatcher comments on G. W. Brown, *Lawrence Republican,* 15 October 1857, quoted by *Connelley* whose book is devoted to the fights between free-soil factions. When *Richardson,* 87, said, 'ordinarily the Free Soilers were divided into cliques and factions,' he put it mildly.

LANE'S DANITES — *Robinson,* 379–81, says he refused to join this order and quotes Redpath's exposé of it in his short-lived *Crusader of Freedom,* established at Doniphan, K.T., 4 March 1858. *Snider,* 222–3, also discusses the Danites. They are not mentioned by Speer or by Redpath in their books.

II

TOPEKA LEGISLATURE VS. TERRITORIAL LEGISLATURE — *Wilder,* 159, says, 'The Free State Legislature meets at Topeka . . . Governor Robinson, in his message, urges the keeping of the state organization. It is published in the *Quindaro Chindowan.'* *Spring,* 257, mentions the resistance of the Topeka government to the reconstituted Territorial Legislature but gives no names. *Robinson,* looking back, 383–90, strongly intimates that he opposed a continuance of the Topeka government — hindsight, perhaps, because this proved the wise course. *Wilder,* who was a K.T. newspaperman himself by that time, likely had at hand a copy of *The Chindowan* containing Robinson's message. It is one document Robinson does not reprint.

MINNEOLA, NEW CAPITAL — *Richardson,* one of the newspapermen offered town shares, 104–5; *Spring,* 258–9; *Robinson,* 383.

CONSTITUTIONAL CONVENTION AND OTHER LEGISLATIVE MATTERS — Denver speech, made in 1884 and quoted by *Robinson,* 381–2, apparently is *Spring's* source, 260. *Speer,* 175–86, quotes the speech, too, but devotes his chapter to refutation of it. Speer introduced Bill 41 calling for a constitutional convention, and he claimed that Denver received the bill an hour and ten minutes before the three-day deadline. *Speer* could not bear Governor Denver, called him, 170, 'a usurper, attempting to exercise judicial and military control.'

MINNEOLA AND LEAVENWORTH CONVENTIONS — *Spring,* 261; *Richardson,* 108; *Robinson,* 383.

III

JAYHAWKING BACKGROUND IN THE SOUTHEAST — *Spring,* 237–44; *Redpath,* 208–12; *Speer,* 163–74; *Richardson,* 126, gives the Montgomery quote; *Andreas,* 878, 1102–4.

– 31 –

BI-ANNUAL MAY MASSACRE

Kansas in '58 (1859), William Tomlison.
Kansas, Leverett Spring.
Life and Letters of Captain John Brown, James Redpath.
Kansas Conflict, Charles Robinson.
Life Beyond the Mississippi, Albert Richardson.
Annals of Kansas, D. W. Wilder.

CHARLES HAMILTON — A new book author now appears. William Tomlison got a job as correspondent for the *Lawrence Republican* to cover what were being called 'the Fort Scott difficulties.' He joined Montgomery's guerrillas and wrote his *Kansas in Fifty-Eight* to extol that leader. *Tomlison,* 63, says Hamilton came to Kansas in 1855; *Spring,* 244, says 'he was caught by the Kansas Crusade proclaimed in Georgia in 1856.' *Tomlison,* 195–201, tells of Montgomery's killing of the federal dragoons. Also *Redpath,* 211. The *Herald of Freedom,* 22 May 1858, carries a letter telling some of Montgomery's depredations on proslave residents early in May. *Andreas,* 878. Montgomery's raid on Hamilton, quoted by *Robinson,* 393.

MARAIS DES CYGNES MASSACRE — *Tomlison,* who arrived at Trading Post next day, 71–6; *Richardson,* who came down later with Governor Denver, 245–7; *Spring,* 245–7.

RAYSVILLE MEETING — *Tomlison,* who was there, 120–38; *Spring,* 247–8.

MARCH ON FORT SCOTT AND LATER ATTACK — Basic story, *Tomlison,* 139–62, 205–20; *Spring,* 248–9, adds Walker quote.

DENVER'S TRIP TO THE TURBULENT AREA — *Richardson,* who went along, 120–30; *Tomlison,* who was around, 228–58; *Spring,* 250–51.

– 32 –
FIVE GOVERNORS DOWN

Annals of Kansas, D. W. Wilder.
Pike's Peak Gold Regions (1860), Henry Villard.
Kansas, Leverett Spring.
Public Life of Captain John Brown, James Redpath.
Harpers Ferry Committee Report.
John Brown and His Men, Richard Hinton.
Kansas Conflict, Charles Robinson.

TELEGRAPH — *Wilder* entry, 25 January 1859.
RAILROAD SURVEY — *Wilder* entry, 13 February 1859.
DISCOVERY OF GOLD — *Wilder,* 184, 188 ('September, 1858 — "Pike's Peak" becomes the leading subject of the Kansas press'). *Villard* opens his book with the story of the discovery of gold.

II

JOHN BROWN'S RETURN — *Spring,* 351–2, Old Brown's talk with Robinson and his appeal to Amos Lawrence for private financial help. *Robinson,* 413. *Redpath,* 196–8, 200–206, gives the whole setup of the Canadian Republic and details on the Harpers Ferry plan as they were told him in June, 1858. Kagi quite frankly said that 'their visit to Kansas was caused by the betrayal of their plans, by Colonel Forbes to the Administration, and that they wished to give a different impression from what these disclosures had, by coming West.'

DENVER TO SECRETARY CASS AND OTHER CURRENT EVENTS —
Wilder, 188–190.

THE JAYHAWKERS RIDE AGAIN — Letter of an incensed free-soiler,
Herald of Freedom, 15 January 1859, writing about the raid on Fort
Scott in December, 1858, points out that the liberated Rice had been
indicted for murder by a free-soil jury. *Robinson*, 405. John Brown's
Kagi, correspondent of the *New York Post*, sent a eulogy of Montgomery to his paper. Tomlison had gone back east by this time. *Redpath*,
216, tells how the portly Epaphroditus Ranson, former Governor of
Michigan and now a dignitary in the land office, dressed 'in his drawers
and nightdress,' was made to trot down the street 'by a boy nineteen
carrying a musket longer than himself.'

JOHN BROWN'S SLAVE-FREEING RAID INTO MISSOURI — *Redpath*,
217–21. Reports vary on the number of slaves freed. Redpath says
eleven and tells of a baby's being born, later. *Wilder*, 192, says fourteen.
Robinson, 406–7, prints in full Crawford's letter to Eli Thayer. Sam
Walker's report on the raid and other difficulties, *Herald of Freedom*,
1 January 1859. Old Brown to A. Wattles, *Harpers Ferry*, 223. *Hinton*,
198–288, covers jayhawking triumphs in the Southeast, including the
Battle of the Spurs.

BAIN'S FORT — *Redpath*, 221, says that in Old Brown's stronghold
'fifty men could have resisted five hundred.'

– 33 –

THE TIME IS AT HAND

Annals of Kansas, D. W. Wilder.
Kansas Conflict, Charles Robinson.
Public Life of Captain John Brown, James Redpath.
Kansas, Leverett Spring.
Life Beyond the Mississippi, Albert Richardson.
Narrative of John Doy, John Doy.
John Brown's Body (1930), Stephen Vincent Benét.
Cooper Union Speech, 27 February 1860, Abraham Lincoln.
Emergence of Lincoln, ii, Allan Nevins.
John Brown, Oswald Garrison Villard.
History of the State of Kansas, A. T. Andreas.
Life of Gen. Jas. H. Lane, John Speer.

JAYHAWK REVIEW — The *Herald of Freedom* followed up its New Year's Day report from Sam Walker on troubles in southeast Kansas Territory, 15 January 1859, with a review of free-soil excesses the year past, largely with an eye to throwing blame for them on Lane and the pen-and-tongue-wielding abolitionists, Conway, Phillips, Thatcher. Editor Brown mentions Montgomery's amnesty message to Governor Medary. *Wilder,* 196–7, quotes Sam Walker and tells of the convening of the legislature and Medary's report of Montgomery's note, giving text.

CAPTAIN SNYDER'S RAID — *Redpath,* 217, is the only source for this story. It may not have happened.

OFFICIAL PROTESTS FROM MISSOURI — *Spring,* 253–6.

MEETING OF THE TERRITORIAL LEGISLATURE — *Spring,* 262; *Wilder* entries, 195–8. *Richardson,* back from the gold fields of west Kansas to take up his duties as a legislator, reports on the lighter side of lawmaking. There was a midnight trial 'of a jovial member from Coffey county' who had been 'discovered kissing a chamber-maid in his hotel.' The fine was 'twelve cans of oysters and two baskets of champagne.'

REWARDS FOR THE ARREST OF JOHN BROWN — *Richardson,* 152; *Wilder,* 197; *Spring,* 256; *Redpath,* 221.

'BATTLE OF THE SPURS' — *Redpath,* 222–4; *Richardson,* 282–4.

PROSLAVE REPRISALS — Crawford letter, *Robinson,* 407.

BURNING OF THE 'BOGUS LAWS' — *Spring,* 262; *Richardson,* 184–9.

JOHN DOY, ARREST AND TRIAL — *Wilder,* 198; *Richardson,* who covered the trial, 152–3; most important, *John Doy,* who was tried, 31–115.

II

LICENSED JAYHAWKING — *Robinson,* 411–12.

FIRST MURDER PUNISHED BY LAW — *Wilder,* 274.

HARPERS FERRY — *Stephen Vincent Benét,* 33–43; *Redpath,* 238–383; *Nevins,* 70–97; Wattles quote, *Robinson,* 413. Letter from Mrs. Doyle, *Robinson,* 399; also *Villard,* 164. *Cooper Union Speech.*

III

PROGRESS ITEMS — *Wilder* entries, 198–201. *Richardson,* 115, says the 600-mile Kaw was at first thought navigable but 'proved to be adapted only to that traditional steamer which could run wherever there was a heavy dew.'

Greeley's Visit — *Wilder* entries, 203–4. *Richardson,* 161–95, reports his trip to the gold fields with the editor.

New Indian Treaties — *Wilder* entries for 16 July and 5 October 1859.

Wyandotte Convention and Constitution — *Wilder,* 208–24, extracts proceedings and gives constitution in full.

Abe Lincoln's Visit — *Wilder,* 231; *Speer,* 244.

Wyandotte Constitution in Congress — *Spring,* 264–5.

Drouth and Kansas Relief — *Wilder* entries, 241, 261; *Spring,* 271; *Andreas,* 178.

Acting-Governor Beebe Quote — *Wilder,* 253.

– 34 –
THE GIANT IS TWINS

True History of the Civil War, Guy Carleton Lee.
Rise of the American Civilization, ii, Charles Beard.
History of the United States, Samuel Eliot.
Kansas, Leverett Spring.
Kansas Conflict, Charles Robinson.
Annals of Kansas, D. W. Wilder.
Life of Gen. Jas. H. Lane, John Speer.
Appeal to the Record, William Connelley.
Kansas Historical Collections, xii, referred to as *KHC,* xii.

Tariff as Campaign Issue — *Lee,* 150; *Beard,* 31–2; *Eliot,* 362–8.

Jefferson Davis Quote — *Spring,* 265.

II

Room No. 7, Eldridge House — *Spring,* 266, 270, says, 'there followed an impromptu jollification, to which buckets of whiskey, freely circulated, lent inspiration.' Judge Simpson was to remember it thirty-five years later, according to *Robinson,* 425–6.

Area of the State of Kansas — *Wilder,* 256.

III

Kansas in the Civil War — Governor Carney to President Lincoln, *Spring,* 272.

KANSAS-MISSOURI BATTLEGROUND — *Wilder,* majority of entries, 260–425. *Robinson,* 435–63, reported the Civil War only to prove what a louse Jim Lane was. Sol Miller, of *The Kansas Chief* at White Cloud (called by *Robinson,* 449, 'the best-informed editor in Kansas'), said that Lincoln's treatment of Robinson 'at the instance of Lane' had 'left a stain upon his Administration that even his martyrdom cannot efface.' And *Speer,* 247–301, to establish Gen. Jas. H. Lane as 'Liberator of Kansas'; also *Connelley,* 58–63.

BRIGADIER GENERAL LANE — *Spring,* 268–305, inclines toward the Robinson point of view on Lane but also lays considerable responsibility for the Quantrill raid on the Redlegs. Speer makes Lane a great friend of Lincoln's and a trusted and extremely able commander.

QUANTRILL'S RAID — Included in the *Spring, Robinson,* and *Speer* references above. Two of Speer's young sons were burned to death in the raid. See letter from O. W. McAllaster, *KHC,* XII, 401–4.

IV

ROBINSON'S IMPEACHMENT — *Spring,* slides over, 283–4. *Connelley,* 22–54, gives a considerable body of damning evidence.

LANE SUICIDE — *Speer,* 313–26, includes eulogies.

Index